John P. Senning

HARVARD STUDIES IN ADMINISTRATIVE LAW

VOLUME IV

LONDON : HUMPHREY MILFORD

OXFORD UNIVERSITY PRESS

THE

PARLIAMENTARY POWERS
OF ENGLISH
GOVERNMENT DEPARTMENTS

BY

JOHN WILLIS

CAMBRIDGE

HARVARD UNIVERSITY PRESS

1933

PRINTED AT THE HARVARD UNIVERSITY PRESS
CAMBRIDGE, MASS., U.S.A.

CONTENTS

THE PARLIAMENTARY POWERS OF ENGLISH GOVERNMENT DEPARTMENTS

INTRODUCTION

WHEN the Lord Chief Justice of England descends from Olympus to launch an attack upon the "lawlessness" of the government departments, the Bar must listen in respectful silence and the average man of intelligence, less submissive but more mindful of his ignorance, does not presume to question facts or conclusions. But when those facts and those conclusions are cited as authoritative in Parliament and the Press, and are adduced to prove anything from the intolerable oppression of excessive legislation to the arbitrary methods of the departments in enforcing the law, it is time to call a halt and to look more closely into a few of the extraordinary powers criticised by Lord Hewart.

The New Despotism did not purport to deal exhaustively with any of these powers, but was intended to direct the attention of Englishmen at large to the significant changes which have come about in the constitution since the publication of Dicey's classic work. That the departments had in many instances power to issue rules, some of them with statutory force, to modify Acts of Parliament, to approve schemes, and to decide disputes without recourse to the courts was well known to legal scholars. C. T. Carr had dealt in his *Delegated Legislation* with their legislative aspect, and W. A. Robson's *Justice and Administrative Law* had shown how many questions of vital import to large sections of the community were being decided by government officials. Neither Carr nor Robson was concerned to arouse admiration or disgust, but to make an orderly exposition of what in fact was going on behind legal shibboleths.

It would be out of place to criticise *The New Despotism* as a work of legal scholarship. Lord Hewart knows more of law in action than law in books: as a barrister, member of Parliament, Attorney-General, and finally Lord Chief Justice he has been active in public life for many years. Even as a judge it is only one of his multifarious duties to preside over the Divisional Court to which application is made for the prerogative writs, the instruments for controlling the discretion of inferior governmental bodies. As he sat on that court he came to find that the King's Bench was losing its historic control over the powers delegated by Parliament to inferior bodies, and like Juvenal to feel that "si natura negat facit indignatio versus" — hence *The New Despotism*.

But "indignatio" invites research. Could it be that these extensive powers had grown up overnight? Did they represent nothing but a nefarious bid for dominion by calculating civil servants — or had they sprung from some pressing necessity? Were the powers always as extensive as they seemed? These were the doubts which crept into my mind as I read. And they were doubts which could only be confirmed or quelled by an investigation, partly historical, partly critical, of delegation of powers. And so it was that stirred to action by *Yaffe's Case*, the locus classicus for judicial truculence, I began a search of the statutes in an effort to discover to what extent Parliament had in the past permitted the departments to stand in its place and above the control of the courts in issuing legislative rules and orders, and then made reference to the volumes of Statutory Rules and Orders and the Law Reports to view the departments in action.

With those rules and orders which on their face were subject to the control of the courts and could if ultra vires be annulled by them I was not concerned: there was nothing to be gained by adding to Carr's survey of the general topic of delegated legislation. Nor am I now disposed to canvass as a matter of political theory where delegation should stop, or as a matter of practical politics to prophesy its career during the next few years. My interest is in the more extraordinary powers of the departments discussed in this essay, the power to issue rules of statutory finality, to modify Acts of Parliament, to build up executive private bills — in discovering how the departments came to possess these powers and what has in fact been done under them. For it is here that the constitutional shoe pinches.

It is common knowledge that with the flight of James II there disappeared the last pretensions of the Crown to legislate by the prerogative. That left a Parliament that was not only in theory but in fact supreme. But just because Parliament is supreme and uncontrolled by the dead hand of a written constitution, it has been able to restore to the executive many of those powers which in 1688 seemed to have gone for ever. The wheel has run full circle. Once more the departments lay claim to powers as great as those once exercised under the prerogative, but this time they shelter from the courts behind the cloak of Parliament. Once more the Crown is in conflict with Parliament, but now the Crown can reply, "The powers we exercise are of your granting; take them away — if you can." "If you can" — these are the words which tell. In this essay I shall try to show to what extent the departments have replaced Parliament as the sole creator of new rights, but shall not dare to guess the future.

In the appointment of the Donoughmore Committee there was a tardy recognition by the powers that be of the importance of the practice of delegating legislative and judicial power to the departments. A long period of imperceptible growth, a quickening to meet the felt needs of the new Social State, a sudden flowering during the War, and after the War the full fruition — such is the history of delegation in England, not difficult to trace out after the event, but, except for a voice here and there, crying in the wilderness, disregarded in its making by lawyer and statesman alike. Indeed there was little to catch the eye. The statesman, looking to the end to be achieved, is not much interested in the procedural complexities attendant on the execution of his project, while the English lawyer, with his strange but quite intelligible aptitude for divorcing life from law (economic and political controversies are, in England, decided at the polls and not at the bar), failed to realise the significant changes going on beneath the trappings of legal theory.

In the United States it has been quite otherwise. That fundamental human instinct which leads men to cling to the tried wisdom of the past, in law exalted to what is perhaps an uncritical reverence for judicial pronouncements made in settlement of conflicting interests long since reconciled, gave birth to an institution from which there is now a struggle to escape — "a government of laws and not of men." The colonial governments had long been accustomed to a paternal scrutiny of their legislative innovations by a superior sovereignty ready, if necessary, to enforce its will by force of arms or by trade boycott. After a revolution fought to free them from shackles believed to be injurious to full development, they found themselves unable to cast out the notion of a higher power guiding their destinies. Enabling Acts gave place to Constitutions enforced, it was thought, not from without, but by their own inherent force as interpreted — no more — by the judges of the day; a political fact no longer true became canonized as a legal doctrine. Whatever may have been the designs of the constitutional conventions of the thirteen States and of the Federal arm, the judges accepted their handiwork as a declaration of the absolute nature of the political concepts of 1789. Among these concepts was preëminent the doctrine of the separation of powers.

There is no need for me here to enlarge on that doctrine or to point out how far short — even if one accepts the traditional definition of the nature of the three powers — the newborn States fell of realising their own ideal. But with the acceptance of the doctrine of separation as a doctrine of law, and with the assumption that the new governments as constituted measured up to it, it became possible to resist any new development in the distribution of the functions of government. Meanwhile events did not stand still. Interests unknown to the Common Law came into being, interferences heretofore out of its ken showed their heads. There was a trend to the towns, there was specialisation, and, as a necessary consequence, an increasing interdependence which called for regulation — problems very much the same as those which had to be faced in England, but with this difference: in England the legislature is omnipotent and its commands are conclusively binding on the subject in all matters, and it was precisely by reason of this omnipotence of Parliament that the process of delegation remained unnoticed for almost a century; in the United States a legislature must first ask itself whether constitutionally it has the power to act, and, if so, in what manner it may act. If the members of an aggrieved public can induce the passage of an Act to regulate a monopoly business, it is still open to that business, beaten at the polls, to have recourse to the courts and claim that it has been deprived of some inalienable right guaranteed it by concepts supposed to be inherent in the State or Federal Constitution. If it is unsuccessful in its challenge of the fundamental principles of the legislation, the machinery of the Act may still afford a loophole, more generally granted fifty years ago than today. For then the courts had decreed that the setting up of a new standard was exclusively within the power of the legislature, a notion which still persists in England as a political tenet of the extreme Right. But when that prejudice was endowed with all the dignity of a constitutional doctrine, a State was at its wits' end to discover a practicable method of regulation. How could it fix the rates for an intrastate railroad or public utility? To perform the work itself was not within the realms of possibility; to delegate its power elsewhere was unconstitutional. Thus delegation early received the attention of politicians and lawyers in the United States.

As long as the pressure of public need and public opinion was not

too great the courts remained adamant in "upholding the Constitution," but at length, as the irritation increased, by the judicious
choice of a word — "administrative" — they found themselves
able to grant the fact of delegated legislation and still to deny the
name — subject however to judicial review of such a nature that
in such matters as rate regulation it is in effect the courts which
under cover of passing on constitutional rights exercise legislative
power. Delegation is normally to a commission rather than to
one of the executive departments of government, and to this extent
separation of powers still rules as a quasi-legal doctrine. But the
main battle is now won, and no counsel would now challenge delegation itself, but would confine himself to showing that in the Act
concerned the legislature had virtually abdicated in favour of the
commission.

Separation of powers is, of course, fully recognised in England
as a political doctrine and, just as in the United States, is as much
honoured in the breach as in the observance. In the United States
the power of the judges over executive and legislative branches
alike, elementary in American constitutional law, gives the lie to
the very doctrine which those judges are zealous to enforce, while
in England a supreme Parliament which constitutionally might
tomorrow abolish the office of judge, and has in fact reversed judicial decisions, which controls the actions of a department by
criticism of the departmental head, himself an important initiator
of legislation, illustrates with what striking reservations the doctrine must be understood. It is interesting to notice that although
a supreme Parliament in England and a supreme judiciary in the
United States have both been directed to the same end, that of
restricting the scope of the executive, the outcome has been very
different: in England today a theoretically supreme Parliament is
in practice swayed by the will of the Cabinet, itself profoundly in-
fluenced by the permanent Civil Service, while in the United
States the judiciary have gathered into their own hands the power
to direct the streams of legislation, to regulate rates, to make and
unmake combinations of capital, to say to what extent and in what
manner a workman may constitutionally defend himself against
his employer. So much for the separation of powers, which has done
much to retard the intelligent development of governmental
methods.

It is still the fashion in the United States to put a great deal
of detail into legislation. A glance at any Act of Congress,

particularly at a budget, is sufficient to make that clear. However, there is a marked tendency on the part of the Federal Government to delegate a larger discretion to the departments: the rules of the Patent Office, of the Department of Agriculture with reference to interstate shipments of fruit and cattle, of the Interstate Commerce Commission anent safety devices and methods of accounting, each form a substantial code. But State laws still go deeply into specific detail; deeply rooted habit has not yet been forced to bow to convenience where there is little business of importance to be done.

To the special aspects of the English problem taken up in this essay there can be no American parallel — such is the power of the Fourteenth Amendment. A rule of statutory finality is unthinkable in a country where an Act may not even go so far as to make the determinations of a commissioner final on questions of fact, but must go on to exclude "jurisdictional fact" from that finality: any legislature which sought to prevent the courts from passing on the question of ultra vires would be told that by so doing it was depriving the individual adversely affected of "due process," of a constitutional right to challenge "illegal usurpation of power" before the courts. About a power in the executive to modify legislation, it is not possible to be quite so positive, although such a power is markedly legislative. The Tariff Commission, with the concurrence of the President, may modify an enacted import duty within limits and according to a standard prescribed by Congress; but it is at least doubtful whether Congress could empower the Commission in the case of a difficulty to modify the substantive provisions of the Act "so far as it may deem it necessary or expedient for carrying its orders into effect." In such a case the court would probably do one of two things, declare that part of the Act unconstitutional or so interpret it as to make it read in effect "so far as this court may deem necessary."

The development of the scheme procedure through procedure by private bill and Provisional Order, and the emergence of the Special Order, is so wrapped up in the peculiarities of the procedure of the English Parliament that it is difficult to make comparisons. The power of the Interstate Commerce Commission to approve railroad consolidation must rest ultimately on much the same philosophy which has inspired the Coal Mines Acts and the Transport Acts during the last decade in England — economic planning. The Commission was directed to "prepare and adopt a plan for the consolidation of the railway properties of the continental United States into a limited number of systems," and to approve the consolidation if it found that the public interest would be promoted thereby; it could enter an order "approving and authorizing such consolidations . . . with such modifications and upon such terms and conditions as it may prescribe." But there was this limitation upon the power of the Commission (clearly marking it off from the power of the Minister under the highly socialistic Coal Mines Acts to coerce an unwilling minority): that it could only be exercised "if all the carriers involved assent thereto." Nevertheless it is only the Interstate Commerce Commission which at all approaches the position of an English department in the powers it may exercise.

There is, then, little to be gained from any attempt to compare the extraordinary powers discussed in this essay with American practice, there being nothing in the United States to set alongside them. Even the general topic of the delegation of legislative power is not apt for comparison; for while in the United States delegation is intimately concerned with questions of judicial review and constitutionality, the English problem is one of control, — by Parliament, the courts, or any other feasible method, — an issue which is clearly one of practical politics rather than of law.

This essay is mainly concerned with procedure — trivial stuff, it might be thought. But the controversy which at present rages around delegation of legislative power is not in essence concerned with anything more exciting than procedure. That slums must be cleared and safety devices made compulsory in factories has never been in dispute. The issue is solely by what means Parliament shall carry its declared policy into effect. Must Parliament itself define the details and prescribe the methods? Or shall a subordinate authority be charged with those duties? How far shall the performance of those duties by a department be supervised by the courts? Thus stated, questions of procedure become questions of power. But in practice the full significance of procedure and procedural change does not so clearly appear. A change in the procedural provisions customarily inserted at the end of a statute does not challenge inquiry, is not political capital — until there comes a day when trivial changes of procedure, cumulative in their effect, each precedent going a little further than the one before it, have gnawed their way into the fabric of substance, and the elaborate, supposedly perpetual, edifice of a constitutional theory is seen to be tottering to its fall. Then and only then is a cry raised, and, as if to compensate for their former blind apathy, party leaders open the flood gates of oratory and swamp the issues in swirling rhetoric.

It is pleasant at such a moment to stand apart from political passions and to view from the standpoint of the law — which is the formal statement of the living ambitions and aspirations of mankind — the structure of government as it is. Accusations, fears, ideals, war cries, fade insignificant into the distance, and one is left face to face with something that is tangible, some starting point for discussion, something that is a symbol of an idea greater than itself: a point of procedure.

CHAPTER I

THE GROWTH OF DELEGATED LEGISLATION

THE history of the delegation of legislative power in England falls into four main periods. The first is a long one of slow growth, going hand in hand with the growth of the paternal element in government, and culminates in the Housing Act of 1909 and the National Health Insurance Act of 1911. Then comes the World War, the first war in modern European history in which the armies were citizen armies, in which every person, man, woman, and child, was directly concerned: in this pressing emergency Cabinet dictatorship was set up, and every detail of daily life was subject to regulation by executive orders and rules issued under the Defence of the Realm Acts. After the War, there was a return to pre-war ideals of government, but with a difference; for the years of war had not only resulted in unprecedented dislocation of industry and social conditions, they had revealed unsuspected deficiencies in the physique of the nation and had shattered once and for all, as far as England was concerned, the once popular doctrine of rugged individualism. With increasing governmental interference and increasing trust in the expert there went naturally an increasing delegation of legislative power. But the English are by tradition admirers of the amateur, and this feeling, as much as any reverence for the Constitution, contributed to the attempted reassertion of parliamentary control which began in 1929, only to be rudely interrupted in September 1931 on account of what appeared to many an emergency more terrible even than the World War.

A. THE PERIOD OF GROWTH

At the beginning of the nineteenth century the central government was chiefly of importance in matters international: it was responsible for defence and regulated exports and imports. Any effect it had upon the lives of the common people was either indirect or by a control exerted through the criminal law in matters of the peace. That public welfare and public order might stand roughly in the relation of cause and effect was an idea foreign to the legislators of that date. The more kindly side of government, poor-relief and education, was in the hands of local bodies: poor-relief under the direction of overseers of the poor; education, as far as there was any, still in the hands of the Church. As intermediaries merely between local authorities and a supreme Parliament stood certain rudimentary government departments headed by committees of the Privy Council or a secretary of state: and local autonomy, within a statutory framework and subject to control by the prerogative writs, was still a very real thing. But with the industrial revolution and the consequent specialisation of function — not to speak of the loss of local feeling occasioned by the flock to the towns — when dislocation at the Port of London might result in untold misery in Staffordshire, there grew up wider interests and wider loyalties. Simultaneously the pressure of events began to force the central government to take an interest in local affairs; by the Reform Act the landed gentry lost their control over seats in the Commons, and in retaliation began to inquire into factory conditions. They then gradually extended the principle of control over the morals and living conditions of the apprentice, — a principle cast into law by the millowners, — in order to safeguard the health and safety of workmen against the niggardly spirit of the owners themselves. The smashing up of the new agricultural machinery by the starved and apprehensive laborers of 1830 led gentry and manufacturers to join in the defence of what were mutual interests, and to put an end to the old system of the Poor Law. With the gradual extension of the franchise, it became the practice for parties to vie with each other in promising reforms, and so from 1870 onwards a new note creeps into legislation.

Before that date drastic reorganisation of the courts had begun with the delegation to the judges of the power to regulate their own procedure, and a series of Public Health Acts, at first adoptive but later compulsory, were the first steps in a fight against disease; to the same end were directed the Housing Acts. Nevertheless, until the end of the century Government only interfered where the shoe pinched hard: Merchant Shipping Acts arose from the capitalists' desire to keep the means of export working smoothly, and the recognition of Trade Unions in 1871 came not from any love of collective bargaining but only because the repressive measures of the criminal law were no longer adequate to dam the movement.

Measures inspired by "distributive justice," such as regulation of the hours of labour, were, however, at the end of the century beginning to replace reliance on "inexorable economic law." [1]   Till

[1] E. g. Railway Regulation Act, 1893.

then attempts to protect the weak had been based rather on senti-
ment than on any general policy of public welfare.[1] But with the
coming to power of the new government in 1906 a new era set
in: the Education (Provision of Meals) Act of 1906, the Old Age
Pensions Act of 1908, the National Health Insurance Act of 1911,
the Shops (Early Closing) Act of 1912, all show a sense of responsibility in the State for the well-being of its citizens, while the Trade
Boards Act of 1909 and the Coal Mines (Minimum Wage) Act of
1912 are recognitions that economic civil war is not only disastrous to workmen and expensive for employers but is against the
interest of the community at large.

Whatever the motives for its interference, it is clear that during
this period the State had changed its character, had ceased to be
soldier and policeman, and was rapidly becoming protector and
nurse. The central government therefore draws closer to the local
authorities, and begins by interfering haphazard to deal with
matters that had aroused popular indignation or political spite,
such as factories and the Poor Law, or with matters where local
authorities could of themselves do nothing (the prevention of the
spread of cattle disease, for instance), but ends by directing the
social policy of the whole country. And this direction is carried on
at first only on the petition of the local authorities,[2] later by the
control exercised through grants-in-aid [3] and the power of refusal,
and finally by direct intervention.[4]

Since this period is one of transition one would naturally expect
to find new methods of legislation existing side by side with the old.
And that is the case here. The essence of Blackstone's ideas of the
State, carried on by Dicey, the supremacy of Parliament as the
only department of government entitled to create new rights, is
reflected in at any rate a formal inability to distinguish between
the different types of legislation, general, local, and special Acts all
being printed in the body of the Statute Book,[5] in the effort to
provide for every conceivable case that might come up under the
Act, and in the treating of each situation as if it were removed toto

---

[1] E. g. An Act to Prohibit the Payment of Wages to Workmen in Public
Houses, 1883; Prevention of Cruelty to Children Act, 1889; Compulsory Load
Line Act, 1890; Shop Assistants Seats Act, 1899.

[2] E. g. Public Health Act, 1848. 11 & 12 Vict., c. 63, sec. 10.

[3] E. g. Education Act, 1902. 2 Ed. 7, c. 42, sec. 7 (4).

[4] E. g. Housing Act, 1925. 15 Geo. 5, c. 14, sec. 23.

[5] The writer of course realises the essential differences in parliamentary
procedure.

coelo from any other situation, however familiar. As a result, the grant of a pension, the setting up of a new local authority, and a survey of the whole field of local government are all put under the same head; for is not Parliament the source of all? But it is the wealth of detail in the Acts, and the apparently needless repetition of the same provisions in Act after Act upon the same subject matter that is the most striking. The machinery necessary for the erection of any new public building in London cannot differ materially with the site, and yet for each new building Parliament would pass a brand-new Act.[1] But this practice was not invariable; Parliament had already begun to generalise. The Public Health Act, 1875,[2] is a generalisation of this nature upon the health powers of local authorities, and the Electric Lighting (Clauses) Act, 1899,[3] is by its very title "An Act for Incorporating in one Act certain Provisions usually contained in Provisional Orders made under the Acts relating to Electric Lighting."

The bewildering statement of masses of detail was one of the slowly passing legacies from the old land law, but this characteristic is more than one of form. In the Thames Navigation Act, 1866,[4] savings are made in respect of "the trees at Temple Lock" (sec. 46) and "George Cherry's land" (sec. 47); in the Burgh Police (Scotland) Act, 1892,[5] every conceivable by-law that might strike the fancy of a whimsical local authority is set out at length; and who but a statistician can take any pleasure in a list of tolls and of all that may or may not be done in Harwich Harbor,[6] or in an exposition of the rates and the method of collecting the malt duty?[7] How far we have travelled since then is shown by the chaste austerity of the Seeds Act, 1920,[8] and the delegation in 1930 to the Minister of Transport of the power to frame a new highway code.[9]

The number of trivial amending Acts, and Acts "to remove doubts" or "to remove difficulties," made their collection im-

[1] Houses of Parliament Act, 1867. 30 & 31 Vict., c. 40; National Gallery Act, 1867. 30 & 31 Vict., c. 41, and a series of enactments dealing with the new courts in the Strand and the new offices in Whitehall.

[2] 38 & 39 Vict., c. 55.

[3] 62 & 63 Vict., c. 19.

[4] 29 & 30 Vict., c. 89.   [5] 55 & 56 Vict., c. 55.

[6] Harwich Harbor Act, 1865. 28 & 29 Vict., c. 120.

[7] Malt Duty Act, 1865. 28 & 29 Vict., c. 66.

[8] 10 & 11 Geo. 5, c. 54, sec. 7 (1).

[9] Road Traffic Act, 1930. 20 & 21 Geo. 5, c. 43, sec. 45.

practicable. But there can be no other way out where no modifying power is delegated. Likewise, in default of a power of adding to the things as to which an Act has effect, Parliament must itself by an Act passed through all three stages in each House and submitted for the royal assent add "cockles" to an Act expressed only to deal with "oysters and mussels." [1]

But it was during this period that the central government was taking new functions upon itself, and further using new methods to have its wishes carried into effect. The traditional methods of control through the criminal law, or through suits for penalties instituted by common informers, were no longer satisfactory, the first because you cannot put a corporation in gaol, and the second — even apart from the difficulty of finding the common informer — because it is often less expensive to pay penalties than, say, to install safety devices. Hence the appointment of inspectors under the Factory and Workshop Acts,[2] and of analysts,[3] and the device whereby when a local body makes default upon its statutory obligations the central government may step in and charge the cost to the local body.[4] This is, of course, the rational method of impressing Parliament's wishes upon the recalcitrant individual or local authority, and is now so familiar that it is easy to forget how radical a departure it is from prior practice. For one thing, it is fundamentally at variance with the general principles of the Common Law, which like the nineteenth-century God waits for you to commit the sin and then pounces. And how can there be inspectors, or how can the central government step in, if there is no apt executive machinery?

This difficulty was met in either of two traditional ways, the appointment of ad hoc commissioners or the setting up of a new committee of the Privy Council — for Orders in Council were not then, as now, a more picturesque type of departmental order.

These ad hoc bodies were normally independent of the central government; their awards or rules might be subject to confirmation by Order in Council and to be laid before Parliament, and the commissioners might be under a duty to lay an annual report of their proceedings before the Houses, but their policy, once they were appointed, was subject to no control unless they exceeded

---

[1] Fisheries Amendment Act, 1884. 47 & 48 Vict., c. 27.
[2] E. g. 1878. 41 Vict., c. 16, sec. 67.
[3] Sale of Food and Drugs Act, 1875. 38 & 39 Vict., c. 63, sec. 10.
[4] Seed Supply (Ireland) Act, 1880. 43 Vict., c. 1, sec. 10.

their statutory jurisdiction. Their field of action was narrow, but within that field immense grants of power were made to them; in 1801 the Enclosure Commissioners were empowered to make regulations with respect to allotments to be held in common "for the equitable enjoyment thereof or the participation of any produce growing or to grow thereon as such Commissioners may think beneficial and proper for the parties interested therein";[1] and by the Act of 1845 confirmation by the Commissioners of the valuer's award was declared to be "conclusive evidence that all the directions of the Act in relation to such an award . . . have been obeyed."[2] The Commissioners of Encumbered West Indian Estates could even alter the provisions of the Act under which they functioned whenever there was a conflict between the laws of England and the laws of the colony.[3] Some of these bodies were semi-permanent and of considerable importance, those for instance which regulated the Poor Law, supervised enclosure, or fixed railway rates; others were temporary, but still important, among them being the Oxford University Commissioners[4] and later the Electricity Commissioners,[5] involving as they did, respectively, the reorganisation of Oxford University and the rationalisation of electricity supply in England. A commission is, however, by its very nature anomalous; for it combines all three powers, legislative, executive, and judicial, and is in its own field a government in miniature. And since its true value lies in the application of the special knowledge and skill of certain named persons to a task of narrow scope and limited duration, such a body tends to be absorbed into the departmental system; this was the fate of the Land Commissioners[6] and the very recent Insurance Commissioners.[7] The history of the Railway Commissioners is rather different: this Commission is a very august body and is presided over by a judge of the King's Bench Division specially assigned.[8] It continued to combine rate fixing and judicial powers until 1921,

[1] Enclosure Act, 1801. 41 Geo. 3, c. 109, sec. 13.

[2] Enclosure Act, 1845. 8 & 9 Vict., c. 118, sec. 105.

[3] West Indian Encumbered Estates Act, 1854. 17 & 18 Vict., c. 117, secs. 66–68.

[4] Oxford University Act, 1860. 23 & 24 Vict., c. 23.

[5] Electricity Supply Act, 1919. 9 & 10 Geo. 5, c. 100.

[6] Their duties were transferred to the Board of Agriculture in 1889.

[7] Their duties have been transferred to a machinery supervised by the Ministry of Labour.

[8] E. g. 1913–1923, Lush, J., 1923–1928, Sankey, J.

but in that year the rating powers were transferred to a new Railway Rates Tribunal.[1]

There are still persons who favour government by statutory commission as less "bureaucratic" than the departmental system.[2] Surely the reverse is the case if by bureaucracy is meant the "new despotism." There may be excellent reasons for setting up a statutory commission, — to deal, for instance, with matters which must at all costs be kept free from any hint of political pressure,[3] — but there can be no doubt that a commission is outside even that control exerted by Parliament over the departments.[4]

The other method by which new problems were met was to entrust the new duties to the Privy Council, and it was thus that much of the machinery of justice was reorganised.[5] During the nineteenth century the Council goes once more through much the same process as its more vague counterpart did in the twelfth and thirteenth, when the Courts of Common Law began to sit apart at Westminster; but this time the movement is to Whitehall. In the days when the extent of delegation was slight the rule-making powers would be entrusted either to the Home Office [6] or to the Council.[7] If the delegation was to the Council, the powers would be exercised nominally by the issue of an Order in Council, but in reality by an office subject to the control of a committee: thus was exercised control over trade and education, besides the ancient disease powers. But in 1889 the powers over diseases and destructive insects passed to the Board of Agriculture, and in 1899 the Board of Education was set up. As for the trade powers, the Board of Trade is no different from any other Department and its President has a seat in the Cabinet, but in legal theory still the Board of Trade is a committee of the Privy Council. Now Orders in Council are employed only to give a departmental order a more than departmental sanctity; [8] but they are still the only orders which have any operation outside England.

[1] Railways Act, 1921. 11 & 12 Geo. 5, c. 55, sec. 20 (1).

[2] Lord Dawson, 80 Lords Deb. (5th Series), p. 314, March 12, 1931.

[3] E. g. the Interstate Commerce Commission in the United States, the Electricity Commission and the British Broadcasting Corporation in England.

[4] See Major Elliot, 254 Com. Deb. (5th Series), p. 2116, July 8, 1931.

[5] E. g. Judicature Act, 1873. 36 & 37 Vict., c. 66, secs. 27 and 32; Judicature Act Amendment Act, 1875. 38 & 39 Vict., c. 77, sec. 23.

[6] E. g. under the Factory Acts.

[7] E. g. under the Contagious Diseases (Animals) Acts.

[8] E. g. under the Defence of the Realm Acts — although incidentally in that case this gave the Inner Cabinet a chance to scrutinise the rules.

It is only after 1850 that there is a marked increase in the number of general legislative powers delegated to the executive. But it must not be supposed that the practice of delegation is as recent as that. After all there is the famous statute of 1539, — the Statute of Proclamations, — by which the King was given power with the advice of the majority of the Council to set forth proclamations to be obeyed, observed, and kept, as though they were made by Act of Parliament. It was passed, as the preamble states, "because sudden occasions arise when a speedy remedy is necessary," but it has been the fashion of late years to abuse the statute, and the phrase "Henry VIII clause" is now a vituperative way of describing, whether from the Bench or in Parliament, the "conclusive evidence" or the "have effect as if enacted in this Act" clauses. C. T. Carr points out, however, that despite the passage of the statute Parliament continued to function as before, that the proclamations contained nothing of importance, and that the Act should really be regarded as a parliamentary victory, as limiting the use of the prerogative to accord with the spirit of the Act.[1]

I have already made casual mention of the disease powers of the Privy Council, but Parliament early found it necessary to delegate them further than the Privy Council. By an Act of 1603 [2] "for the charitable relief and ordering of persons infected with the plague" it was provided (sec. 9) that it "shall be lawful for the justices of the peace, mayors, bailiffs and other head officers . . . to appoint [various special sanitary officers], to administer unto them oaths for the performance of their duties [which were specified in the Act] and give them other directions as unto them for the present necessity shall seem good in their discretions." This Act by section 9 (2) was only to last until the end of the first session of the next Parliament, and contemplated presumably that by then the duties might be described with more particularity. But no new Act was passed, and it was upon the model of the 1603 Act that the Lord Mayor of London founded his orders in the terrible year of 1665.[3]

Carr cites an Act of 1710 [4] by which the Privy Council was given power to make rules establishing quarantine during a plague of cholera, and the case of R. v. Harris in 1791 [5] shows the authority

---

[1] Delegated Legislation (1921), chap. 6.
[2] 1 Jac. 1, c. 31.
[3] Daniel Defoe, A Journal of the Plague Year (1928), pp. 45–47.
[4] 9 Anne, c. 2.   [5] 4 T.R. 202.

of such rules. There the prisoner was indicted for having come into England from abroad without performing quarantine, contrary to Orders in Council issued under section 1 of 26 Geo. 2, c. 6: section 5 of the Act, which established a penalty of £200, exactly covered the prisoner's case, but the Court nevertheless upheld the contention of the Crown, and convicted and sentenced him to imprisonment for an offence against the Common Law, the Court saying at p. 205 that "this Statute gave authority to the King in Council to make the order in question, and the disobeying it becomes an indictable offence at Common Law."

But the power to make rules and orders did not remain confined to the Privy Council or to this narrow class of occasions. The whole purpose of the appointment of bodies of commissioners was to remove what were then called purely administrative matters from the hands of Parliament, and so in 1801 the Enclosure Commissioners are found exercising a power which approximates to private bill legislation.[1] By the Glass Act, 1819,[2] the Treasury Commissioners are empowered to alter the regulations established by law for the protection of the revenue in the manufacture of glass, and the Poor Law Commissioners of 1834 "for executing the powers given them by this Act . . . are authorized . . . to make rules orders and regulations for the management of the poor . . . and for carrying this Act into execution in all other respects as they shall think proper."[3] By the middle of the century this practice is well established: in 1851 appear rules made by the local authority for the proper regulation of common lodging-houses,[4] and rules of the General Board for Scottish Prisons as to the carrying out of sentences of hard labor.[5] Under statutes passed during the next year the Council was to prescribe rules for preserving order on vessels bound for the colonies,[6] and the Secretary at War was to make regulations with respect to the militia, their pay, and what men are to be received [7] — not to mention those occasions whereon matters of procedure might be so prescribed.[8] In each of these

[1] Enclosure Act, 1801. 41 Geo. 3, c. 109, sec. 13.
[2] 59 Geo. 3, c. 115, sec. 4.
[3] Poor Law Amendment Act, 1834. 4 & 5 Wm. 4, c. 76, sec. 15.
[4] Common Lodging Houses Act, 1851. 14 & 15 Vict., c. 28, sec. 9.
[5] Prisons (Scotland) Act, 1851. 14 & 15 Vict., c. 27, sec. 7.
[6] Passengers Act Amendment Act, 1852. 15 & 16 Vict., c. 44, sec. 55.
[7] Militia Act, 1852. 15 & 16 Vict., c. 50, sec. 13.
[8] E. g. Appointments Act, 1851. 14 & 15 Vict. c. 82, sec. 7; Patent Law Amendment Act, 1852. 15 & 16 Vict., c. 83, sec. 3.

cases the rules had to be laid before Parliament after they were made, and were subject to annulment. Henceforward instances of delegation become progressively more frequent, until in 1919 sixty out of the one hundred and two Acts passed delegate legislative power.

But it is upon the more striking powers of the executive that I wish to touch, pointing out how respectable is their antiquity. When Lord Hewart speaks of the encroachments of the executive (majestic assumption!), or appeals to the public to see that the control of Parliament is reasserted, the man on the Clapham omnibus, unless he is unusually acute, might be tempted to believe in a bureaucratic plot newly hatched by the Civil Service after an excess of D.O.R.A. What control? Twenty years ago Parliament never did more than discuss the general principle of a bill; today it laboriously goes through the clauses one by one, and when the bill has become law bombards the Minister with intimate questions about its operation.[1] And there is no evidence that members were then less careless about the orders lying on the table. Nor is it safe to assume that there were then no grants of arbitrary power; for the nineteenth-century Statute Book reveals that any prostitute near a military camp who refused to submit to a physical examination might be imprisoned,[2] and that when the Board of Trade had reason to believe that any British ship was unfit to proceed to sea the Board might without more ado detain the ship for a survey.[3]

It is true that before 1900 there are only three instances in which a difficulty might be removed by order,[4] but it is not until the twentieth century that any drastic schemes of reorganisation are put into action to cause such difficulty to arise. And when in 1855 it was provided that "upon petition to Her Majesty in Council that by reason of the provisions of any local Act of Parliament difficulties have arisen, it shall be lawful for Her Majesty by Order in Council to suspend or alter any of the provisions of such local Act,"[5] there were heard no "ancestral voices prophesying war."

[1] See Sir Thomas Inskip, 226 Com. Deb. (5th Series), p. 2510, March 27, 1929.   [2] Contagious Diseases Act, 1866. 29 & 30 Vict., c. 35, sec. 28.

[3] Merchant Shipping Act Amendment Act, 1873. 36 & 37 Vict., c. 85, sec. 12.

[4] Local Government Act, 1888. 50 & 51 Vict., c. 41, sec. 108; Local Government Act, 1894. 56 & 57 Vict., c. 73, sec. 80; Metropolis Local Management Act, 1855. 18 & 19 Vict., c. 120, sec. 248.

[5] Metropolis Local Management Act, 1855. 18 & 19 Vict., c. 120, sec. 248.

As far as modification goes, on only four occasions [1] has Parliament permitted direct alteration by order of general directions laid down in a public Act, and three of those cases were before the beginning of the present century. Sections 371–383 of the Merchant Shipping Act, 1854,[2] are actually headed with the words "Subject to any alteration to be made by Trinity House," while section 33 of the Explosives Act, 1875, permits the Secretary of State to make rules altering the quite general provisions contained therein.[3]

Parliament felt no qualms, apparently, about the putting into operation of a statute by order,[4] or the addition by order to the schedule of more persons, places, or things as to which the Act was to have effect,[5] and the Bill of Rights did not deter it from reviving again the powers of dispensation and suspension — rightly, for rigid application of any principle will at its extreme result in hardship or nonsense. So that where the injunctions of the statute are in a particular case impossible of performance,[6] or unnecessary,[7] or work hardship,[8] an exemption may be granted. The same is true of the more general power of suspension: there is nothing to be said for punishing a newly created statutory nuisance unless the local authority has had time to put matters right,[9] and even the rights of labour may well be waived in an emergency.[10]

The Seeds Act of 1920 has come in for some criticism as a legislative novelty, but the principle upon which it is founded is correct and by no means new. There are some problems which are best dealt with by fashioning the remedy and then applying it where experience dictates; that is the rationale of the Act of 1876,[11] which directs the Secretary of State to prescribe by order what classes of

[1] Courts of Justice Salaries Act, 1869. 32 & 33 Vict., c. 91, secs. 14, 16; Judicature Amendment Act, 1875. 38 & 39 Vict., c. 77, sec. 24; Day Industrial Schools (Scotland) Act, 1893. 56 Vict., c. 12, sec. 3 (9); Motor Car (International Circulation) Act, 1909. 9 Ed. 7, c. 37, sec. 1 (b.)

[2] 17 & 18 Vict., c. 104, secs. 371–383.   [3] 38 Vict., c. 17, sec. 33.

[4] E. g. Copyright Act, 1852. 15 & 16 Vict., c. 12, secs. 2 and 4; Deserting Seamen Act, 1852. 15 & 16 Vict., c. 26, sec. 1.

[5] E. g. Carriage of Dangerous Goods Act, 1866. 29 & 30 Vict., c. 69, sec. 9; Salmon Fisheries (Scotland) Act, 1863. 26 & 27 Vict., c. 50, sec. 4; Notice of Accidents Act, 1894. 57 & 58 Vict., c. 28, sec. 2 (2).

[6] Coal Mines Regulation Act, 1872. 35 & 36 Vict., c. 76, sec. 22 (2).

[7] Truck Act, 1896. 59 & 60 Vict., c. 44, sec. 9.

[8] White Herring Fishery (Scotland) Act, 1861. 24 & 25 Vict., c. 72, sec. 5.

[9] Pollution of Rivers Act, 1876. 39 & 40 Vict., c. 75, sec. 3.

[10] Coal Mines Regulation Act, 1908. 8 Ed. 7, c. 57, sec. 4.

[11] Prevention of Crimes Amendment Act, 1876. 39 & 40 Vict., c. 23, sec. 2.

prisoners shall come under an Act of 1871 whereby prisoners generally were to be registered and photographed. The Cotton Cloth Factories Act which the House of Lords was so reluctant to pass in 1929 [1] has an exact counterpart in 1897. The problem before the Government in these cases was how to pass effectively into law the complicated report of a departmental committee on artificial humidification, and the solution they adopted was to provide by statute that "the Secretary of State may by order make regulations for giving effect to such of the recommendations contained in the report as he may deem necessary for the protection of health in cotton factories." There is no need to go all the way with Lord Banbury [2] and imagine the civil servants saying to themselves, "We do not care twopence for the House of Lords or the House of Commons: we are going to do them," in order to see the objection to delegating a power to select recommendations and put them into the form of regulations which cannot afterwards be questioned by the courts. Nevertheless there was no alternative, for any debate upon the technicalities of a bill of this nature would have been farcical; and it may well be that in the circumstances any objection at all is academic, for the committee was agreed to by both employers and employees, and they were the only persons conceivably to be affected.

What of the now famous Henry VIII clauses? Excluding consolidating Acts [3] and occasions where nothing but procedural trivialities are thus weightily safeguarded, [4] there are in all about twenty-two cases [5] in which it is provided that the making of a rule or an order or the confirmation of a scheme shall be conclusive evidence that all the requirements of the Act have been complied with; of these twenty-two cases seventeen are in statutes passed before 1900, among them being section 5 of the Extradition Act of 1870, [6] which is franker than them all, providing as it does that the Order in Council putting the Act into force with regard to nationals of other powers "shall not be questioned in any legal proceedings whatever."

Rules and orders expressed to "have effect as if enacted in the

---

[1] 72 Lords Deb. (5th Series), p. 930, February 14, 1929.
[2] 72 Lords Deb. (5th Series), p. 1187, February 28, 1929.
[3] E. g. Housing Act, 1925. 15 Geo. 5, c. 14, Sched. III, 2.
[4] E. g. Land Titles and Transfer Act, 1875. 38 & 39 Vict., c. 87, sec. 111.
[5] This does not include cases of quasi-judicial decision.
[6] 33 & 34 Vict., c. 52, sec. 5.

Act" fall sharply into two classes, the one where the department is itself the author of the rule or order and so — si parva licet componere magnis — performs roughly the functions of Parliament in enacting a Public General Act, the other where the department confirms, with or without modification, a scheme submitted to it by some body, — commissioners, local authority, or trustees, — and replaces Parliament in private bill legislation.

To deal with the first class first. It is true that the precise effect of the phrase in this connection is doubtful, *Lockwood's Case* [1] having lately lost what general significance it ever had; [2] true also that there is often a bewildering lack of coherence among those occasions wherein it occurs and those wherein it does not. [3] But taking it, despite Scrutton, L. J., [4] to be something more than a pleonastic expression of "what every schoolboy knows," in a search of the statutes from 1848 to 1931 I have been able to discover over 150 instances of this executive power to make miniature Acts of Parliament. Twenty-four of these cases, however, concern the power of the judges to make rules governing the issuance and form of writs or their own procedure, and should be counted as one. No less than eighty-two out of the remaining 130 odd are contained in statutes passed before 1900. They range in importance from rules regulating the manner of registering titles to land, [5] or the procedure before a maritime court of survey, [6] to an order in effect fusing the historic Courts of Common Law, the Exchequer, the Common Pleas, and the King's Bench into one division of the High Court, [7] or special rules to be made by the Secretary of State to govern special conditions in any mine. [8] Sometimes the rules and orders thus protected were far-reaching in their effects, Orders in Council declaring an area infected, or ordering the slaughter of a herd, [9] but it is not until after the close of the century that the code-making power

---

[1] Institute of Patent Agents *v.* Lockwood, [1894] A.C. 347.

[2] R. *v.* Minister of Health ex parte Yaffe, [1931] A.C. 494, *passim.* See also R. (Conyngham) *v.* Pharmaceutical Society of Ireland, [1899] 2 I.R. 132.

[3] Compare for instance 19 & 20 Vict., c. 56, which has no such phrase (sec. 44) with 18 & 19 Vict., c. 90 which has (sec. 3).

[4] *Ex parte Yaffe*, [1930] 2 K.B., p. 146.

[5] Transfer of Land Act, 1862. 25 & 26 Vict., c. 53, sec. 125.

[6] Merchant Shipping Act, 1876. 39 & 40 Vict., c. 80, sec. 30.

[7] Judicature Act, 1873. 36 & 37 Vict., c. 66, sec. 32.

[8] Coal Mines Regulation Act, 1887. 50 & 51 Vict., c. 58, sec. 51.

[9] Contagious Diseases of Animals Act, 1878. 41 & 42 Vict., c. 74, secs. 10 16, and 58 (2).

appears under this head,[1] and only after the World War is found wholesale delegation of so tremendous a power as that delegated in the Emergency Powers Act, 1920,[2] or the National Economy Act, 1931.[3]

It is during this period also that just as procedure by Provisional Order was beginning to replace procedure by private bill, so Provisional Orders were, in the interests of cheapness and despatch, beginning to give way to procedure by scheme in which the final approval rests with a department. In 1870 there were only twelve Acts confirming Provisional Orders, issued under the authority of seven principal Acts; in 1890 there were passed sixty-three such Acts, and the orders confirmed rested upon eleven enabling Acts, while during the year 1930 seventy-eight sets of Provisional Orders were confirmed. By 1899 the advantages of this procedure were so well recognised that the Private Legislation Procedure (Scotland) Act [4] was passed, and thereafter almost all Scottish measures in the nature of private bills have been submitted to Parliament in this manner. But the mere figures, unexplained, give no just indication of the extent of legislation thus in effect handed over to the executive. For while each private Act deals only with one situation, a confirmation Act consists normally of one section directing that the orders set out in the schedule shall take effect, and in the schedule there may be many orders.

Where the procedure is by Provisional Order it is Parliament, at least in form, which gives the orders their force, but in procedure by scheme the department stands in the place of Parliament and, in at least one case, is under no duty to lay the scheme with its confirming order on the tables of the two Houses.[5] It must not be forgotten that this procedure has its genesis very early; in 1855 the Commissioners for building new churches are empowered upon certain representations to draw up a scheme uniting the duties and revenues of neighbouring parishes, and upon approval by Order in Council and publication in the Gazette the scheme goes into force.[6] But in this class of cases the most striking developments take place

---

[1] E. g. Cremation Act, 1902. 2 Ed. 7, c. 8, sec. 7; Air Navigation Act, 1919. 9 Geo. 5, c. 3, sec. 1.

[2] Emergency Powers Act, 1920. 10 & 11 Geo. 5, c. 55; see also Restoration of Order in Ireland Act, 1920. 10 & 11 Geo. 5, c. 31.

[3] See also Abnormal Importations (Customs Duties) Act, 1931.

[4] 62 & 63 Vict., c. 47.

[5] Housing Act, 1909. 9 Ed. 7, c. 44, sec. 24.

[6] Union of Contiguous Benefices Act, 1855. 18 & 19 Vict., c. 127, secs. 2–7

in comparatively recent times. Not only did the nineteenth-century scheme deal merely with matters of trifling importance, such
as confirmation of voluntary agreements between railways[1] and
schemes by fiduciary bodies with respect to the trust property;[2]
it was also liable upon objection to give way to procedure by Provisional Order,[3] or sometimes even by private bill.[4] Beginning with
the Light Railways Act in 1896,[5] in which "by the application for
an Order authorizing a light railway something equivalent to a
railway Bill promoted in Parliament is intended,"[6] the procedure
was extended to create rights which twenty years before it would
have been unthinkable to create except by private bill. The chief
purpose of that Act was to save expense in small projects, but the
further new idea contained in the Scots Act of 1899 — to emphasize
the local nature of local legislation — was carried on in the 1909
Housing Act: under that Act[7] the improvement scheme drawn up
by the local authority is submitted to the Local Government
Board; the Board appoints an officer to hold a public local enquiry,
and upon his report confirms the scheme with or without modifying it — but as critic, not author.[8] After the War the device is
used for national reorganisation, not merely to solve the problems
of slum property in the cities but to rationalise industry; unemployment insurance schemes in special industries,[9] amalgamation
of mine-owners,[10] the regulation of coal production,[11] the re-group-
ing of the railways,[12] are all effected by ministerial orders not
subject to any confirmation by Parliament.

[1] Railway Companies Powers Act, 1864. 27 & 28 Vict., c. 120, secs. 4–17;
Railway Construction Facilities Act, 1864. 27 & 28 Vict., c. 121, secs. 6–17.

[2] See Endowed Schools Act, 1869. 32 & 33 Vict., c. 56, secs. 31–47; Endowed Schools Act, 1873. 36 & 37 Vict., c. 87, sec. 15.

[3] See Military Tramways Act, 1887. 50 & 51 Vict., c. 65, sec. 10 (2);
Public Health (Scotland) Act, 1897. 60 & 61 Vict., c. 38, sec. 145 (5).

[4] Railway Companies Powers Act, 1864. 27 & 28 Vict., c. 120, sec. 8.

[5] 59 & 60 Vict., c. 48.

[6] Per Phillimore, L. J., in R. v. Light Railway Commissioners, [1915]
3 K.B. 536, p. 554.

[7] Housing Act, 1909. 9 Ed. 7, c. 44, sec. 24.

[8] Per Lord Dunedin in R. v. Minister of Health ex parte Yaffe [1931]
A.C. 494, p. 504.

[9] Unemployment Insurance Act, 1920. 10 & 11 Geo. 5, c. 30, sec. 18.

[10] Mining Industry Act, 1926. 16 & 17 Geo. 5, c. 28, sec. 7 (4).

[11] Coal Mines Act, 1930. 20 & 21 Geo. 5, c. 34.

[12] Ministry of Transport Act, 1919. 9 & 10 Geo. 5, c. 50, sec. 3 (1) (d).
Subject to the requirement that the order must not involve an estimated expenditure of more than a million pounds.

Private bill legislation by the scheme procedure had thus attained recognition long before the close of the century; indeed in mere number the instances of the grant of such powers by statute between 1850 and 1900 immeasurably outweigh the instances between 1900 and 1931. But their scope is less sweeping. Before 1900 the schemes tend to be purely local, the union of parishes, the setting up of new bishoprics, readjustment of charities; it is only in the period following 1911 that on a general policy sketched out by Parliament are built by the executive branch gigantic new structures of social life. The same is true of the power to make general rules, although this has always been kept within narrower bounds, since on its face it bears more resemblance to the work which Parliament has in the past been accustomed to do than does the procedure by scheme.

Nevertheless by the 1890's the number and scope of statutory rules had become sufficiently great to require not only that they should be collected and made accessible, but that some regularity should be imposed on the procedure prior to their issuance. So that in 1893, despite opposition from several departments, the Rules Publication Act became law.[1] This Act, like much good legislation, laid down no new principle but merely made generally applicable principles which heretofore had governed the making of orders under the Statutes which set up the specific requirements. The provisions of (2) and (1) of section 1, giving opportunities of objection by persons likely to be interested, had already appeared in the series of Factory Acts, and it is probable that even where no such consultation was required the departments were in the habit of asking for advice; for a department has to act through human beings, and even the most hostile critics of the Civil Service must admit that the civil servant likes to tread softly. Again there were very few rules which were immune from publication in the Gazette, and fewer still not subject to be laid before Parliament. There is this grave difficulty, however: the Act does not catch either statutory rules which are required to be laid before Parliament for any period before the rules come into operation, — and these may often be of grave importance to private persons, — or rules made by the Local Government Board, the Board of Trade, or the Revenue Department, the first two of which have since 1893 become just those two departments which closely touch the life of every subject. To say that in such cases Parliament still has the

[1] 56 & 57 Vict., c. 66.

control does not meet the difficulty. The purpose of the Act was
not to increase that control, but to insure that draft rules should be
accessible for objection by all those members of the public who
might in any way be affected by their subsequent operation.
Worse even than that, as time and unexpected circumstances have
shown, is the fact that the Act does not apply to rules made under
the authority of other statutory rules; for most of the war-time
legislation of the departments was made under a code issued under
D.O.R.A., the Act itself being nothing but a grant of general power
to make rules.

Carr points out [1] that section 2, which permits the making of
"provisional rules" in case of urgency, has in at least one instance
been abused, for in 1920 certain provisional rules made in 1911
under the Old Age Pension Act were still in operation. The purpose
of the section is to insure that a scheme shall not be wrecked as the
result of delay occasioned by following the procedure of the Act
with regard to the issuance of rules, and in such a case the section
permits the rules to be issued without compliance with the formal-
ities, and provides that they shall remain valid until rules have
been properly issued under section 1. But clearly it is the duty of
the departments to regularise their proceedings as soon as possible;
section 2 should be amended to provide for the cessation of provisional rules at the end, say, of three months.

The objections here made are levelled not at any use made by
the departments of the gaps in this Act, but at the parum elegan-
tiae, as Gaius would say, in the legislation itself. The Act should
be amended to conform with experience, and no doubt will be so
amended when the Donoughmore Committee reports.

B. WAR PERIOD

From 1900 to 1914, as government entered more deeply into
everyday affairs, providing houses, old-age pensions, health insurance, and national education, the process of delegation, more
especially that of quasi-judicial power, steadily went on. The slow
change from sectionalism to centralisation, and all that that means
to the governmental process, was suddenly precipitated in 1914.
During the next four years, and for those years only, the nation
lived under what was in effect a central despotism. On August 7,
1914, Parliament passed the first Defence of the Realm Act [2] with

---

[1] Delegated Legislation (1921), p. 36.   [2] 4 & 5 Geo. 5, c. 29.

only one question asked, "Is the Act to be retrospective?" This Act was mainly declaratory of the royal prerogative, providing as it did by section 1 (1) that "his Majesty in Council has power during the continuance of the present war to issue regulations for securing the public safety and the defence of the realm." Orders in Council were immediately issued in the form of a code defining the powers in more detail and allotting their exercise to the several departments. Government was by a small inner cabinet, which set up new departments and "competent authorities," mainly military, to carry the regulations into effect. A committee, appointed by the Government and representing all the departments interested, prepared for submission to His Majesty in Council successive batches of regulations dealing with each situation as it arose. By the end of 1917 the regulations were 205 in number,[1] many of them mere covering authority for the making of departmental orders, orders by the Ministry of Food, for instance, under the regulations dealing with control of the food supply. By the Munitions of War Act of 1915[2] all labour, and by the Foodstuffs Act of 1914[3] all food, was in effect commandeered, and later by a series of emergency Acts[4] the export of all articles whatsoever, the slaughter of animals, and the sale of liquor were made subject to regulation by the executive. New machinery — Ministries of Food, Labour, Shipping, National Service, Munitions, and Reconstruction — was set up to deal with the duties thus thrust upon the central government. In all these cases the new ministries were shaped by Orders in Council;[5] Parliament gave *carte blanche*. By the Trading with the Enemy Act, 1914,[6] power was given to a secretary of state or the Board of Trade, in case of emergency, to authorise by written order any person appointed by him or them to inspect the books or documents of any person or company suspected of dealing with the enemy; by a similar Act of 1915,[7] dealings with any person not resident in the United Kingdom might be interdicted by mere proclamation.

[1] Review of Legislation (U.K.) (1917), 1 J.S.C.L. (3rd Series), Part II, p. 17 (1919).   [2] 5 & 6 Geo. 5, c. 54.   [3] 4 & 5 Geo. 5, c. 51.

[4] 4 & 5 Geo. 5, c. 64; 4 & 5 Geo. 5, c. 75; 4 & 5 Geo. 5, c. 77.

[5] New Ministries Act, 1916. 6 & 7 Geo. 5, c. 68; Ministry of Munitions Act, 1915. 5 & 6 Geo. 5, c. 51; Ministry of National Service Act, 1917. 7 Geo. 5, c. 6; New Ministries Act, 1917. 7 & 8 Geo. 5, c. 44.

[6] 4 & 5 Geo. 5, c. 87.

[7] Trading with the Enemy (Extension of Powers) Act, 1915. 5 & 6 Geo. 5, c. 98, sec. 1 (1).

Of course there were abuses, and of course there were complaints; and no doubt certain courses taken by the Government may not have been within the strict letter even of those liberal war-time grants of power.[1] But Scrutton, L. J., spoke for all the judges when he said in court that "a war could not be carried on according to the principles of Magna Charta,"[2] and in the Rhodes Lecture for 1918 that "the judges do not consider it their duty to run the war, and they take the view that the responsibility for the infringements of the previous liberties of British citizens rests with Parliament, who authorized those infringements, and with the executive, who exercise the powers conferred by Parliament."[3] The final word on the subject comes from a writer in the 1919 Journal of Comparative Legislation when it was all over: "Whilst the interference with individual liberty and private property, which was undoubtedly effected by these regulations, gave rise naturally to no little complaint and criticism, experience amply proved that in times of national emergency such as existed throughout the year under review [1917] some process of legislation on important matters, which is not subject to the delay and publicity of parliamentary procedure is vitally necessary for accomplishing the national purpose."[4]

C. The Period of Extension (1918–1929)

Conditions during the War everywhere gave rise to inflated conceptions of the supposed liberties enjoyed by the British subject before 1914, and when after the official end of the War in August 1921 good Tories dimly perceived that there was to be no immediate return to the halcyon days of Lord Coke's supremacy, they resolutely applied themselves to denouncing from the Bench, the the Lords, or the Press the wickedness of "bureaucracy" as a system abhorrent to the principles of the Constitution. And this is the real importance of the period, a growing consciousness that governmental organization no longer squared with legal theory. Thinkers parted into the two familiar camps of those who argue from what is and what might be, and those who argue from what was and what therefore ought to be. Both sides agreed that some-

[1] The Rule of D.O.R.A. 1 J.S.C.L. (3rd Series), Part I, p. 37 (1919).
[2] Ronnfeldt v. Phillips, (1918) 35 T.L.R., p. 47.
[3] The Rhodes Lecture, 1918. 34 L.Q.R. 130 (1918).
[4] Review of Legislation (U.K.) (1917), 1 J.S.C.L. (3rd Series), Part II, p. 17 (1919).

how or other a guiding principle for the future must be worked out, but as yet the subject was not ripe for popular indignation to bring it within the realm of practical discussion.

It was impossible, however, that this indignation should be long delayed. While the growth of delegation had been steady ever since 1850, its development had been so piecemeal, and the belief in parliamentary supremacy and the control of the courts through the prerogative writs so firmly founded, that it was not until 1915 that Dicey published his short article with its startling title.[1] Lawyers in the United States had not been so naive, and even in England there had been voices crying in the wilderness.[2] But in general the attitude was one of criticism directed against bureaucracy, and there was little realisation that to deal with new problems a new technique had been adopted, or that not all the laws of England were contained in the Statute Book and the Law Reports. Attention had been directed chiefly to the judicial powers of the departments; for the courts were already familiar with the exercise of legislative powers by subordinate bodies, — their own rules of court, the by-laws of local authorities and railway companies, to go no further, — and as it so happened the position of these legislative powers had been passed on in 1894 by the House of Lords.[3] But when the departments began to be entrusted with the decision of questions which closely touched the liberty and property of the individual the judges no longer held back. In 1911 Cozens Hardy, M. R., said that "he had seen signs of an attempt by the Executive to interfere with the judiciary and against all such attempts he could pledge himself and his colleagues to offer a strenuous resistance";[4] and in 1910 Farwell, L. J., had spoken in court of the "growing tendency" of the departments "to claim the right to act without regard to legal principles and without appeal to any Court."[5] The true nature of such comments is admirably brought out by this after-dinner pronouncement of Vaughan Williams, L. J.: "The greater evil follows that in due course people become accustomed to the idea that the rule of law is and ought to be

[1] The Development of Administrative Law in England, 31 L.Q.R. 148 (1915).

[2] See W. J. Ambrose, The New Judiciary, 26 L.Q.R. 203 (1910).

[3] Institute of Patent Agents v. Lockwood, [1894] A.C. 347. Recent developments, however, have led the Bench to rest the case upon the wording of the Act involved.

[4] 70 Sol. Journ., 534 (1911).

[5] Dyson v. A-G, [1911] 1 K.B., p. 423.

superseded by the discretionary powers of officials, and the tendency grows more and more to disregard the private interests of individuals, the conservation of which constitutes the weal of the community"; he concluded by commenting on "the growth of the new system, which is displacing the even-handed justice of the Courts by the control of Government officials." [1]

A more scientific, less partial attitude to the question was stimulated by C. T. Carr's essay, *Delegated Legislation*. This essay spoke with authority, for it came from one who was then assistant to Mr. Pulling, the inspirer and editor of the annual volumes of Statutory Rules and Orders,[2] and was less concerned to praise or blame than to show the extreme importance of this type of legislation, and to put it in proper historical perspective. Much of the material was descriptive, and went to show that a careful perusal of Statutory Rules and Orders was not only of prime practical importance in every-day life, but also to constitutional lawyers, since only by a clear understanding of the complete legislative process could they avoid vain repetition of unreal and theoretical conceptions of the State. Certain criteria of good rule-making were suggested, and upon a classification of the most familiar classes of rule-making powers the writer concluded that the practice was, subject to control, not only inevitable but positively beneficial. Discussion of the subject from both points of view has also since 1922 been carried on in the Journal of Public Administration.[3]

Leaving then the general question I wish to comment on the practice in this matter during 1918–1929. The period was one of social reconstruction and hence of great legislative activity; after the war-time experience of central control it was no longer felt possible to go back to sectionalism, and accordingly the task of reconstruction fell to the central government. The vast majority of important statutes deal with unemployment and health insurance, housing conditions, and the overhauling of every corner

[1] 20 Madras Law Journ., p. 285 (1910).

[2] Carr is now editor of S.R. & O.

[3] Sir Josiah Stamp, Recent Tendencies Towards the Devolution of Legislative Functions to the Administration, 2 J.P.A. 23 (1924); M. L. Gwyer, Powers of Public Departments to Make Rules Having the Force of Law, 5 J.P.A. 404 (1927); Harold Potter, Legislative Powers of Public Authorities, 6 J.P.A. 32 (1928); Sir John Anderson, Bureaucracy, 7 J.P.A. 3 (1929); Charles Christie, The Legislature and the Administration, 8 J.P.A. 367 (1930); B. M. Laing, The Legislative Functions of Government Departments, 8 J.P.A. 335 (1930); G. D. H. Cole, The Method of Social Legislation, 9 J.P.A. 4 (1931).

of local government; and the social aims of government were officially recognised in the names of three new ministries, Labour, Transport, and Health.

The Ministry of Health was set up in 1919 to succeed the Local Government Board and to take over from the departments their health powers. This new creation was destined in the space of a few years to gather into its hands perhaps the most extensive powers ever intrusted to one department: the new housing plans, the new rating scheme, the new structure of local government, the new poor law, were all first put into operation and administered by the Ministry of Health, and all this in addition to the control over the whole panel system of the country. For better or for worse the Minister controlled the financial policy of local authorities by means of the auditor,[1] could himself step in and create a housing scheme where the local authority made default,[2] and could even demand the dismissal of any paid officer of a board of guardians "who at any time refuses to carry into effect any rules orders and regulations made by the Minister." [3] By reason of his very power, and also because by the nature of his functions he was enabled to interfere in what had theretofore been considered the private life of the citizen, the Minister by his mere presence in the House drew attention to the extent of delegation. Parliament never had before it any of the housing schemes; [4] Acts of Parliament might be modified by his orders; [5] the Minister might by order "remove difficulties" and for that purpose do "any other thing." [6] None of these powers were in fact so extensive as they seemed, but when it was always the Minister of Health who rose to answer the questions of the "anti-bureaucrats," and always the Minister of Health who had to pilot through the more autocratic bills, the cry went up, "How long?" [7]

In the other departments the powers were no less extensive, but they were less concentrated. To the Ministry of Transport fell in

---

[1] Roberts v. Hopwood, [1925] A.C. 578.

[2] Housing Act, 1925. 15 Geo. 5, c. 14, sec. 52 (1).

[3] Poor Law Act, 1927. 17 & 18 Geo. 5, c. 14, sec. 31 (1).

[4] Housing Act, 1925. 15 Geo. 5, c. 14, sec. 52 (2).

[5] Rating and Valuation Act, 1925. 15 & 16 Geo. 5, c. 90, sec. 66; Public Health Act, 1925. 15 & 16 Geo. 5, c. 71, sec. 6.

[6] Rating and Valuation Act, 1925. 15 & 16 Geo. 5, c. 90, sec. 67 (1); Local Government Act, 1929. 19 Geo. 5, c. 17, sec. 130.

[7] 224 Com. Deb. (5th Series), p. 970, January 29, 1929. Speech by Mr. Greenwood in reply to the Minister of Health.

1919 the reorganisation of the railways,[1] and in 1924 of London traffic;[2] in 1930 this department was commissioned to draw up a new Highway Code,[3] and to supervise the road system from Whitehall. The dole, with its far-reaching effects on the lives of all workmen and their families, and its corollary, the attempted placing of workers through a centrally administered system of employment exchanges, was in the hands of the Ministry of Labour,[4] while the Board of Trade administered the schemes which dealt with the struggling coal industry.

The widening of the field of government brought to the departments new legislative powers, for who else could deal effectively with matters that required special knowledge of conditions and special skill? So that the words recurring most often in any postwar enactment are "The Minister may, if he thinks fit," and departmental regulations almost maintain their war-time numerical level. Half of the Acts passed during this period — almost all those that contemplate any great change in national life — delegate legislative power. A comparison in any year [5] of the bulk of the annual volume of Statutory Rules and Orders, closely printed on thin paper, with the bulk of the volume of Statutes, the print widely spaced and the paper thick, gives some idea of the disparity. Mr. Baldwin's average figures for 1926–1929 [6] were 50.6 statutes passed and 1408.6 rules and orders; an Act of Parliament was amended, adapted, extended, or otherwise affected by a statutory rule or order in eighty instances during 1921 and in sixty-six instances during 1930.[7] It must be remembered too that ministerial orders of a local character are not always printed: during 1921, 1400 orders of this type were made, in 1922 1000, approximately half of which were printed. Local schemes, those, for instance, made under the Housing Acts or the Mining Industry

[1] Ministry of Transport Act, 1919. 9 & 10 Geo. 5, c. 20.

[2] London Traffic Act, 1924. 14 & 15 Geo. 5, c. 34.

[3] Road Traffic Act, 1930. 20 & 21 Geo. 5, c. 43, sec. 45.

[4] See the Schedule to New Ministries Act, 1916, and the series of Unemployment Insurance Acts.

[5] Except 1925, when the new Property Acts, the Judicature Act, the Rating Act, and the Housing Act went through.

[6] 226 Com. Deb. (5th Series), pp. 24–26, March 4, 1929. Reply to Sir John Marriott.

[7] For figures in any year see the annual volume of the S.R. & O. and the yearly review of the legislation of the United Kingdom in the Journal of Comparative Legislation.

Act of 1926, are naturally never included, although they are as much legislation as is a private bill. The departmental regulations are often of so vast an ambit that they must be printed in the form of a code; in 1926, for instance, there were published the following codes: Emergency Powers Act Regulations and Orders, Army Act Rules of Procedure, and Workmen's Compensation Rules.

This is the scientific method of legislation, and the departments are not a little scientific in carrying it out. The "intent of Parliament" is not that shy modest virgin with whom the judges sometimes like to flirt; the department concerned knows her well. Legislation can only start in one of two ways: either the Government has promised a specific course of policy to the electorate, or else the department, acutely conscious of existing defects and anomalies, wishes a remedy to be applied. In either case the department will hold consultation with the Minister and the department will draw up the bill.[1] Many an ardent Minister must have cooled off about his precious measure when confronted by his right-hand man with facts and figures and "what happened last time," and must have consented to considerable modification. A civil servant is all the time behind the Minister, gives those written answers which look so pretty after the Minister's name in Hansard, and is ready at any moment to pop out from behind a pillar in the House to whisper urgently required information in his ear. And when the measure has passed into law, it is not enough for the department to make clear what it does not mean, but the legal jargon of the statute has to be interpreted in words of one syllable so as to be intelligible to the minor officials, perhaps in outlying districts, who are charged with the duty of administering it, of carrying out in fact the most difficult task of all, the creating of events out of words. To this end long pamphlets are published and distributed to those concerned, giving explanations and suggestions; in the Orange Book issued by the Ministry of Agriculture on the Marketing Act of 1931 the text of the Act itself takes up twenty-six pages, the irreducible minimum of interpretation takes fifty-seven. And if ever again the British Government has any money to spend and action is taken under the Act, pamphlets of suggestions will naturally be added.[2]

[1] Parliamentary counsel, however, will put it in proper legal form.

[2] For a collection of the more important pamphlets issued by the Ministry of Health see the Local Government Reports.

The characteristic feature of this period, then, is an ever-in-creasing reliance on the departments. For now procedure by scheme deals with projects more novel than any dealt with in a private bill;[1] out of the twelve instances that I have discovered of the use of the "power to remove difficulties" clause five are to be found in Acts passed between 1920 and 1930,[2] and the power to modify substantially an Act of Parliament is granted in no less than twenty statutes [3] between 1915 and 1929.[4] A torrent of rules pours forth, and on occasion "before the ink on the Act is dry" the department issues under it regulations more bulky than the Act itself.[5] But it does not follow, as some writers have thought, that power leads to arbitrary methods; at no other time has such an effort been made to take action on the basis of fact rather than conjecture. Not only has there been in the field of parliamentary legislation a steady stream of special commissions on the coal in-dustry, the machinery of government, the Poor Law, and local government, but a new star has appeared in the departmental firmament, the advisory committee.

The first definite reference in a statute to a departmental ad-visory committee, as opposed to a district committee, is found in the Board of Education Act, 1899;[6] even before 1914 Parliament had begun to take an interest,[7] and during the War, according to

[1] Housing Act, 1925. 15 Geo. 5, c. 14 (housing schemes); Mining Industry Act, 1926. 16 & 17 Geo. 5, c. 28 (district amalgamation); Coal Mines Act 1930. 20 & 21 Geo. 5, c. 34 (regulation of production); Housing Act, 1930. 20 & 21 Geo. 5, c. 39; Land Drainage Act, 1930. 20 & 21 Geo. 5, c. 44 (flood control); Agricultural Marketing Act, 1931. 21 & 22 Geo. 5, c. 42 (regulation of marketing).

[2] Unemployment Insurance Act, 1920. 10 & 11 Geo. 5, c. 30, sec. 45; Widows, Orphans and Old Age Contributory Pensions Act, 1925. 15 & 16 Geo. 5, c. 70, sec. 36; Rating and Valuation Act, 1925. 15 & 16 Geo. 5, c. 90, sec. 67 (1); Poor Law Act, 1927. 17 & 18 Geo. 5, c. 14, sec. 13 (1); Local Government Act, 1929. 19 Geo. 5, c. 17, sec. 130.

[3] See London Traffic Act, 1924. 14 & 15 Geo. 5, c. 34, sec. 10 (2); Local Government Act, 1929. 19 Geo. 5, c. 17, sec. 138 (3); Bridges Act, 1929. 19 & 20 Geo. 5, c. 33, sec. 3 (2) (e).

[4] Excluding those recent instances where the rule modifying has no effect until affirmatively approved by both Houses.

[5] See Marriott, Prologue to Crisis of English Liberty (1930), p. 10, where he uses these words in respect of the issuance by the Secretary of State of six rules and orders under an Act of two short clauses covering half a page; Factory and Workshop (Amendment) Act, 1929.

[6] 62 & 63 Vict., c. 33, sec. 4.

[7] See Census of Production Act, 1906. 6 Ed. 7, c. 49, sec. 9; Merchant

J. A. Fairlie,[1] no less than sixty such committees were set up by Order in Council or regulations. Since 1919 the practice has been continued and extended by statute.

An advisory committee is normally composed of very diverse elements, to represent the interests affected; it is sometimes composed of experts, and always of persons with some special knowledge. Take the three advisory committees contemplated in the Ministry of Transport Act, 1919.[2] The Rates Advisory Committee, set up according to section 21 (1) "for the purpose of giving advice and assistance to the Minister with respect to and for safeguarding any interests affected by any directions as to rates," was to be composed of five persons, a lawyer nominated by the Lord Chancellor, two representatives of trade and agriculture nominated by the British Chamber of Commerce, one representative of transportation interests nominated by the Minister of Transport, and one representative of labour interests nominated by the Minister of Labour jointly with the Trades Union Congress. In this case the Minister was directed before revising any rate to refer the matter to the committee for their advice, but it is more often left wholly within the discretion of the Minister to refer the matter or not as he chooses.[3] This type of committee has permanent duties, and is appointed and paid by the department.[4]

The Roads Advisory Committee by section 22 (1) was to advise the Minister with respect to "interests affected by the exercise of the powers . . . in relation to roads, bridges, and vehicles and traffic thereon," and was to consist of three types of persons, five representatives of highway authorities, five representatives of users of mechanical and horse traffic, and one representative of labour. Clearly this was not like the Rates Advisory Committee,

Shipping Act, 1906. 6 Ed. 7, c. 48, sec. 79 (1); Pilotage Act, 1913. 2 & 3 Geo. 5, c. 31, sec. 9.

[1] Advisory Committees in British Administration, 20 Am. Pol. Sci. Rev. 812 (1926).

[2] 9 & 10 Geo. 5, c. 50.

[3] London Traffic Act, 1924. 14 & 15 Geo. 5, c. 34, sec. 2; Therapeutic Substances Act, 1925. 15 & 16 Geo. 5, c. 60, sec. 4 (2); Unemployment Insurance (No. 3) Act, 1931. 21 & 22 Geo. 5, c. 36, sec. 2.

[4] With the Rates Advisory Committee compare Importation of Plumage Act, 1921. 11 & 12 Geo. 5, c. 16, sec. 3; Unemployment Insurance (No. 3) Act, 1931. 21 & 22 Geo. 5, c. 36, sec. 2; Tramways (Temporary Increase of Charges) Act, 1920. 10 & 11 Geo. 5, c. 14, sec. 2; Trade (Credits and Insurance) Act, 1920. 10 & 11 Geo. 5, c. 29, sec. 1 (1).

a collection of experts who might well expect to have work to do, but a sort of "grievance cabal."

Last of all, by section 23 (1) the Minister was directed to set up the most typical and most important of the Committees,[1] "a panel of experts, and of impartial persons of wide commercial and trading experience, appointed from nominees, after consultation with the various undertakings and interests concerned, of the various classes of undertakings affected by this Act, and of labour, trading interests, local authorities, and such other interests as he may deem desirable." Most advisory committees are of this nature. They are not paid, and meet seldom, but when they do meet are treated to a speech from the Minister,[2] and if there is business to be done they then proceed to discuss it, with the help of a public inquiry if necessary.

This new body is intended to effect two main objects, to provide the Minister with expert information, and to increase public confidence, possibly in two ways; for decisions and rules will be more kindly received when it is known that they have been taken on the advice of persons not concerned with the policy of the department, and the members of the committees will gain a valuable insight into the governmental process. They may even discover that civil servants, like most people, are anxious to be helpful.

The position of the committee with respect to the department is an odd one: it is there to advise at need; it can neither require that it be consulted nor ensure that the advice will be carried into effect. Indeed the words of the statutes, "may submit recommendations," "for the purpose of giving advice," are conclusive to the contrary. It is difficult to see how Parliament could provide

[1] With this committee compare the local consultative health councils under the Ministry of Health Act, 1919 (9 & 10 Geo. 5, c. 21, sec. 4), and the consultative committee of the Board of Education constituted by Order in Council of August 7, 1900, under the Board of Education Act, 1899, sec. 4. This latter committee was dropped during the War, but was revived by Order in Council of July 22, 1920, and re-established by statute in 1921 (Education Act. 11 & 12 Geo. 5, c. 51, sec. 2).

See also Agricultural Land (Utilization) Act, 1931. 21 & 22 Geo. 5, c. 41, sec. 16 (2); Mining Industry Act, 1920. 10 & 11 Geo. 5, c. 50, sec. 4; Dyestuffs (Import Regulations) Act, 1920. 10 & 11 Geo. 5, c. 77, sec. 2 (3) and (6).

See on the whole matter Encyclopedia of the Social Sciences, under Advisory Boards; J. A. Fairlie, Advisory Committees in British Administration, 20 Am. Pol. Sci. Rev. 812 (1926).

[2] See London Times, November 27, 1931, p. 10, col. 3, for an account of the meeting of the Consultative Cinematograph Committee.

otherwise: to make the report of the committee binding on the Minister would be to remove to it the real power of decision, and thus the Minister would be enabled to shelter behind the committee. Worse still, administrative interpretations of the Act might be made by persons in no way intimate with the problems of administration. As it is, this new development has been attacked as encouraging irresponsibility in the Minister: for at any rate in theory, delegation to a department is merely delegation to the Minister, while the insertion of an advisory committee over which the Minister had little if any control would make the theory too transparent even for the rigid parliamentarian. But this opens up the whole question of parliamentary control, which I do not propose to canvass, beyond agreeing with Mr. Maxton that the real vice lies elsewhere.[1] Another valid criticism is their uselessness;[2] but advisory committees may well achieve just those results which some writers claim are attainable only by the hardly practicable method of functional devolution, and their present defects may well be overlooked if their mere existence — which should be more widely known — has the effect of increasing public confidence in the executive.

D. PERIOD OF REGRESSION (1929 TO THE PRESENT)

This period marks a slight regression, not in the extent of the powers delegated to the departments — for this is the period of the Land Drainage Act, the Local Government Act, the Road Traffic Act, and the Agricultural Marketing Act — but in the freedom to use them, and is interesting for the increasing animus with which Parliament, judges, and public alike speak of the "bureaucracy."

[1] 254 Com. Deb. (5th Series), p. 2182, July 8, 1931. "Every hon. member knows that our troubles in this House do not arise because power is distributed in too many hands, but because, in actual practice, in this Chamber power is concentrated in far too few hands. The one man who is responsible for the financial affairs of this Parliament can dominate and dictate and direct the whole policy of Parliament."

[2] 254 Com. Deb. (5th Series), p. 2139, July 8, 1931. Mr. Stanley: "The Committee set up under this Bill is absolutely powerless: it has absolutely no functions whatever. Unless the right hon. Lady chooses to send certain matters to it for reference, it will never have a job of work to do. If she does send certain recommendations to it, she can ignore its report when it makes it. These men may be selected for their knowledge and experience of the working of these Acts. They may see under their noses anomalies and abuses continuing which they know ought to be remedied but they are absolutely powerless to do anything in the matter. They have no power to investigate and no power to report."

In 1925 Professor J. H. Morgan introduced a pleasing moral note into the controversy when he wrote, "No one can accuse our own [judiciary] of having encroached on the proper functions of the Executive — a fact which to my mind makes the recent usurpations of judicial functions by the Executive all the more unwarrantable." [1] C. T. Carr chimed in from the side of the angels and confessed to his "disillusionment" at being "shown the other side of the picture" to Dicey's Rule of Law. [2] On three occasions in April 1928 [3] the Law Lords gathered en masse to defend the Constitution against an innovation introduced by a lawyer greater than them all. [4] On January 30, 1929, not even the efforts of Sir Henry Slesser could prevent the passage of the "power to remove difficulties" clause in the Local Government Bill [5] — although later the wording, but the wording only, was amended. On March 27 Sir John Marriott, having failed to shock Mr. Baldwin, [6] introduced the subject sideways into the debate on the Easter adjournment. [7] On October 30 Lord Sankey appointed a committee to consider "the powers exercised by or under the direction of Ministers of the Crown by (a) delegated legislation, (b) judicial or quasi-judicial decision, and to report what safeguards are desirable or necessary to secure the constitutional principles of the supremacy of Parliament and the supremacy of the Law." On November 2 the Lord Chief Justice published *The New Despotism*, and was universally applauded for what has been called extravagant rhetoric with a core of truth. [8] On March 6, 1930, the Court of Appeal delivered their unanimous judgment in the case of Yaffe, a judgment less remarkable for what was said than for how it was said, [9] and from comments on legislative technique the same court had advanced by March 28 of the next year to gratuitous criticism of social policy. [10] In Sir John Marriott's prologue to a book of his

[1] Remedies against the Crown, an introductory chapter to Robinson's Public Authorities and Legal Liability, p. xliv.

[2] Review of (1) by C. T. Carr in 42 L.Q.R. 265 (1926).

[3] Debates on Advisory Opinions, 70 Lords Deb. (5th Series), pp. 614, 756, 795; and see p. 914.

[4] Lord Birkenhead.

[5] 224 Com. Deb. (5th Series), p. 969, January 30, 1929.

[6] 226 Com. Deb. (5th Series), pp. 24–26, March 4, 1929.

[7] 226 Com. Deb. (5th Series), p. 2505, March 27, 1929.

[8] 1 Political Quarterly (1930), p. 127.

[9] R. *v.* Minister of Health, ex parte Yaffe, [1930] 2 K.B. 90.

[10] R. *v.* Minister of Labour, ex parte National Trade Defence Association

published in 1930, *The Crisis of English Liberty*, words like "ambitious civil servants," "autocracy," "danger" stand out from the page. Finally in April 1931 a volume of essays by Mr. C. K. Allen was published entitled *Bureaucracy Triumphant*, in which occurs the following sentence: "The regulations of departments and local authorities are created by the tortuous processes of the official mind, and curtained from the vulgar gaze by departmental discretion."[1] No wonder that with the students of constitutional law so partial in their judgments the Government found their most harmless measures obstructed by ill-placed criticisms.[2]

There is little doubt that by reason of the extension of principles long recognised a minor revolution had taken place in the framework of government — and this in the short space of ten years. But there had been a major revolution in the expectations of every British subject; for the first time in English history an avowedly Socialist party was in the ascendant, and its ideas coloured, even directed, the policy of the Liberals and the Conservatives. Government, no longer content with reducing order out of present chaos, tried to go back to first causes and by opportune regulation to prevent the occurrence of tragedies long accepted as the will of God. So Westminster came to deal with the problems of the individual trade, but being unsuited by its very nature to do anything except enunciate a series of those "abstract principles which do not decide concrete cases," left with Whitehall the practical side of the process, which had always been the latter's concern but had theretofore been more a mechanical carrying out of precise orders. Now the process became preëminently one of creative interpretation.[3]

But the picture put before the public has been incomplete. The civil servant, bound by the Franciscans' "triple vow of poverty, anonymity, and obedience," was unable to reply to the charge of arbitrary dealing; a few, having retired, could meet the attack in

(reported in London Times March 28, 1931), per Scrutton, L. J.: "One might doubt whether it would really be any better when anything a British citizen wanted to do was regulated for him by orders of the Minister on the advice of the Civil Service, but that was a matter for Parliament and not the Courts."

[1] At p. 8.

[2] See 247 Com. Deb. (5th Series), p. 1939, February 4, 1931. Comment of Mr. Attlee.

[3] Compare the Trade Boards Act, 1918, with the Trade Boards Act, 1909; or the machinery of the Widows Orphans and Old Age Contributory Pensions Act, 1925, with the machinery of the Old Age Pensions Act, 1908.

general terms.[1] The highest court in the land on each of the four occasions in which the general question has come up has discharged the department concerned without a stain on its character, and has reversed or varied vitriolic judgments of the Court of Appeal, one of which went on the basis of denial of natural justice;[2] and the Attorney-General was forced to remind Sir John Marriott that "sometimes the learned Lords in the final court of appeal have expressed disagreement with criticisms of the use of departmental powers in particular cases."[3] Indeed the silence of the House of Lords in *Yaffe's Case*, and the fact that they found themselves able, while denying the general contention, to uphold the scheme as modified and confirmed by the Minister, is instructive as a comment upon Mr. Allen's statement that "a study of the narrative of facts . . . will show the reader how arbitrary and inquisitorial was the administrative procedure throughout."[4]

Nevertheless the "drive" instituted by the legal profession left its mark on the legislation of this period (despite a tendency to wait for the Donoughmore Committee to report[5]) in the attempted reassertion of parliamentary control. Whether real control of detail is practicable, or if practicable, to be desired, is another matter.

The provision so strongly objected to which makes the orders or the rules of the Minister to "have effect as if enacted in the Act" is not found in the Housing Act of 1930, the Land Drainage Act of 1930, or the Agricultural Marketing Act of 1931 — finality being attained otherwise. Instead, it is provided that within a certain specified time after the making of the confirming order an application may be made to the High Court to question its validity on the ground that it is not within the powers of the Act or that any requirement of the Act has not been complied with; if the Court is satisfied upon the hearing of the application that the order is not within the powers of the Act, or that the interests of the applicant have been substantially prejudiced by the require-

[1] E. g. Stamp, Recent Tendencies Towards the Devolution of Legislative Functions to the Administration, 2 J.P.A. 23 (1924).

[2] See the whole course of litigation in *Lockwood's Case*, 20 S.C. (4th Series) 315, [1894] A.C. 347; Board of Education *v.* Rice, [1909] 2 K.B. 1045, [1910] 2 K.B. 165, [1911] A.C. 179; Local Government Board *v.* Arlidge [1913] 1 K.B. 463, [1914] 1 K.B. 160, [1915] A.C. 120; *Yaffe's Case*, [1930] 2 K.B. 90, [1931] A.C. 494.

[3] 226 Com. Deb. (5th Series), p. 2512, March 27, 1929.

[4] Allen, Bureaucracy Triumphant (1931), p. 78.

[5] 77 Lords Deb. (5th Series), p. 759, May 19, 1930. Earl de la Warr.

ments of the Act not having been complied with, it may quash the order.[1] After that the order is not subject to certiorari. This provision (which is not new,[2] but has only in the last year or two been generally adopted) is eminently sensible, for it combines that finality which is essential for every scheme involving much thought and money with an adequate protection to the individual owner. The scandals from a social point of view of the *Derby Case* and *Yaffe's Case*, whereby great improvement schemes were held up for months by slum owners upon technical points,[3] are now less likely to be repeated.

The "conclusive evidence" clause, which has an even stronger effect than the clause dealt with above,[4] has also met with criticism and amendment. In the Land Drainage Bill the House of Lords on the representation by Lord Dynevor that "the Minister says everything is all right whether it is within the law or without" substituted "prima facie" for "conclusive," [5] and by section 90 (8) the confirmation by the Minister of Transport of an order establishing a parking place under the Road Traffic Act of 1930 [6] is "evidence" merely that the requirements of the section have been complied with. However, the clause turns up again in the Agricultural Marketing Act, 1931,[7] — wherein there is nowhere any opportunity for review by the courts: but the scheme cannot come into operation without the positive approval of Parliament, and there is plenty of opportunity given to persons aggrieved to register their disapproval on the poll as to whether the scheme shall remain in force.[8]

Another bone of contention has been the grant of power to a department to modify the provisions of an Act of Parliament; members clearly recognized the necessity of such a provision to

[1] Housing Act, 1930. 20 & 21 Geo. 5, c. 39, sec. 11 (3); Land Drainage Act, 1930. 20 & 21 Geo. 5, c. 44, Sched. II, Part III, 2; Public Works Facilities Act, 1930. 20 & 21 Geo. 5, c. 50, Sched. I, Part III, 2; Poor Law Act, 1930. 20 Geo. 5, c. 17, sec. 142.

[2] E. g. Educational Endowments (Scotland) Act, 1882. 45 & 46 Vict. c. 59, secs. 21–32.

[3] R. *v.* Minister of Health, ex parte Davis, [1929] 1 K.B. 619; *Yaffe's Case,* [1930] 2 K.B. 90, [1931] A.C. 494.

[4] *Ex parte Ringer,* (1908) 25 T.L.R. 718; and see the judgment of Scrutton L. J., in *Yaffe's Case,* [1930] 2 K.B. 144.

[5] 77 Lords Deb. (5th Series), p. 932, May 20, 1930.

[6] 20 & 21 Geo. 5, c. 43.

[7] 21 & 22 Geo. 5, c. 42, sec. 1 (8).

[8] 21 & 22 Geo. 5, c. 42, sec. 3.

prevent the introduction into the Act of needless special detail, but it seems probable that in the future such an order will require the affirmative approval of Parliament before coming into force.[1] But it is early yet to prophesy, for the Agricultural Land (Utilisation) Bill provided for the application to proposed corporations of the Companies Act "subject to such modifications as may be expressed by Order," and there was no provision for anything except annulment by Parliament,[2] while schemes under the Town and Country Planning Bill, 1931, were to be enabled to suspend the operation of any statutory enactment.[3] In any case it is difficult to decide when a rule does or does not adapt or modify an Act of Parliament, and to meet this difficulty the whole of the Mental Treatment Rules, 1930, had to be thus approved.[4] Neither does it seem probable that the traditional inertia of members will fail to extend to such resolutions; when the resolution to carry into effect certain modifying rules under the Local Government (Scotland) Act was made in the House of Commons, a mere handful was there, and the Speaker was asked to take notice that there were not forty members present.[5] A suggestion was once made that the Minister of Transport's regulations under the Road Traffic Act, 1930, should be subject to modification by Parliament when laid before it, but was dropped because in case of a difference between the two Houses on the regulation there was no machinery for settling the dispute.[6]

The practice of requiring the positive approval of Parliament whenever the rules or confirmed schemes are likely to be far-reaching in their effects [7] was continued in the Road Traffic Act, 1930, and applied to the Highway Code,[8] an elaborate series of rules by the Minister on good driving and good road marking, and

---

[1] Local Government Act, 1929. 19 Geo. 5, c. 17, sec. 130; Local Government (Scotland) Act, 1929. 19 & 20 Geo. 5, c. 25, sec. 76 (1); Road Traffic Act, 1930. 20 & 21 Geo. 5, c. 43, sec. 10 (4); Mental Treatment Act, 1930. 20 & 21 Geo. 5, c. 23, sec. 15 (2).

[2] 247 Com. Deb. (5th Series), p. 1936, February 4, 1931.

[3] 251 Com. Deb. (5th Series), p. 299, April 15, 1931.

[4] See Lord Sankey, 80 Lords Deb. (5th Series), p. 486, March 24, 1931.

[5] 247 Com. Deb. (5th Series), p. 1588, February 2, 1931.

[6] 76 Lords Deb. (5th Series), p. 321, January 27, 1930.

[7] See Electricity Supply Act, 1919. 9 & 10 Geo. 5, c. 100, sec. 7 (2); Safeguarding of Industries Act, 1921. 11 & 12 Geo. 5, c. 47, sec. 2 (4); Land Drainage Act (20 & 21 Geo. 5, c. 44) with reference to approval on the promotion of or opposition to bills creating new catchment areas.

[8] Road Traffic Act, 1930. 20 & 21 Geo. 5, c. 43, secs. 45 (2) and 10 (4).

the Commons finding that, in spite of the recommendation of the Royal Commission, it was quite impracticable to fix the speed limit by statute, scheduled a limit and provided that it could not be varied except by regulations thus affirmatively approved.[1] In the original draft of the Agricultural Marketing Bill the schemes were to be laid in draft before both Houses for a twenty day period; and thereafter the confirming order of the Minister gave them binding force, but the clause was amended in committee and section 1 (8) of the Act demands a resolution of approval by each House. A like approval is necessary for the revocation of any scheme.[2] It is interesting to note that this procedure was adopted only once in the Statutes of 1926, not at all in 1927, once in 1929, but nine times in 1930: of those nine, seven are cases in which a resolution is necessary to bring schemes or rules into operation; the other two are respectively concerned with disapproval, and continuing the validity of a set of rules after the expiration of three months.

The Government showed symptoms of a desire to tread softly and proceed by Provisional Order in the Land Drainage Bill, where any addition, subtraction, or alteration was to be made in the grouping of the catchment areas contained in the schedule, and was not to be turned from the path of reverence for the Donoughmore Committee by any representations of expense or inconvenience.[3] And a new variation in this time-honored procedure was inserted in the Public Works Facilities Act, 1930,[4] when it was provided by section 1 (9) that the confirming bill "shall be deemed to have passed through all stages up to and including committee, and when the Bill has been read and passed a third time the like proceedings shall be taken in the second House of Parliament."

A suggestion was made in the debate on Housing (No. 2) Bill that where the Minister confirmed a scheme with a modification not recommended in the report of the person who held the inquiry he should lay the report before Parliament with the reasons for his variation and modification; but the Government refused to accept the amendment on the ground that it would be a reversal of all prior practice dealing with these confidential reports, and for authority referred to the late Lord Moulton and Lord Shaw.[5] Never-

---

[1] Sched. I.   [2] Sched. I, Part II (6).
[3] 77 Lords Deb. (5th Series), p. 755, May 19, 1930.
[4] 20 & 21 Geo. 5, c. 50.
[5] 78 Lords Deb. (5th Series), p. 656, July 21, 1930.

theless the Land Drainage Act forces the Minister to lay before Parliament a report giving particulars of any question referred to him, and the reasons for his decision,[1] there being no question here of a confidential report made to the department by a person not in the employment of the department. That is a new departure, but there is nothing new in section 10 of the Agricultural Marketing Act by which an annual report of all schemes then in operation must be presented.[2]

Thus, although there was no slackening off in the number and the extent of the powers granted to departments it is clear that there was a substantial reassertion of parliamentary control — at any rate on paper.

But the control thus begun was not destined to be continued. In September 1931 England found itself in the midst of a financial crisis, a National government was rapidly formed, and the Socialist party, at whose allegedly bureaucratic measures some of these drastic controls may have been aimed, went into opposition. The Government then introduced and passed the National Economy Act. This measure empowered the Government to issue Orders in Council to reduce expenditures in certain services scheduled to the Act: this power was to last for only one month, but the orders when made were to stand until revoked by an Act of Parliament. The extent and nature of the cuts nowhere appeared in the Act, but were set out in a White Paper to which the Government pledged itself — and this although the economy plans included not only a ten per cent reduction in all salaries and pensions but also an increase in the rate of contribution to the unemployment insurance fund. The Prime Minister in the House of Commons [3] and Lord Reading in the Upper House [4] were insistent on the fact that the measure was to be justified on the grounds of emergency alone, and from this point of view it does not differ greatly from the Emergency Powers Act.[5] But that Act was passed not in the middle of a crisis but to anticipate one, and did not grant what are in effect taxing powers; nor was there in the 1931 Act any provision for laying any of the orders before Parliament. That there was an

[1] Land Drainage Act, 1930. 20 & 21 Geo. 5, c. 44, secs. 7 (5) and 12 (2).

[2] See Ecclesiastical Commissioners (Amendment) Act, 1850. 13 & 14 Vict., c. 94, sec. 26; Contagious Diseases (Animals) Act, 1878. 41 & 42 Vict., c. 74, sec. 59.

[3] 256 Com. Deb. (5th Series) p. 419, September 11, 1931.

[4] 82 Lords Deb. (5th Series), p. 169, September 30, 1931.

[5] 1920. 10 & 11 Geo. 5, c. 55.

emergency and that intelligent discussion of the matter might —
but might not — have precipitated disaster is beyond dispute.
Nevertheless, so uncontrolled a grant of power had never till then
been made to the executive.

This emergency government then found that it was not sure of
its position in the country, and after a general election a new
National government was returned to power. On the 17th of November the Abnormal Importations (Customs Duties) Bill came
before the House of Commons in committee.[1] By this bill the
Board of Trade was empowered to impose by order duties up to
100 per cent upon any article or articles in Class III of the Imports
and Exports List; the Act was to be in force for six months, and
any orders made under it were to take effect at once but were to
be laid before Parliament and be subject to revocation for the space
of twenty-eight days.[2] These orders were to have all the force of
statute. The bill passed and duly became law. Its passing is remarkable for three reasons. The powers delegated are more nakedly
powers of taxation even than those of the Economy Act. Second,
it is by executive action that a vital change in the policy of the
country is being inaugurated. Finally, it is difficult to see just what
emergency there is — except an emergency created by fears of
traders abroad as to the tariff policy of the Government.

Delegation can go no further; but how far a precedent is created
by these Acts depends upon the meaning that may in the future be
put on the word "emergency."[3] One thing is certain: at the very
moment when the whole question of the scientific method of legislation was to come up for review, that method has been used to
mask just that irresponsibility most deplored by its Tory critics,
and to enable a dictatorship — perhaps a necessary and benevolent
dictatorship — to be set up within the legal frame work of the
Constitution.

[1] 259 Com. Deb. (5th Series), p. 723.

[2] But this provision was not very material, for two reasons: first the over-
whelming majority commanded by the Government, even on financial policy;
and second, the fact that the Act had only been in operation about a fort-
night when Parliament went into recess for nearly two months.

[3] See Mr. Clynes in 256 Com. Deb. (5th Series), p. 436, September 11, 1931.

CHAPTER II

DELEGATED LEGISLATION TODAY

ANYONE who sets out to inquire into any aspect of the work of the government departments in England today is faced with a difficulty raised by the use of the phrase "administrative discretion." It has always been difficult, and with the increasing scope of governmental interference it has become almost an impossibility, to discriminate between a legislative and a so-called administrative discretion. The task is not lightened by the fact that the courts have tended to give the name "administrative" to any acts of subordinate bodies with which they did not feel justified in meddling. Owing to the existence of a great number of semi-autonomous bodies, the Guardians of the Poor, the Enclosure Commissioners, and the licensing justices, for instance, whose discretion was within its limits absolute, control by the courts has always taken the form of defining those limits, and the judges in order to put into force their ideas of how the machine should run — and that is a factor to be reckoned with, if we follow the school of "hunch jurists" [1]— have been forced to correct the decisions of these bodies on the ground that they erred in law in mistaking the limits of their powers. The law of ultra vires is curious not only for the very different uses to which it has been put, anything from the testing of a State statute by the standard of the Constitution of the United States to the testing of the issue of new shares by the corporate charter, but also because in applying it the courts stand as it were apart from the body whose actions they pass in review. "The situation in England," it has been said, "is affected in every direction by the fact that the modern bureaucratic departments have succeeded to local self-governing bodies with mixed administrative and legal attributes, and that the control of the High Court is still exercised mainly by writs of mandamus and certiorari, i. e. still from the point of view of an outside jurisdiction." [2] The system has its advantages, among them that of ensuring substantial freedom of action to the administrative bodies, but on the other side of the account must be placed the lack of coherence between the

[1] See Jerome Frank, Law and the Modern Mind (1930).
[2] Vinogradoff, Collected Papers, vol. II, p. 381.

various lines of cases, the fortuitous nature of the interference, and worst of all the apparent inability of the courts to look through questions of technical procedure to questions of substance — and this though in matters strictly legal they have travelled far since the days of Baron Parke.

An "administrative discretion" means then in law any discretion with which the courts will not interfere. But there are two other senses in which the word administrative is commonly used. It has become fashionable ever since Dicey's famous article [1] to institute comparisons between the law which in England clusters around the prerogative writs, and the system of French administrative law — comparisons usually unfavourable to the English procedure.[2] It is a pity that a term applied to a system which has but few resemblances to the English method of judicial control of governmental agencies should have been imported to give a label to a heterogeneous collection of decisions on sharply distinct lines of cases; but the vice lies deeper than that, in the connotation to a lawyer of the word "law." Hooker defined law as rules whereby actions are framed, Salmond as the rules enforced in the courts. In Salmond's definition the courts play an essential part, but Hooker, looking more, I suppose, to the custom from which all ancient law took its origin, — and upon which even modern statutory law depends for its observance, — laid his emphasis upon what we should now call its social and psychological aspects, and implicitly recognised law as a formal statement of what men habitually do in the manifold relations of life. Lord Hewart was only adopting the traditional standpoint of a lawyer when after an examination of the functions of the modern government departments, in which he found that no more than half of the picture could be seen in the Statute Book and the Law Reports, he characterised the whole process as administrative lawlessness. If his premises are correct, if, that is, Dicey's Law of the Constitution is read without attention to his acknowledgment of the existence of extra-legal factors, then Lord Hewart's conclusion inevitably follows. But when he assumes in his premises that a court is competent to pass upon all matters involving the application of standards, and that, because in the past courts have exercised powers

[1] The Development of Administrative Law in England, 31 L.Q.R. 148 (1915).

[2] See The New Despotism, chap. 3, Administrative Law; chap. 4, Administrative Lawlessness.

remaining to them from a period in history when justices in eyre exercised taxing powers, and justices of the peace were in substance if not in form a part of the executive, they should be granted the control of any new powers which resemble those now controlled by the King's Bench, it is impossible to agree.

When, however, the phrase "administrative discretion" is used in contradistinction to "legislative discretion" it is supposed to mean a discretion which is of the same nature as legislative discretion, but to be exercised in matters of detail and pursuant to the general order. All action implies discretion; the only question, but the all important question, is how much. When a mother tells the nurse that the children must not get their feet wet she legislates; but so far nothing has happened except disturbance of the air by sound waves. It is for the nurse to carry out those orders, and she may do it in one of two ways. She may keep the children by her side, and if she sees a puddle she may keep them away from it vi et armis. She is then acting in a true executive capacity, like the sheriff on an attachment of goods. But if the children are intelligent and old enough to go far afield she will tell them of their mother's orders, and direct them not to walk near ponds or puddles. If the mother had not given the prior order, we should say that the nurse was legislating — and in any case to the children the nurse is here the legislature. In the field of government it is clear that to give to a department the power to regulate its own internal procedure, or to prescribe the forms upon which statutory returns to it must be made, is to grant the power of legislation, no less than when, for instance, the Secretary of State is commanded to draw up a Cremation Code,[1] clear also that important as procedure may be, the interests affected by procedural regulation are normally less vital than those we call substantive rights. But in essence the laying down of a general rule, whether in obedience to a superior body and upon local procedural or exceptional matters, or as a sovereign command conclusively binding upon all persons in every sphere, is legislation, and delegated legislation is the best name for the process when carried out by an inferior body at the command of a superior — and so will be the name given it throughout this essay. For the use of the word administrative raises more problems than it solves, and is a relic of the days when sound legal doctrine held that to issue general commands was the exclusive privilege of an elective legislature.

[1] Cremation Act, 1902. 2 Ed. 7, c. 8, sec. 7.

There are few questions about which it is more difficult to be humbly impartial or to keep a proper sense of proportion than that of the delegation of legislative power. Natura nihil facit per saltum, and most institutions, even those of our modern institutions which seem to have leapt straight from limbo to the pages of the Statute Book, are necessarily the outcome of long periods of growth, and are where they are only by the divine right of successful competition. From its very beginning the executive, the one indispensable arm of government, had given general orders, but later by the growth of a legislative body, the acquisition by it of power over money matters, and the increasing expenses to be met by the Crown, the latter was forced to defer in matters of policy. It ceased to issue commands except in the sphere of foreign relations or to meet emergencies at home, and during the early part of the seventeenth century the definition of "emergency" and the powers that might be therein exercised were still further restricted; for that is the meaning of the *Case of Ship Money*, and the subsequent special Act, concealed though it was by the now-familiar judicial device of declaring the Common Law. The minority judges, faced with a clash between old and new methods of doing business, gave what we should now applaud as a "liberal decision," and chose that which appealed most strongly to the leading spirits of the day. Thus began a movement fraught with consequences more far-reaching than they are represented by some writers of history; the issue was not one of morals between Stuart despots and English lovers of liberty, but of legislation, both parliamentary and judicial, against a Common Law which recognised only too clearly the rights of the prerogative, the rights of the community against the individual. Because the time had gone by when a strong central government was necessary to protect the weak against robber barons, old learning was bent to new ends; the scene changes, and now the villain is a king, Piers Plowman the hero. Freedom of speech, freedom from arrest, from "illegal" exactions, from martial law — the liberty of the individual is now the central theme. But in the theatre of history applause does not mean that the play is over. Again the scene changes: time, the twentieth century; scene, the slums of an industrial city. Piers Plowman may still go where he likes and say what he likes, or at least the law says he may; the "inalienable rights of man" are his to exercise. But this time he is living cheek by jowl with maybe a million other free men; he would like to work reasonable hours, be paid a living wage, sleep in a sanitary house. This time "sic utere tuo ut alienum non laedas" cannot help him, for now the issue is one of distributive justice, and the courts, guardians of the past, are powerless. Again the servants of the Crown are mustered against robber barons, — the captain of industry and the slum owner, — but their position and function are changed. They act only on the direction of a supreme Parliament and to secure what in their opinion and the opinion of their director is to the economic and social advantage of all. Again the rights of the community bulk larger than the rights of the individual.

But then there arises a conflict with the underlying notions of lawyers. Statutes, it is true, have authorised the Crown to take notice of changed conditions and to say "thou shalt" where formerly it was the business of the law to regulate by the magic formula "thou shalt not," but to a lawyer a statute does not speak the living language of the day. Lawyers' ears are attuned to the accents of the forgotten past, new commands are faintly apprehended through the fog of the Common Law. So comes about the doctrine that statutes are to be interpreted strictly, that there is a presumption in favour of the liberty of the subject, and the result of the doctrine, that it is not thought *mal à propos* to measure modern development by the yardstick of the *Case of Proclamations*.

However, it is now undoubted law that the Crown may not legislate by the prerogative in England — not even to bind the prize court which is set up under the prerogative and administers international law.[1] But it is no less clear that where Parliament grants to the Crown the power to issue rules or orders under an Act, any rule or order "made under a power given in a statute is the same thing as if the statute enacted what the order directs or forbids: the statute delegates to others . . . the power to say what shall or shall not be done."[2] Provided, that is, that the rule or order is within the power granted. And the only body competent to pass on the question of ultra vires is a court. Most people will admit that "where delegated legislation is subject to judicial control, it is perhaps not open to the most serious kind of objection."[3] What of those cases where the jurisdiction of the court is ousted by an apt form of words? For whether the phrase used is to the effect that "the rules . . . shall have the same effect as if enacted in this

[1] The Zamora, [1916] A.C. 77.
[2] Reg. *v.* Walker, (1875) 10 Q.B. 355, p. 358.
[3] The New Despotism, p. 64.

Act," or "shall be deemed to have been duly made and to be within the powers of this Act," or "shall be conclusive evidence that the requirements of this Act have been complied with," in each case the most determined court will find it hard work to get behind the face of the rule or order.[1] A question may well be asked why such phrases were ever allowed to get into an Act of Parliament, and this is one of the questions which I shall try to answer later by setting out the chief instances of their use: for I do not here propose to describe the rule-making power except in so far as it has been extended to permit the departments to draw up codes or exempted them from control by the courts.

One of the reasons for delegating power to make rules to the departments is, put shortly, to enable questions of detail to be removed from the consideration of Parliament. Right up to the middle of the nineteenth century Parliament not only took care to provide for every exceptional case within the purview of the Act, but appended lengthy schedules of forms or tables of fees. Nothing was left to the imagination; even the methods of tax collection were strictly laid down in the body of the taxing Act.[2] Now it was not from choice that Parliament obscured the generality of its enactments by a cloud of petty details; the Civil Service as we know it today had not yet been born, and there were then no departments upon which to rely. But if a mass of cumbersome detail was not then a burden it would be a burden today. Those were the halcyon days of Benthamite liberalism, when there were few friends for legislation, halcyon days too for lawyers and legal jargon. A glance at any volume of the Statutes will show that there is now a genuine attempt to state the intention of Parliament in plain language that shall be intelligible and unambiguous for lawyer and layman alike. Further, even though it were practicable for Parliament to give up its time to discussion of details, there is no guarantee that it would be competent. Some writers are more than doubtful of the competence of Parliament: G. D. H. Cole suggests that "whenever possible we should put less detail into our laws, and aim at providing only a general framework, to be built upon by regulations capable of amendment without passing a new Act."[3] The

---

[1] See for instance in *Ex parte Yaffe*, [1930] 2 K.B. 90; [1931] A.C. 494, the emphasis placed on the words "when made" in "the order of the Minister when made shall have effect as if enacted in this Act."

[2] E. g. Malt Duty Act, 1865. 28 & 29 Vict., c. 66.

[3] The Method of Social Legislation, 9 J.P.A. 13 (1931).

germ of his suggestion is contained in an Act of 1863 which empowered the Commissioners of Customs to make regulations, among other things, "for the purpose of carrying out the object and intention of this Act in all cases not herein expressly provided for." [1] There is much to be said for it. The floor of the House may be an excellent place for the debate of questions of general policy, but matters of procedure do not command the interest of the average member; with the result that, as the State comes to deal more and more with technical questions of economics and social welfare, Parliament must inevitably become at best a mouthpiece for informed opinion, and a chamber for criticism of the executive.

Whatever the reasons for delegation, the importance of departmental rules and orders cannot be over-estimated. That they have a long history of slow growth I have already shown, but their first appearance in the lime-light was during the Great War. Before that date every barrister must have known of the Rules Committee of the Supreme Court, and every member of the general public have been familiar with the by-laws of his rural or urban district council. Members of the Civil Service were certainly conscious of taking part in great events; hear the evidence of the Chairman of the Board of Customs: "The work of a taxing department today is an absolutely different thing from what it was twenty or even ten years ago. In those days Parliament when it fixed a tax fixed every detail, leaving to the department only the administration of the tax on the lines laid down by Parliament. The tendency of Parliament nowadays is to lay down only principles, leaving matters of difficulty in the discretion of the department. I think it fair to say that a department like mine nowadays exercises powers . . . which sometimes get very near being legislative." [2] That was in 1914. But it remained for war-time experience of D.O.R.A. to awaken some curiosity in the breast of the average Englishman; when he was liable to be knocked up of nights and roughly told to show less light, he must sometimes have asked himself by whose authority he was restrained from exercising the immemorial rights of Englishmen. The War ended in November 1918; in 1921 C. T. Carr published his essay on delegated legislation. The very first page demonstrates how dependent we have become upon executive orders: that we have a statute authorising the Government to put

[1] Tobacco Act, 1863. 26 & 27 Vict., c. 7, sec. 11.
[2] Fourth Report of Royal Commission on the Civil Service (1914), Cd. 7338, p. 281.

summer time into effect we all know, but who decides each year on which day it shall come into force? [1] On the second page he turns his attention to their quantity: "The annual volume of public general statutes for 1920 occupied less than 600 pages: the two volumes of statutory rules and orders for the same period occupy about five times as many. This excess in mere point of bulk of delegated legislation over direct legislation has been visible for nearly thirty years." Here were facts startling enough, but Sir Josiah Stamp's testimony opens up horrid possibilities. According to an article of his in the Journal of Public Administration for 1924 [2] it became necessary in 1914 to double the income tax for the second half-year, but it was found too difficult to phrase a formula that could be understood by the House of Commons. The remedy adopted was to grant power to the Commissioners of Inland Revenue to make rules for the situation. But there is worse to come: the statute imposing an excess profits duty was framed in deliberately vague terms, and a rule-making power was granted under them; for if it had been too clear John Citizen would have been able to evade it.

Such a use of the rule-making power is open to criticism, but so far as I know the method is peculiar to the Inland Revenue,[3] and this department has already received more than its fair share of the hard knocks which are the inalienable right of a taxing body.[4] However questionable the ethics of being obscure in order to stop evasion, it is common knowledge that much of the department's time is spent in stopping up holes, and it is inherently more probable that the form of legislation in question is directed to that end rather than to "usurping the proper functions of Parliament." The peculiar difficulties which face the State as "trustee" of the public moneys, and as collector of the same, are sufficient justification for methods criticised in this connection as tyrannous, and in any case the sins of the Inland Revenue should not be visited on the heads of the other departments.

[1] This is now the principle upon which a census is ordered. Before 1920 Parliament passed a special Act each census year. In 1920 the Census Act — following the Census of Production Act of 1906 — provides by subsection 1 of section 1 that "it shall be lawful for his Majesty by Order-in-Council from time to time to direct that a census shall be taken for Great Britain."

[2] Recent Tendencies Towards the Devolution of Legislative Functions to the Administration, 2 J.P.A. 23 (1924).

[3] See comments of W. A. Robson in 169 L.T., p. 230.

[4] Appendix II to C. K. Allen's Bureaucracy Triumphant, p. 132.

After the War the control of the central government continued to spread at the expense of local freedom of action. Local government had long been local in name only. When a municipality finds it necessary to obtain new powers there are only two ways open to it of realising its wishes: if the powers are such that they may be obtained by Provisional Order under a particular statute, application may be made to the department concerned; if they are not, the town must proceed by private bill. A Provisional Order is, of course, settled by the department and comes to Parliament under its aegis; but even a private bill has little chance of passing into law unless it has the stamp of departmental approval. To adopt a new by-law might seem preëminently a matter for the local Council, but here too Whitehall steps in, and all by-laws other than those affecting the prevention of nuisances must be submitted to the Home Office for sanction. More often than not the Council will decide to adopt one of the model by-laws from the Home Office's list.[1] During the years 1920–1930 the whole structure of local government was overhauled to meet modern requirements. This meant standardisation, as the Poor Law Act, the Rating Act, and the Local Government Act abundantly show; and in this matter, the subordination of local elective bodies to the consistent policy of the Minister of Health, the judiciary were in thorough accord with Parliament.[2] Indeed one judge went so far as to limit the discretion of a local authority to "such matters as the necessity for a urinal and the choice of its position."[3] The power of the Ministry of Health to demand the dismissal of any paid officer of a Board of Guardians "who at any time refuses to carry into effect any rules, orders, and regulations made by the Minister,"[4] and the power to constitute a new Board of Guardians in place of those "who have ceased, or are acting in such a manner as will render them unable, to discharge all or any of the functions exercisable by the board,"[5] both show which way the wind is blowing.

But this tendency was not confined to local government; it ex-

[1] Harold Potter, Legislative Powers of Public Authorities, 6. J.P.A. 32 (1928).

[2] See Roberts v. Hopwood, [1925] A.C. 578, and the other Poplar Cases; see also Laski in 39 Harv. Law Rev. 832.

[3] Lord Sumner in Roberts v. Hopwood, p. 605. See also a remark of the same judge, "There is nothing about a borough council that corresponds to autonomy."   [4] Poor Law Act, 1927. 17 & 18 Geo. 5, c. 14, sec. 31 (1).

[5] Board of Guardians (Default) Act, 1926. 16 & 17 Geo. 5, c. 20, sec. 1 (1);

tended also to business, to housing, and to unemployment. However mistaken the policy of all three parties may seem to some, however sad the decay of local institutions and the spread of standard socialism, England has now set her feet firmly in the path of governmental interference, and even the Tory reaction of 1931 used Socialist tools to carry out the new policy. Both the Emergency Tariff and the Economy Act rested on executive orders.

Hand in hand with this increasing scope of executive regulation has gone an unwillingness to set hard and fast limits to the power to make rules, and a tendency to leave untouched any action taken by the department under a rule or order later annulled by an address to the Crown or declared ultra vires by the courts. But even today the courts would not hesitate to penalise, as they did in 1910, a money lender for acting on a rule made by the Commissioners of Inland Revenue which was declared to be ultra vires when it later came before the court. The interpretation placed upon the Act by the Commissioners was eminently reasonable, and yet the money-lender relying on the rule of the Commissioners was remediless against a debtor who chose to set up the technical defence of non-registration.[1] Parliament has not yet provided against the patent injustice of a situation like that, but there has at least been a realisation that where a local authority changes its position in obedience to an order of the Ministry of Health it would not be sound sense to demand that, because of an ex post facto declaration of technical invalidity, all that has been done must incontinently be undone. Section 219 of the Poor Law Act of 1927 meets the case of ultra vires, and provides that the rule shall thereupon be void "without prejudice however to the validity or legality of anything previously done thereunder," and the same disposition is made in the Board of Guardians Default Act of 1926 of any acts done under any order of the Minister annulled by address to the Crown — though there is nothing new in this latter practice.[2] Again, recent enactments have emphasised the generality of the rule-making power in so far as it seeks to carry out the primary purposes of the Act. G. D. H. Cole's suggestion, referred to above,

and see 1926 S.R. & O., p. 1426, for orders under this section superseding boards at West Ham and Chester-le-Street.

[1] Staffordshire Financial Co., Ltd. v. Valentine, [1910] 2 K.B. 233.

[2] Board of Guardians (Default) Act, 1926. 16 & 17 Geo. 5, c. 20, sec. 1. See also Court of Chancery Funds Act, 1872. 35 & 36 Vict., c. 44, sec. 19; Factory and Workshop Act, 1901. 1 Ed. 7, c. 22, sec. 84; National Health Insurance Act, 1924. 14 & 15 Geo. 5, c. 38, sec. 93 (2).

is therefore on its way to becoming the law of England; but so strong is the hold of the ejusdem generis rule on the minds of the courts that they will not, presumably, feel at liberty to take a broad view unless the statute under which the rule is made contains some such provision as that in subsection 1 of section 7 of the Seeds Act, 1920. The subsection empowered the Minister of Agriculture to "make regulations generally for the purpose of carrying this Act into effect and in particular and without prejudice to the generality of the foregoing provisions for prescribing . . .," and then followed a list of cases in which the power might be exercised. Such a provision is now pretty generally inserted.[1]

Since I do not propose to deal with the rule-making power in general, but only with some of its extreme instances, these introductory remarks may seem unduly copious. But it is just these extreme instances which are most likely to give rise to misconceptions unless they are viewed in proper perspective as part of a movement springing from a real need. Bare quotation from statutes can be oddly misleading. The words of grant are not in themselves important; it is the action taken under them which should as a practical matter decide the case for or against such delegation. But action is determined by the attitude of mind of the actor. And so, at the risk of appearing irrelevant, I will try to show in what light the Ministry of Health, for instance, regards its functions.

After the Ministry has given its advice on a projected bill, has primed the Minister with facts and figures to produce in Parliament, and the bill has successfully passed all three readings in each House, much still remains to be done. Any far-reaching piece of legislation needs considerable explanation before it can be carried into effect. More important still, there may be many areas affected by the Act which are totally opposed to the policy of the Government in power, and these the department, in its historic position of intermediary between local feelings and the commands of Parliament, must conciliate by an exposition of the conditions which called forth the new Act and the benefits which may reasonably be expected to flow from it.[2] Directly the Local Government

---

[1] See Air Navigation Act, 1919. 9 Geo. 5, c. 3, sec. 1 (1) and many others.

[2] See 224 Com. Deb. (5th Series), p. 822, January 28, 1929. Mr. Hopkinson: "Anyone who has had no experience of local government in this country would think after listening to the speeches of the Opposition that the local authorities are in a perpetual state of guerilla warfare with the Ministry of Health. I have taken an active part in the work of local government for a number of years, and during that period I have come into contact with Ministers of

Act had become law in 1929, there issued from the Ministry of Health to all local authorities a circular, analysing in quite general terms the difficulties with which the Act was supposed to deal — illustrated by quotations from a speech of the Minister — and explaining the remedies which had been adopted to meet them. Later circulars took up each remedy in detail.[1]

The Public Works Facilities Act, 1930, introduced a speedier method for the obtaining of new powers by local authorities, and for the compulsory acquisition of land by order. The general circular issued under it explained briefly the purpose of the Act, the relief of unemployment, and set out in plain and unambiguous language the niceties of the new procedure.[2]

Nowhere does this "air of sweet reasonableness" appear to greater advantage than in the statement of the purposes of the Milk and Dairies Order, 1926. This order made it compulsory among other things for a cowman to wash his hands before milking. To soften what must have appeared to the average rustic an injustice that cried to heaven for redress, the penal provisions of the Order were linked up with the functions of the Agricultural Education Authority, "whose educational work, so far as it deals with the production of clean milk, is designed to secure substantially the same objects as the Order."[3] A new note is sounded in the enforcement of law.

This point, it might be said, does not need to be laboured — these are just the duties for which the Civil Service exists. Nevertheless in recent years the nation has been in danger of forgetting how far it depends upon the routine work of the departments, and has concentrated upon their more controversial activities, the exercise of legislative and judicial power. Important as these powers are, they are an infinitesimal part of the work done. Parliament might tomorrow set up a statutory commission to make rules and orders; the judicial powers of the executive might, as Lord Sankey suggests, be turned over to a Judge of the High Court with a technical assessor;[4] and still there would be plenty of work for the depart-

Health of all parties, including the Labour Minister of Health: and I think I am right in saying that never yet have we had to complain of any interference of any kind whatsoever."

[1] Circular 1000, April 10, 1929. 27 L.G.R., Part II, p. 87.

[2] Circular 1141, August 22, 1930. 28 L.G.R., Part II, p. 648; see also the Home Office circular on the Shop Hours Act, 1904. 2 L.G.R., Part II, p. 222.

[3] Circular 757, January 20, 1927. 25 L.G.R., Part II, p. 5.

[4] The Principles and Practice of the Law Today (1928), p. 18.

ments, in their unending efforts to reach a compromise between the
airy generalities of the Statute Book and the multiplicity of awk-
ward situations and recalcitrant persons to which the Acts must
be applied.

Many Acts, however, are not compulsory, and here the Ministry
is charged with the grave responsibility of seeing that some action
is taken under them. The Housing Acts, except in certain rare
circumstances, depend for their effect upon the energy of local
authorities. But the Minister of Health, the parens patriae of today, has found the authorities too dilatory for his liking, and sometimes stimulates advance by advertisement, or by arousing a spirit
of competition. He suggests, for instance, in a circular urging
rural authorities to get to work under the Housing (Rural Workers)
Act, 1926, that leaflets, giving briefly the effect of any scheme they
may have prepared, be distributed in their district to persons who
might be expected to avail themselves of the Act, and encloses —
allegedly for information — a copy of the leaflet issued by the
Worcestershire County Council.[1]

The functions of a department do not end with the administration of law. Long before the Agricultural Marketing Act of 1931
there was a Bureau of Marketing in the Ministry of Agriculture:
men were sent to spy out the land, and free advice was given. Educational displays are given at the fairs — illustrating anything
from the amount of fat which London demands on its sirloin of
beef to the effect of worms on pigs. Statistics are drawn up on
seasonal fluctuations in the price of foodstuffs, and invaluable reports made on wheat acreage. In the same way the Ministry of
Health supervises the health of school children, advises expectant
mothers, issues pamphlets on influenza and how best to avoid it;
and even where it is concerned with the administration of law it
makes suggestions that go deep into human nature and accord ill
with the popular conception of autocratic officialdom.[2] Such are
a few of the activities of the executive to which Parliament has
delegated the legislative power.

Delegated legislation in England falls, like parliamentary legislation, into two main classes, that which corresponds to a public
general Act, the rule-making power, and that which is in the nature
of a private Act, the power of confirming schemes by order. Given

---

[1] Circular 839, January 4, 1928. 26 L.G.R., Part II, p. 1.

[2] See particularly Circular 1069, January 3, 1930. 28 L.G.R., Part II, p. 197,
which deals with the proper treatment of casuals.

the strict line of cleavage between the effect of, and the necessary procedure for passing, a public Act and a private Act, it would have been, to say the least, extraordinary if the distinction had not been reproduced in the new field. A public Act is in the nature of a burden imposed on the nation at large; it is debated before the full House in each chamber, is passed by a strictly party vote of the members, and no power on earth short of consistent lobbying can stop the consideration of it when once it has started on its journey through Parliament. A private Act, on the other hand, is in the nature of a grant of special privileges over and above what the general law allows and is granted on the petition of a particular person or organisation. It is for the promoters to press their suit before a Committee in each House: counsel are employed to speak for them, and the members appointed to sit in judgment on the bill are expected to make their decision in a judicial frame of mind. The Committee may administer an oath and listens to the evidence; there is examination and cross-examination; and if the promoters decide to withdraw their bill, there is no power in the Committee to bring it before the House and have it passed.

Both these functions of Parliament were early delegated to the executive; but Parliament has always been chary of extending the scope of the rule-making power, and chary of giving the rules finality. General legislation is, as a matter of history, peculiarly the function of the full House: and in these days of democracy a government stands or falls by the sort of legislation it brings forward. Under these circumstances, and bearing in mind the wide effects that will flow from the new Act, it will not readily surrender these powers. The attitude towards private bills is different. No great issues are involved; if the Act proves unsatisfactory the promoters have only themselves to thank, while, if some new experiment in local legislation turns out a success, Parliament can acquire merit by incorporating it in a later public Act. Further a private Act, even an Act involving the organisation and expenditure of a great city, deals only with local affairs: what could be more natural than to relax the requirement that the evidence for and against the grant of special privileges must be presented in London? Apart from questions of expense, it is unsatisfactory for a municipality to be forced to present its case for, say, a new scheme for relieving unemployment, through counsel who are not very familiar with the problems of the municipality, before members who regard their duties with regard to private bills as unimportant and burdensome.

Considerations of this type, coupled with the realisation that investigation — and that is what the Committee does — is no real part of parliamentary labours, have led through a slow process of evolution to the procedure by scheme. No such process of evolution is apparent in the rule-making power.

Since, however, it is the business of the law to see the likeness in unlike things and to proceed by "artificial reason," the discussion in *Yaffe's Case*, in which was involved the effect of an order purporting to give finality to a scheme allegedly ultra vires, centred in *Lockwood's Case* — which at most amounted to a decision on the finality of certain rules. Because in each case the form of words in the statutes involved was nearly alike — the rules of the Board of Trade were to have effect as if enacted in the Act, and the order of the Minister of Health when made was to have effect as if enacted in the Act — the question was treated as one of statutory interpretation, and would have been solved without difficulty had it not been that between 1894 and 1930 the attitude of the Bench to the executive had suffered a sea change. Statutory interpretation rests in theory upon the intent of Parliament, the court having to decide what provision Parliament would have made for the situation before it if Parliament had ever adverted to the question. The distinction — all-important as it seems to me — between Parliament's attitude towards private bill legislation by the departments, as manifested in the statutes passed by Parliament, and its attitude towards the rule-making power was not treated with the attention it deserved. But if *Lockwood's Case* went off as it did, a fortiori in *Yaffe's Case* certiorari should have been denied upon precisely the same grounds. Accordingly I propose to treat as separate questions the delegation of power to make general rules and the delegation of power to confirm schemes.

CHAPTER III

FINAL STATUTORY RULES

I

HOW FAR DOES A PROVISION THAT THE RULES SHALL HAVE EFFECT AS IF ENACTED IN THE ACT EXCLUDE REVIEW?

A. *According to the Decisions of the Courts*

THE first occasion on which the courts were forced to take notice of the increased legislative power of the departments brought to the fore both those aspects of it which have since met with considerable criticism. For the decision of the House of Lords in *Lockwood's Case* [1] rested on the ground that the legislation was a piece of skeleton legislation, left to be filled up in all its substantial and material particulars by rules of the Board of Trade, and that hence a rule levying fees for registration was intra vires the Board, although there was no mention of such a power in the statute itself, while all the Lords went on to discuss the effect of a provision that "general rules . . . made under this section shall be of the same effect as if they were contained in this Act." Neither aspect was, even in 1893, wholly unfamiliar to the courts; they had dealt with the rules of the Park Commissioners,[2] — a pretty extensive code, — and beginning in 1880 with the first mention in court of a clause declaring rules to be part of the Act there had been several suggestions, but no decision upon its meaning.[3] Since the code-making power may or may not be exercised under a statute which provides that the rules when made shall have effect as if enacted in the Act, it will be best to consider now the difficult question of the meaning of those words.

The casual dicta thrown out by judges before 1893 are too short to be illuminating. The question came up first in two cases under the Bankruptcy Act, 1869, cases which involved nothing more than

---

[1] Institute of Patent Agents *v.* Lockwood, [1894] A.C. 347.

[2] Bailey *v.* Williamson, (1873) 8 Q.B. 129.

[3] Reed *v.* Harvey, (1880) 5 Q.B.D. 184; *ex parte Foreman,* (1887) 18 Q.B.D. 393.

the effect of a rule under section 78 if inconsistent with an express provision of the Act. Section 78 of the Act empowered the Lord Chancellor, with the advice of the chief judge in bankruptcy, to make general rules "as to any . . . matter . . . in respect to which it may be expedient to make rules for carrying into effect the objects of this Act," and provided that "any rules so made shall be deemed to be within the powers conferred by this Act, and shall be of the same force as if they were enacted in the body of this Act." In *Reed* v. *Harvey* [1] Rule 28 of the Bankruptcy Rules of 1871, forbidding a trustee in bankruptcy to execute a disclaimer of a leasehold interest without the leave of the Court, was alleged to be inconsistent with section 23 of the Act itself, which gave the trustee leave to disclaim onerous obligations. A divisional court decided that in the case before them the rule was inoperative, since it was not intended to do more than regulate the conduct of the trustee as between him and the court, but went on to say that if the rule had in terms gone further than that they would have been prepared to hold it ultra vires "being inconsistent with the enactment itself. . . . The power to make rules is a power given in order to carry into effect the enactments of the Statute, and the Act says that the disclaimer by the trustee shall be operative and have effect." So much for section 78. *Ex parte Foreman* [2] was also a case of apparent inconsistency. Section 104 of the Bankruptcy Act of 1883 gave a right of appeal in bankruptcy from the county court to the Divisional Court, and section 104 (2) (*d*) provided that "no appeal shall be entertained except in conformity with . . . general rules." Rule 111 (2) of the Bankruptcy Rules of 1883, made under section 127 of the 1883 Act, a section identical in form and effect with section 78 of the Act of 1869, allowed no such appeal except where the amount involved was more than fifty pounds. The trustee contended that, the Act having granted a right of appeal, any rule which diminished that statutory right was ultra vires. The other side rested their case partly on section 127 and argued, in Lord Bowen's happy summary, that its effect was "to clothe the rules, when they have been laid before Parliament and issued, with legislative authority, and that the court cannot go behind them, and examine into the scope of the authority under which they purport to have been made." Both the Divisional Court and the Court of Appeal decided against the trustee on the strength of section 104 (2) (*d*), which to them indicated that the

---

[1] (1880) 5 Q.B.D. 184.   [2] (1887) 18 Q.B.D. 393.

legislature had granted only such right of appeal as the rules chose to define. The Divisional Court referred to section 127 — which they called "a very reasonable provision" — and said, "So in fact there is given to the rules the same effect as if they were enacted by the Act," but the Court of Appeal expressly refused to venture an opinion on the section. Lord Esher, however, was on dangerous ground when he stated that "whenever the objection is taken that a general rule made by such a great judicial officer with the concurrence of a great officer of state [here the Secretary of State] is ultra vires . . . we should be strongly inclined to the view that such high functionaries had not exceeded their authority," and yet, presumably with section 127 in mind, went on to say that "if we thought that they had, we should be bound to say so." Particularly is this so in view of his statement in *Dale's Case*,[1] when he said of certain forms, which under the statute before the court were to be laid before Parliament for a certain time, and if not objected to, to be "binding": "Whenever that provision is introduced into an Act of Parliament it seems to me that the rules and orders, if not objected to by Parliament, become part of the Statute." If in *Dale's Case*, where there was no provision similar to that of section 127, he could go that far, why the excessive caution in *Ex parte Foreman*? And why rely on the high authority of the Lord Chancellor to validate rules to which it is improbable that the Lord Chancellor ever contributed anything but his signature, when there was a provision like section 127 to hand?

Although these cases do not directly touch our point, they are nevertheless interesting. For one thing, they foreshadow the judicial technique which was employed in *Lockwood's Case* and later cases which have distinguished it. The unwillingness to believe that a judge is capable of promulgating an ultra vires rule,[2] the reliance on the fact that the rules were laid before Parliament,[3] the ready loophole provided for an unsympathetic court when the rules are "for carrying into effect the objects of the Act" and a court can treat this general description as a condition precedent to the legal existence of a rule,[4] or for a sympathetic court when they

---

[1] (1881) 6 Q.B.D. 455.

[2] Commissioners of Public Works v. Monaghan, [1909] 2 I.R. 718, per Lord O'Brien, L.C.J., p. 744.

[3] Glasgow Insurance Committee v. Scottish Insurance Commissioners, [1915] S.C. 504, *passim*.

[4] E. g. the use of the words "when made" in *ex parte Yaffe*, [1930] 2 K.B. 90.

may refer to the "generality of the words used"[1] — all are foreshad-
owed in these brief suggestions. For another thing, *Reed* v. *Harvey*
illustrates one point of which there can be little doubt, whatever
the interpretation of *Lockwood's Case*: even if rules declared to have
effect as if enacted in the Act are to be treated on exactly the same
footing as the express provisions of the Act, they will give way in
the event of irreconcilable inconsistency with any express provision. The power to modify must be expressly granted in order
to justify its exercise, and in this respect, at any rate, rules with
statutory force stand on a lower plane than the enactment itself.

Lockwood's Case is difficult to discuss. The House of Lords was
not required to decide — and did not claim to decide — anything
except the question of ultra vires,[2] but the meaning of the words in
controversy was so fully examined at the bar that the Lords felt
justified in expressing an opinion upon it. In a strictly technical
sense no decision was given on the point, but the considered dicta
have always been treated as decision, and the same court felt bound
to distinguish the case in *ex parte Yaffe*.

On the other hand, if the House of Lords had to make a ruling
today upon facts that were the same as those in the principal case,
except that the rule was clearly ultra vires, they might be anxious
to reach an opposite conclusion to Lord Herschell,[3] and they would
indeed be fortunate if they could succeed in this without treating
most of his speech as mere dictum. Again the dual aspect of the
case, involving as it does consideration of skeleton legislation and
of rules with statutory effect, has enabled both courts and text
writers to mould it to their own uses, and the multiplicity of possible grounds upon which the case may be upheld has seriously im-
paired its value as a precedent.

The Patents Act of 1888 forbade any person to describe himself
as a patent agent unless he was registered as a patent agent in
pursuance of the Act. By subsection 2 of section 1 the Board of
Trade was directed to make "such general rules as are in the opinion of the Board required for giving effect to this section," and by

---

[1] See the judgment of Palles, C. B., in R. (Conyngham) v. Pharmaceutical
Society of Ireland, [1899] 2 I.R. 132.

[2] The actual decision can be made even narrower than that, *viz.* even assuming without deciding that the rules were intra vires, the action of declarator
and interdict was incompetent, subsection 4 having provided a remedy by
way of summary prosecution.

[3] Lord Dunedin calls *Lockwood's Case* "the high water mark of inviola-
bility of a confirmed order." *Ex parte Yaffe*, [1931] A.C. 494, p. 501.

reference to section 101 (3) of the Act of 1883 the rules, after lying before both Houses of Parliament for forty days, and being subject during that time to annulment by resolution, were to "be of the same effect as if they were contained in the Act." Subsection 3 provided that every person practising as a patent agent before the passing of the Act should be entitled to be registered as a patent agent in pursuance of the Act. Subsection 4 provided a summary penalty of twenty pounds for any person who knowingly described himself as a patent agent in contravention of the section.

The Board of Trade made certain rules, known as the Register of Patent Agents Rules, 1889, which were laid before Parliament and were not annulled. They provided for registration on payment of a fee of five guineas for entry on the register, an annual fee of three guineas, and erasure of the name from the register if the fees were not duly paid. According to a note in Rettie [1] these fees were employed for the provision of an Institute Library and kindred purposes.

The defendant, a patent agent who had practised before 1888, and had been registered under the new Act and paid the fees, later declined to pay these annual fees, maintaining that he had by subsection 3 a statutory right to describe himself as a patent agent. The Institute brought an action for a declaration that he was not entitled to practise as a patent agent and for an injunction.

The Lord Ordinary gave the declaration and granted the injunction. In his view the Board of Trade could not do what it was directed by the Act to do, establish a register, without the power to levy fees, and so came to the conclusion that in levying the fees the Board was not acting ultra vires or subjecting the defendant to illegal taxation.

The Court of Session reversed his decision,[2] on the ground that, since the Act gave no express power to levy fees, and since in fact the fees were used for a library and not a register, the rule was ultra vires. The Court was then forced to deal with the contention that by section 101 (3) of the Act of 1883 Parliament had ousted the jurisdiction of the Court to consider the question of ultra vires. They rejected the contention, and took the "plain meaning" of the subsection to be that only if within the powers conferred by the statute should the rules have the same operation and effect as if expressed in the statute. Lord Young reached his conclusion by

[1] XX S.C. (4th Series), p. 324, footnote 3.
[2] Institute of Patent Agents v. Lockwood, XX S.C. (4th Series), p. 315.

a process of reductio ad absurdum. Someone, said he, must have power to decide the question of ultra vires: not the Board of Trade, "for that was extravagant upon the face of it"; not Parliament during the forty-day period, for "the Legislature has never assumed the power to interpret statutes and constitutionally it has not the power." That left only the courts. But the reasoning not only neglects the legislative history of the subsection, it fails to give an adequate explanation for its insertion in the statute; the draftsman must have known the settled law by which an intra vires rule has statutory effect — why then this tautology? The premise that there must be some person or body entitled to decide every question is hard to justify when we are faced with the "conclusive evidence clause," and in 1932 a decision *cannot* be had upon the legality of the reduction of the judges' salaries by Order in Council.[1] Besides, fundamentally the question is not one of interpretation, it is one of control.

On appeal to the House of Lords [2] the decision of the Court of Session was affirmed on the sole ground that the Institute had mistaken its remedy, and should have proceeded by prosecution before a court of summary jurisdiction (sec. 101 [4]), but the reasoning of the Court of Session was in effect reversed. Lord Herschell summed up his whole attitude towards the question of ultra vires here when he remarked that the judges of the Court of Session "did not sufficiently observe the method of the legislature." [3] He treated the section as a piece of skeleton legislation; Parliament had given orders to establish a register, but had left the details to be worked out by the Board; everybody knows that a register cannot be kept up without money; Parliament, then, having made no money grant for the purpose, clearly intended it to be raised by the Board under the general power. He laid stress on the control exercised by Parliament over the department, and over the rules while they lay on the tables of both Houses.

Upon the meaning of section 101 all the Lords except Lord Morris spoke with one voice. "I own I feel very great difficulty," says Lord Herschell, "in giving to the provision that 'they shall be of the same effect as if they were contained in this Act' any other meaning than this, that you shall for all purposes of construction

[1] Sir William Holdsworth, The Constitutional Position of the Judges, 48 L.Q.R. 30 (1932).

[2] Institute of Patent Agents *v.* Lockwood, [1894] A.C. 347.

[3] [1894] A.C. 347, p. 355.

or obligation or otherwise treat them exactly as if they were in the
Act." [1] And Lord Watson was of the same opinion: "I do not
think I can express my opinion more clearly than by saying that
they mean exactly what they say. Such rules are to be as effectual
as if they were part of the statute itself." Lord Morris dissented
on this part of the case; he rightly pointed out that the rules do
not receive any imprimatur from having been laid before both
Houses, but on the question of jurisdiction to review he went with
the Court of Session, and held that "general rules" could only
mean such rules as the legislature had under section 101 delegated
to the Board of Trade the authority of making.

Not the least remarkable feature of this case is the easy-going
air of tolerance with which it is inspired. Hard things have been
said about the House of Lords as a court, but if it had disappeared
in 1873 as the framers of the Judicature Act intended, England
would have lost what she cannot well do without in these days of
rapid change in the machinery of government: a strong sense for
the realities. They alone among English courts refrained from
standing in the way of administrative decision of disputes,[2] from
confusing the course of Common Law procedure with "natural
justice," [3] from sacrificing reason and justice to ex post facto technicalities.[4] Whether their ability to see through the books to the
present realities is the result of occasional participation in debate,
or of an acquaintance with other systems of law in the Judicial
Committee, it is difficult to say, but there can be no doubt that the
foundations of our modern system of government have been pre-
served unshaken because of the decisions of the Law Lords.

But the generality of the words used by the Lords in the principal case must be subject to some limits. Suppose the Board of
Trade had inserted in the rules a provision that in no circumstances should a person aggrieved thereby have recourse to the
courts, or had levied a fee so unreasonable that none except the
most successful patent agents could ever hope to pay it; taken
literally the words would deny review even here, and yet it is clear
that no court would hesitate to declare such rules beyond the power
of the Board. The most natural method of interpretation, and that
adopted by later courts, was to read the words in close conjunction

---

[1] Id., p. 360.
[2] Board of Education v. Rice, [1911] A.C. 179.
[3] Local Government Board v. Arlidge, [1915] A.C. 120.
[4] Ex parte Yaffe, [1931] A.C. 494.

with the facts — with the result that the questions of skeleton
legislation and statutory finality discussed there have become con-
fused, and the tendency has been to rest the case ultimately upon
its own particular facts.

Two cases decided soon after the principal case allowed rules
made under a provision such as section 101 a latitude that might
have been denied without it. The Privy Council was empowered
to make orders authorising local authorities to make regulations
for prescribing the ventilation of cowsheds: an Order in Council
dealt with ventilation "including air space," but made no express
mention of air space in the article (Article 13) which enabled the
local authorities to regulate ventilation. An order of a local authority made under that article and regulating air space was held
intra vires, by one judge on the ground that ventilation naturally
included air space, but by the other on the ground that under a
"section 101 provision" the subordinate legislation and the Act
itself must be construed as one enactment, and that thereby the
meaning of "ventilation" in the section empowering the Council
to make orders on the subject was enlarged to include air space, and
that Article 13 made under that section must therefore be read as
if it included "air space."[1] A section of the Companies Act, 1890,
providing that the notes of the examination might thereafter be
used in evidence against the person examined was extended by the
Companies Winding Up Rules to cover any of the persons against
whom the application was made who had the opportunity of taking
part in the examination. Vaughan Williams, J., held that since
the rules were to have effect as if enacted in the Act, they must be
read as part of the Act, and that, not being in conflict with any
express provision of the Act, they were intra vires. The rule in
question did not treat the deposition as absolute evidence against
persons other than the person examined, but merely as an affidavit,
yet the judge expressed concern that some of the observations in
Lockwood's Case seemed to tend in the direction of holding that
such a rule would be valid even if drawn in manifest contravention
of the principles on which the law of England is founded.[2] Clearly
these cases do not go far. They do, however, show that in the
presence of a section of this nature a court will be inclined to enlarge rather than restrict the power of the rule-making body. In
each case the rule went beyond what the Act expressly provided,

[1] Baker *v.* Williams, [1898] 1 Q.B. 23.
[2] In re London and General Bank, [1894] W.N. 155.

and in each case the Court found itself able to bring the rule within the penumbra of the powers delegated.

It is where a court finds itself hostile to a rule, and therefore anxious to distinguish *Lockwood's Case*, that difficulties begin to arise. The Pharmacy (Ireland) Act, 1875, empowered the Council of the Pharmaceutical Society of Ireland to make regulations in regard to the examination of candidates. The regulations were to be of no effect until approved by the Lord Lieutenant and the Privy Council in Ireland, and section 17 provided that when so approved they should be of like force and effect as if they had been enacted in the Act. All regulations were to be laid before Parliament within twenty-one days of their making, but there was no provision for annulment. It is remarkable enough to find section 17 applied to the rules of a private autonomous body, — indeed the closest analogy is in three instances where rules of the Bank of England in technical matters of finance were thus dignified,[1] — and here the Council made the onerous requirement that each candidate for the qualifying examination produce a declaration that he had served as apprentice for four years in the employment of a legally qualified pharmaceutical chemist. The Act itself gave no hint of any such requirement, and was designed to increase rather than lessen the number of chemists.

In *Cleeland's Case*[2] the applicant came to court for an interpretation of certain words in the rules, and expressly refrained from raising the question of ultra vires, because he did not wish to prejudice the Council against him. The Court decided the question of interpretation in favour of the Council, and since no other question was raised or argued by the applicant they refused mandamus. But they had something to say on the effect of section 17. It was common ground that the rule was ultra vires, and O'Brien, J., was not alone in thinking that "it certainly is somewhat startling that it should be in the power of any body of persons, by means of an obscure and unnoticed formality, at the suggestion it may be of private interest, to smuggle through Parliament illegal regulations affecting the rights of the public, and to invest them with the force of law."[3] Nevertheless three out of the four members of the Court could not

---

[1] National Debt Act, 1870. 33 & 34 Vict., c. 71, sec. 39; Stock Certificate Act, 1863. 26 & 27 Vict., c. 28, sec. 10; India Stock Act, 1863. 26 & 27 Vict., c. 73, sec. 9. These rules, however, needed no approval.

[2] R. (Cleeland) *v.* Pharmaceutical Society of Ireland, [1896] 2 I.R. 368.

[3] [1896] 2 I.R. 368, p. 376.

distinguish *Lockwood's Case*—although Gibson, J., made the tentative suggestion that it was limited to a skeleton Act. Holmes, J., pointed to several distinctions of fact: here the rule-making body was not a government department responsible to Parliament, but a private society amenable to no control but that of the courts; the possibility of parliamentary control through the power of annulment was absent; finally, the rules of the Council were in direct conflict with the clear purposes of the Act, a monopolistic restriction upon an Act designed to make candidature open to all.

Three years later a candidate had sufficient courage to challenge the validity of the rules.[1] Again the point at issue was not squarely decided, for the rule was held to be validated by a statute of 1890, but the judgments are wholly concerned with the effect of section 17 and *Lockwood's Case*. Palles, C. B., fastened on the unlimited discretion granted to the Board of Trade, "an important government department" ("such general rules as are in the opinion of the Board required for giving effect to the section") and the power of annulment reserved to Parliament, and so succeeded in his distinction. O'Brien, J., had been on the Court in *Cleeland's Case* three years before, and had then refused to distinguish. But now after a full argument he found himself able, while disregarding the verbal differences relied on by the Chief Baron, to distinguish on a broad ground that here the rule was not even made with the intention of executing the main object of the Act; the rules in *Lockwood's Case* whether ultra vires or intra vires were expressedly made for regulating the practice of registration under the Act, but the rule before them was not a rule for the examination of intending candidates, but a "rule avowedly made for constituting a personal status in the candidates reaching back to a period of no less than four years prior to the time when they present themselves for examination, a thing completely and utterly unauthorised, and in my view outside the Act of Parliament altogether." [2]

O'Brien, J., seems to be right in his interpretation of Lord Herschell's speech. That a part of the Act is in skeleton form is important in considering whether the rule is intra vires or not, and is one of the elements to be taken into account in discovering the objects of the Act, but it cannot affect the meaning of the words upon which Lord Herschell rested his judgment in the second part of the case: "shall have effect as if enacted in the Act." As

---

[1] R. (Conyngham) *v.* Pharmaceutical Society of Ireland, [1899] 2 I.R. 132.

[2] [1899] 2 I.R. 132, p. 154.

for the nature of the rule-making authority, this is uncertain ground for legal argument. Can the courts say that the authority is or is not trusted by Parliament, when Parliament has displayed its trust by the very delegation of power?

The provision for annulment by Parliament cannot touch the question of legal power — Parliament is concerned with policy, not legality, and is only likely to annul on the first ground. At any rate no argument on this point can be drawn from *Lockwood's Case*, for there by subsection 5 of section 101 annulment of a rule was to be "without prejudice to the validity of anything previously done thereunder": nothing but the existence in the future of the rule was to be affected. That is no parallel to the power of a court to declare a rule ultra vires, and so upset things done under it in the past; the two species of control are so devoid of connection that it is not possible to argue from the power of annulment to an intention to exclude control by the courts. This notion however did not receive its deathblow until 1916. It was conceded in *Mackay* v. *Monks* [1] that certain regulations of the Secretary of State were ultra vires, but recourse was had to a provision of the Act under which they were made whereby the rules were subject to annulment while before both Houses, and it was contended, relying on *Lockwood's Case*, that if not annulled by either House "these rules automatically become in their own nature legislative and can no more be quashed than the statute from which they are supposed to derive their efficacy." This contention was emphatically denied by the Court. In their opinion the absence of any provision to the effect that the rules should have effect as if enacted in the Act was conclusive against it. In the words of Ronan, L. J., "the principle of that decision appears to me absolutely clear. If the rules had been 'contained in the Act' the Court could not have enquired into the authority of those who made them, the Legislature. Therefore the provision that they 'shall be of the same effect as if they were contained in the Act' amounts to a statutory provision equivalent to an express prohibition of inquiry as to whether the rules were authorized by the Act." And the same judge went on to point out that there was no reason why the provision relied on should preclude the courts from acting; the courts are confined to the question of authority to make rules, and Parliament, although it has power to annul them for any reason, will usually be concerned with policy alone.

[1] [1916] 2 I.R. 241.

But — to return to *Cleeland's Case* — O'Brien, J., realised the necessity for some limit consistent with the generality of Lord Herschell's words, and he thought that as long as the rule-making authority purported to carry out the objects of the Act, — acted, that is, in the general direction to which the Act pointed, — its action could not be questioned, even though that action was not strictly within the bounds of the express words of the Act. His opinion is as significant for what it excludes as for what it includes. That his omission to discuss subsection 2 of section 1 of the Patents Act ("such rules as are in the opinion of the Board necessary") was not made per incuriam is shown by his reference to it in a later case, where that aspect of *Lockwood's Case* is quoted upon a pure question of ultra vires.[1] Here the rule was admittedly ultra vires, and the only part of that case in point was the second. *Lockwood's Case* dealt with two distinct questions, and the great value of this valuable judgment lies in the refusal to confuse the issue of scope of power with the issue of the meaning of a "section 101 provision."

Corporation of Waterford v. *Murphy*[2] does not impair the test of O'Brien, J. A power to make by-laws as to the time and mode of vessels passing through a bridge does not without more ado confer the power to levy fees for opening the bridge, even at unusual hours. And the levying of fees is so different from prescribing times and modes that in making the by-law here in question the corporation can be said to have gone off in an entirely different direction from that to which the statute pointed them; the test protects a rule only where it travels roughly along the trail blazed by the Act. *Lockwood's Case* is easily distinguishable: under the circumstances — the establishment of a new register, a process requiring money, and no money granted by Parliament — a government department, with no private funds of its own, and receiving no privilege in return for the establishment of the register, may well be held to have wandered so little outside the powers granted (assuming that the rule there was ultra vires — which was not the case) in levying a fee for registration that it was bona fide attempting to travel, and in effect was still travelling along the path of the Act — and hence was protected by a section declaring its rules to have effect as if enacted in the Act. The purpose of a grant of power to an Irish city to make by-laws describing the time and

---

[1] Commissioners of Public Works *v.* Monaghan, [1909] 2 I.R. 718, p. 749.
[2] [1920] 2 I.R. 165.

mode of vessels passing through what is in law a nuisance to a waterway legalised by special favour to the city cannot be to make the right of passage still more burdensome, but merely to fit time and mode to local conditions unknown to a Parliament sitting in Westminster; the levying of a fee then is here wholly foreign to the general purpose of the grant of the power to make rules.

An even wider test than that suggested was made an express ground of decision in *Glasgow Insurance Committee* v. *Scottish Insurance Commissioners*.[1] The National Insurance Act set up local insurance committees, but provided that the Commissioners might require, among other things, any insurance committee to combine with one or more other insurance committees. By section 65 the Commissioners were empowered to make regulations for carrying the medical benefit part of the Act into effect; these regulations were to have effect as if enacted in the Act, to be laid before Parliament, and to be subject to annulment within twenty-one days. The Drug Accounts Committee Regulations required insurance committees in Scotland to combine for the purpose of establishing a central organisation to be known as the Drug Accounts Committee. The applicants thereupon claimed that the regulations were ultra vires in that the Act set up local boards, but the regulations set up a central organisation for which there was no warrant in the Act, and they prayed an interdict to prevent the defendants from laying the regulations before Parliament. A majority of the Court of Session refused the interdict; for, said they, since the applicants themselves admit that the regulations were passed to carry into effect that part of the Act, admit then that the defendants were acting in the spirit of the Act when they made them, the Court is precluded by the words declaring that the rules shall have effect as if enacted in the Act from examining their validity. For by them the rules had acquired statutory effect. It was also suggested that Parliament had reserved control to itself by the power of annulment, but, although it was on this basis that Lord Thankerton rested his distinction in *ex parte Yaffe*, the unsatisfactory nature of the proposition has already been shown. The case is important as the first — and only — square holding that in the face of a section such as this a court has no jurisdiction to review, and it is important to discover just what it decided.

Evidently the Court of Session thought that under *Lockwood's Case* it was enough if the rule-making authority acted in the spirit

[1] [1915] S.C. 504.

of the Act, however mistaken the authority might be. What is meant by acting in the spirit of the Act? Is that an objective or a subjective test? If subjective, the heading of every batch of statutory rules will exclude the jurisdiction of the court in a case like this, for it will not be possible to examine the actual author. That is a possible interpretation of *Lockwood's Case*; the Lords were certainly unwilling there to take notice of what the Board did with the fees when received, and assumed — contrary to the finding of the Court of Session — that they were raised to provide, and were used for, a register of patent agents. But no court today would rest content with the subjective test. On the other hand, directly the objective test is introduced you run into difficulties. Stripped of the irrelevancies of legal technique, that was the test used in *Yaffe's Case*, and as used there it effectively deprived the words in controversy of any meaning. It is not stretching language too far to say, as the Court of Appeal did, that directly the authority acts outside the limits of its power as laid down in the Act it is acting also outside the spirit of the Act.

Yaffe's Case is more appropriately dealt with under the power to confirm schemes. But since the principal question there was staged as one of statutory interpretation — the meaning of section 40 (5) of the Housing Act of 1925 ("The order of the Minister when made shall have effect as if enacted in this Act") — it cannot be omitted here. A housing scheme, imperfect according to a prior decision of the Court of Appeal in that it did not specify precisely what was to be done with every parcel of land proposed to be acquired compulsorily, and hence prima facie subject to certiorari, came up to the Minister of Health and was duly confirmed by his order. It was admitted in all courts that the scheme as modified and confirmed was unobjectionable, and the House of Lords later decided that even in the form in which it went to the Minister it was a good scheme under the Act. But in the Divisional Court the Attorney-General admitted that the scheme as submitted was ultra vires, and although this admission was retracted in the Court of Appeal that Court decided against him. The question then was, what effect is to be given to subsection 5 of section 40? Apart from *Lockwood's Case* there was no controlling English decision. A possibility that the schemes might by reason of such a provision later become outside the jurisdiction of the courts had, it is true, disposed the Court in *R.* v. *Electricity Commissioners* [1] and *ex parte*

[1] [1924] 1 K.B. 171.

Davis[1] to grant prohibition at a very early stage in the proceedings; Avory, J., actually stated in the latter case that if the scheme was once sanctioned by the Minister there was no remedy by which the validity of it could be tested; but since in neither case had the schemes progressed far enough "to have effect as if enacted in the Act," there was not much relevant wisdom to be collected from them.

An interval of thirty-six years had not dealt kindly with the attitude of mind that was responsible for *Lockwood's Case*. In 1893 executive interference still operated in the narrow field of the correction of existing abuses, the enforcement of safety regulations in shipping, mines, and factories, the control of disease. Industry had not yet begun to feel the pinch, invention was still to give birth to the motor car and the aeroplane, and interests of property were still deemed superior to interests of personality; there was then no thought of ministries of labour, transport, education, or health. But a growing mass of social legislation brought with it restrictions on individual liberty, and an increase of scope and power to the executive. In 1929 the Labour Party, committed to a program of social betterment by governmental regulation, was in power, and the other parties, solely responsible as they were for health insurance, unemployment insurance, old age pensions, and housing Acts, were now asking the familiar question, "If these things be done in a green tree what shall be done in a dry?" Thus in 1929 began the period of regression to which I have already called attention. At the head of this movement, but for constitutional reasons, marched the legal profession, and as it so happened the Lord Chief Justice had just completed *The New Despotism* when the case of Yaffe with its fundamental question of constitutional law came before a divisional court of which he was a member.[2]

Lockwood's Case itself could have been of little consequence one way or the other. The all-embracing language of Lords Herschell and Watson, the dual aspect of the case itself, the multiplicity of distinctions taken upon it in later cases, and, most important of all, the fact that it was here to be applied to a wholly different situation, all these factors combined to give the courts leave to treat the case as Jack Horner's Christmas Pie, to "put in a thumb and pull out a plum and say 'what a good boy am I.'" Or else to

[1] [1929] 1 K.B. 619.

[2] It will be remembered, however, that Lord Hewart concurred in refusing to grant the writ.

put it aside as wholly indigestible. It is difficult not to feel that this case, particularly as read in the light of the *Glasgow Insurance Case*, did more harm than good to the Crown. From what other repositories of legal learning could the Attorney-General have drawn the argument that "the order of the Minister, however far it may depart from the Act, has effect as though enacted in the Act, if it purports to be made under the Act?" And whence if not from his argument did Swift, J., get the impression that the clause meant "After the passing of this Act the Minister may do what he likes"?[1] That is the subjective test with a vengeance. A less uncompromising line of argument, and one more closely linked with the facts before the Court, would have stood at least a chance of convincing its hearers.

All three courts dealt with the issue in vacuo, as if it were "is a clause of this nature sufficient to exclude our jurisdiction to review Ministerial orders?" Given the hostility of the judiciary to the executive, the answer was easy. In the Divisional Court Lord Hewart was content to hold that, since the scheme as modified and confirmed was within the Act, no relief should be granted. Talbot, J., stood alone in thinking that the only possible motive for the insertion of the clause was to protect the order of the Minister against the action of the courts; otherwise the clause was to him meaningless. In his support he cited those statutes which grant immunity for certain acts "done in pursuance of the statute," and showed how the courts had interpreted "done in pursuance of" to mean "done in bona fide pursuance of"; for acts done within the statute are of themselves lawful and need no validation. The Court of Appeal, in opinions remarkable for the violence of their language, were unanimous in granting certiorari, the decision flowing naturally from their strictures on modern parliamentary methods and "executive encroachment." A specious legal technique was not difficult to find. The judges were agreed that on the words of the subsection, "the order of the Minister when made shall have effect as if enacted in this Act," the order of the Minister must be "made" before the subsection could act upon it, and applying the rigidly objective test they argued that the order was only "made" when there was something upon which it could act. In contemplation of law there was here no scheme; therefore, there being no scheme, no order was in fact "made." What, then, was the mean-

---

[1] London Times, November 6, 1929, quoted in Allen, Bureaucracy Triumphant, p. 77.

ing of subsection 5? Slesser, L. J., thought that it would at least cover a scheme "legally intra vires but administratively imperfect," but went further and agreed with Greer, L. J., in distinguishing ultra vires additions made to a scheme intra vires as submitted; if, for instance, the Minister, in contravention of subsection 4, made an addition to the lands to be taken compulsorily, that would be all right. That clearly is a sound logical conclusion from the premises, and has the virtue of giving some meaning to the words, but is it sound sense? It would be extraordinary to conclude that Parliament intended — and statutory interpretation rests on at any rate a possible intention of Parliament — the Minister to be kept rigidly within the bounds of the law in accepting a scheme for confirmation, but that once a good scheme had been accepted he could play what havoc he chose with it. From the point of view of the aggrieved slum owner, for whose benefit the Court performed its legal acrobatics, the result would be much the same. To Scrutton, L. J., the words were a statement of the obvious, the effect of an order if validly made, and pointing to Schedule III, 2, of the same Act, which provided that a compulsory purchase order "shall . . . become final and have effect as if enacted in this Act; and the confirmation by the Minister shall be conclusive evidence that the requirements of this Act have been complied with, and that the order has been duly made and is within the powers of this Act," he argued that if Parliament had wished to exclude the jurisdiction of the courts they would have used words no less express than those. But to hold that a whole subsection is mere tautology is not a very satisfactory conclusion, and, as for Schedule III, 2, those are the usual words of common form employed to protect an order putting into force the antiquated and complex provisions of the Lands Clauses Acts.[1] A procedure that offers many loopholes may well require more specific words of protection. Further, Scrutton, L. J., refused to take account of — although he did consider — the fact that the Act of 1909 (which the Act of 1925 consolidates with others) marked the completion of the process of Parliament's delegating to a department its control over private bill legislation in matters of housing.

Beginning with the Act of 1875 Parliament gradually relaxes its hold — first Provisional Order, subject on petition to investigation

[1] Compare Local Government Act, 1894. 56 & 57 Vict., c. 73, sec. 9 (7) (c); Small Holdings and Allotments Act, 1907. 7 Ed. 7, c. 54, sec. 26 (3); Education Act, 1921. 11 & 12 Geo. 5, c. 51, Sched. V, 2.

by a Committee of either House; [1] next Provisional Order gives
way in trivial schemes to an order of the Local Government
Board; [2] in the Act of 1903 a confirming order is sufficient where
no compulsory powers are in fact to be exercised; [3] by 1909 the
power of confirmation rests in all cases with the departments. [4]
Facts could not speak more strongly: the department stands now
wholly in the place of Parliament. And to make reasonable inference certain, Parliament expressly states in all these Acts that
the order is "to have effect as if enacted in the Act," and, as if to
underline its intentions, Parliament does not even require the order
to be laid before it. Here then was a situation in which history
spoke more strongly than the words themselves. Scrutton, L. J.,
misses the whole point of counsel's argument on the history of the
Housing Acts when he sets a chasm between procedure by Provisional Order and confirmation by order; it is true that in a confirmed Provisional Order there can be no question of ultra vires
"because Parliament can enact anything right or wrong," but how
does that reply meet the argument that by its step across the chasm
and the use of words aiming at statutory finality Parliament created a new procedure under which the department was to stand
for all purposes in the same position as Parliament itself?

Lockwood's Case and the Glasgow Case were distinguished on the
ground that in those cases the condition precedent to be performed
before the rules came into existence — in the first that they should
be "such rules as are in the opinion of the Board required," in the
second that they should be made "for carrying this part of the
Act into effect" — had admittedly been performed. This is, I
grant, a good verbal distinction; in those cases the section operated as it were sponte sua upon the rules as issued, whereas in our
case it remained for the Minister to invoke it, and on the Court's
reasoning he had no power to invoke it. Nevertheless the fact
remains that if in contemplation of law there was no scheme in our
case, then there were no rules in those others — unless, that is,
they are to be regarded merely as decisions of intra vires. And in
that aspect they are out of point here. From Conyngham's Case
the Court reasoned a fortiori: if in that case the order was repug-

---

[1] Artizans' Dwellings Act, 1875. 38 & 39 Vict., c. 36, sec. 6.

[2] Housing of the Working Classes Act, 1890. 53 & 54 Vict., c. 70, sec. 39
(1) (a) and (b).

[3] Housing Act, 1903. 3 Ed. 7, c. 39, sec. 5 (2) and sec. 6.

[4] Housing Act, 1909. 9 Ed. 7, c. 44, sec. 24 (1) and (2).

nant to the Act, here it is more than repugnant, there being no scheme to be confirmed at all. But what of the fact that there the order was a mala fide detournement de pouvoir? Here the interpretation placed by the Minister upon the Act was not only with reference to the subjective test made bone fide, it was also with reference to the objective test made reasonably, and only became legally wrong by the decision in *ex parte Davis* which was given subsequent to the making of the order in *Yaffe's Case*.

The House of Lords, while reversing on the question of ultra vires, agreed with the Court of Appeal that subsection 5 could not have the meaning contended for by the Attorney-General, and distinguished the cases in much the same manner. Lord Dunedin, who delivered the leading judgment, appeared not altogether satisfied with the reasoning of the Court of Appeal. He admitted that an order had been made and that the order by section 40 (5) had become part of the principal Act, but he reasoned that, assuming the scheme to be ultra vires, the "scheme" part of the Act now formed a section inconsistent with the main body of the Act. As a matter of interpretation the less must yield to the greater: [1] "If one can find that the scheme is inconsistent with the provisions of the Act which authorises the scheme, the scheme will be bad, and that can only be gone into by way of proceedings for certiorari." [2] But Lord Dunedin did not explain how you sue out a writ of certiorari to bring up and quash an Act of Parliament.

I have dealt at length with the legal technique in *Yaffe's Case*, not because legal technique is of any importance in deciding controversial questions in government, certainly not to clear up a decision which rests upon two words in a section now repealed,[3] but in order to illustrate the proposition that they who take the sword shall perish by the sword. That professional and popular opinion alike demanded that the main contention of the Crown be disposed of, and that there may be much to be said for erasing from the statutes any sections which purport to give statutory force to any rules or orders, cannot now be denied. But it is no function of an English court to declare a statute unconstitutional, even by the indirect method of nullifying it through interpretation, and it is distinctly unfortunate that the Court of Appeal should have taken the determined line it did, and used the sort of reason-

---

[1] See Reed *v.* Harvey, (1880) 5 Q.B.D. 184.

[2] *Ex parte Yaffe*, [1931] A.C. 494, p. 503.

[3] Section 40 disappears in the Housing Act of 1930.

ing it did, in a case where the defect was trivial and had in any case been cured under the power of modification before the order in question was issued.

What then emerges from the chaos of judicial opinion? Little except the reflection that in matters of government, where prejudices are strong and passions easily aroused, the deciding factor must inevitably be the personal preferences of the Court before whom the case comes.[1] In this I do not question the impartiality of the Bench, but merely the soundness of their conception of the judicial process as the application of fixed rules of law that move irresistibly to an inevitable conclusion, and their wisdom in treating a great constitutional issue as a matter of interpreting two words in a statute.

As far as legal paraphernalia goes, however, this much is certain:

1. The fact that a rule has been laid before Parliament and has not been annulled will not of itself bar review (*Mackay* v. *Monks*, [1916] 2 I.R. 241), nor will the mere approval of the rules by a "trustworthy body" (*Commissioner of Public Works* v. *Monaghan*, [1909] 2 I.R. 718).

2. Even if an ultra vires rule or order can take effect as if enacted in the Act, it must not be inconsistent with any of the express provisions of the Act itself (*Reed* v. *Harvey*, [1880] 5 Q.B.D. 184 semble), but it may, where not directly inconsistent, enlarge the meaning of a provision in the Act (*In re London and General Bank*, [1894] W.N. 155; *Baker* v. *Williams*, [1898] 1 Q.B. 23).

3. A rule wholly repugnant to the spirit of the statute under which it is made cannot have effect as if enacted in the Act (*R. (Conyngham)* v. *Pharmaceutical Society of Ireland*, [1899] 2 I.R. 132).

4. It is no longer safe to rely on the wide dicta of the Lords in *Lockwood's Case*.

5. The *Glasgow Insurance Case* is the only case which has squarely held that an ultra vires order, made however *by admission* in pursuance of the Act, is saved by a provision that it shall have

---

[1] Compare the historic battles between the courts and the trade unions in the nineteenth century and, later, the decision of Astbury, J., in National Sailors and Firemens' Union *v.* Reed, [1926] 1 Ch. 536. See also Roberts *v.* Hopwood, [1925] A.C. 578. Scrutton, L. J., has some penetrating observations on this difficulty in The Work of the Commercial Courts 1 Camb. L. J. 6, 8 (1921).

effect as if enacted in the Act. The admission seems vital to the case: it prevented the Court from applying an objective standard and enquiring whether the rule was "in fact," i. e. in their opinion, made in pursuance of the Act.

6. The technique employed by the Court of Appeal in *Yaffe's Case*, and not explicitly disapproved by the House of Lords, can be used to nullify the effect of any section declaring that rules or orders shall have effect as if enacted in the Act. The presence of the words "when made" was not vital — merely convenient. The essence of that holding was that there was no scheme to confirm.

There are now two controlling decisions in England on the meaning of such a section: one, on the rule-making power, pointing to an absolute ouster of the jurisdiction of the courts; the other, on the power to confirm schemes by order, which in effect treats the section as superfluous verbiage. Neither are satisfactory as decisions. Not only was *Lockwood's Case* concerned with what even apart from the section was an unusually wide legislative discretion, but the rules were in any case intra vires, and *Yaffe's Case* is liable to be met with the criticism that it was nothing but a decision on a subsection in the Housing Act of 1925, now repealed. In this state of the law it would be rash to prophesy. There must however be some position intermediate between absolute ouster and mere tautology, and I venture to suggest that words of this nature will protect any rule bona fide made to carry out the objects of the section which defines the rule-making power, and directed in the opinion of the Court towards effectuating the general purposes of the Act to be gathered from the terms of the Act as a whole. The same test would be applicable to a power to make orders, except as regards orders confirming schemes. There the words would have at least the force claimed for them by Slesser, L. J., and would validate "an order legally intra vires but administratively imperfect," and perhaps an order made according to a course of procedure not strictly in accordance with the terms of the Act, but affording equally good protection to the individual owner. Beyond that, in the light of *Yaffe's Case*, it is impossible to hazard a guess.

B. *According to the Internal Evidence of the Statutes*

An examination of the statutes themselves has failed to throw much light on either the purpose or effect of a section declaring rules to have effect as if enacted in the Act, and in some cases I am inclined to agree with Scrutton, L. J., that it is mere tautology. It was too much to expect a continuing tradition to run from 1850, where I began my search of the Statute Book, to the present day, but I did not anticipate that it would be beyond my power to draw some general conclusion from the instances collected. If, for instance, the section had been more popular with one department than another it might have been possible to run down the draftsman, and starting from his legal habits of mind (for draftsmen are sometimes sufficiently important to leave their stamp on the memories of others) to speculate on what he and his successors meant to convey, disregarding the intention of Parliament, as to which there is in this matter little or no evidence — or else, perhaps, to point out one department as the chief user of the section and seek to discover the reason therefor. But it is only in comparatively recent years that our departments have become specialised; before 1900 (and there are many more instances of the section from 1850 to 1900 than from 1900 to 1930) the tendency was to delegate powers of rule-making either to the Privy Council or to a secretary of state, authorities so indeterminate, and entrusted with such ill-assorted powers, that it is not possible to argue from the statutes which they were to administer, or from the large number of occasions when their rules were declared to have effect as if enacted in the Act.

The words of a statute sometimes imply — but often do not — that rules which have effect as if enacted in the Act do acquire actual statutory force. There can be no doubt that the Act of 1850, which empowered the judges of the Superior Courts at Westminster to make rules altering the modes of pleading, meant exactly what it said; the rules were to lie for three months before both Houses of Parliament and if not annulled by resolution were to be "of like force and effect as if the provisions contained therein had been expressly enacted by Parliament." [1] This expression of Parliament's intention with time became less definite; all the Acts in 1870 which gave statutory finality to rules provided that any regulation made in pursuance of the section should be "deemed to be within the powers conferred by the Act . . . and of the same force as if enacted in the Act." But presumably the weaker declaration of Parliament's intention which later in subsequent Acts of the same series became common form, that the rules should "have effect as if enacted in the Act," was not intended to cast any doubts

[1] Alterations in Pleadings Act, 1850. 13 & 14 Vict., c. 16, sec. 1.

upon the substitution of the judges themselves for Parliament in matters of procedure. It is interesting to note however that no such protection is thrown over the rules of court issued by the Rules Committee — and this although English practice rests entirely upon them.[1] Was it omitted as unnecessary on the ground that such a committee is unlikely to issue ultra vires rules, or to afford an aggrieved litigant a chance of challenge, or because by 1873 the section was being employed as a statement of the effect of rules if intra vires? In 1870, certainly, out of nine instances in which a grant of rule-making power was made only two were without the section.

There is sometimes recognition of the fact that there may be orders with the force of an Act of Parliament: a section of the Finance Act, 1910, defines "Special Act" as including "any Provisional Order or order having the force of an Act of Parliament," and in this it is not alone.[2] When the words used are that the rules "shall be deemed to be within the powers conferred by the Act, and shall be of the same force as if enacted in the Act," [3] the meaning of Parliament is considerably clearer, and even Scrutton, L. J., admitted that the jurisdiction of the courts was excluded by a declaration such as that in Schedule III, 2, of the Housing Act of 1925, ". . . shall become final and have effect as if enacted in this Act; and the confirmation by the Minister shall be conclusive evidence that the requirements of this Act have been complied with and that the order has been duly made and is within the powers of this Act." A fortiori, then, by the explicit directions of the Protection of Person and Property Act (Ireland), 1881, "every such warrant shall be conclusive evidence of all matters therein contained, and of the jurisdiction to issue and execute such warrant and of the legality of the arrest and detention of the person mentioned in such warrant"; [4] or of the Extradition Act 1870, the most explicit of them all, the sole instance of its kind, "an Order-in-Council shall be conclusive evidence that the arrangements therein referred to comply with the requisites of this Act, and that this Act applies in the case of the foreign state mentioned

---

[1] Judicature Act, 1873. 36 & 37 Vict., c. 66, sec. 74.

[2] See Finance Act, 1910. 10 Ed. 7, c. 8, sec. 38 (4); Tramways (Temporary Increase of Charges) Act, 1920. 10 & 11 Geo. 5, c. 14, sec. 1 (4); Gas Regulation Act, 1920. 10 & 11 Geo. 5, c. 28 sec. 10 (5).

[3] E. g. Irish Land Act, 1870. 33 & 34 Vict. c. 46, sec. 31; Naturalisation Act, 1870. 33 Vict., c. 14, sec. 11.

[4] 44 Vict., c. 4, sec. 1 (1).

in the order, and the validity of such order shall not be questioned in any legal proceedings whatever." [1] But that is another question.

Indirect light is sometimes thrown upon the effect of our section by other provisions in an Act where it is found. No reliance can be placed on the appearance of a saving clause for rules on the repeal of such an Act,[2] for whether the rules acquire the force of statute or not, in either case they must disappear with their Act, but for different reasons. The normal statutory rule hangs as it were from the Act, and with the removal of the Act the rule falls to the ground; the other class, although it has statutory force, has it only because it is engrafted onto the Act itself, and when the Act is swept away the part goes with the whole.

But no one has ever suggested that a rule with statutory force has all the effect for all purposes of a section of the Act; even when it has come into force it may be annulled by resolution, if the enabling Act so provides.[3] Nevertheless it is thought necessary to provide expressly that such a rule may be revoked or amended by a subsequent rule,[4] the notion being that otherwise the Minister might be forced to come to Parliament for an Act to amend or revoke his own rules, and thus the purpose of a rule-making power would be frustrated. And section 6 of the Government of Ireland Act marks out the distinction between regulations "made in pursuance of" and regulations "having the force of" an Act, but conceives it possible that their effect may be the same. This Act (which only partially came into force) declared any provisions of an Irish Act of Parliament to be void if repugnant to any provision of any Act of the United Kingdom, and went on to include in its definition of an Act of the United Kingdom "any order rule or regulation made in pursuance of or having the force of an Act of Parliament of the United Kingdom." [5]

One Act at least, however, contemplates that such a rule may be declared void as ultra vires: section 213 of the Poor Law Act,

---

[1] 33 & 34 Vict., c. 52, sec. 5.

[2] E. g. Foreign Jurisdiction Act, 1878. 41 & 42 Vict., c. 67, sec. 2 (1); Contagious Diseases (Animals) Act, 1878. 41 & 42 Vict., c. 74, sec. 4 (3).

[3] E. g. Irish Free State (Agreement) Act, 1922. 12 Geo. 5, c. 4, sec. 1. Cf. the limitation in Patents and Designs Act, 1907. 7 Ed. 7, c. 29, sec. 86 (2): "General rules shall, *whilst in force*, be of the same effect as if they were contained in this Act."

[4] E. g. Irish Free State (Agreement) Act, 1922. 12 Geo. 5, c. 4, sec. 1 (3); Poor Law Act, 1927. 17 & 18 Geo. 5, c. 14, sec. 211 (2).

[5] Government of Ireland Act, 1920. 10 & 11 Geo. 5, c. 67, sec. 6 (3).

1927, makes every rule to have effect as if enacted in the Act, and then by subsection 3 of section 219 goes on to provide that "if on a rule being . . . removed into the High Court by writ of certiorari *it is quashed as illegal*, the Minister shall notify . . . boards of guardians, and the rule shall from the date of the notice be void." Midway, and in conformity with O'Brien, J.'s test, stands a section of the Factory Act, 1901: "The order, while it is in force, shall, so far as is consistent with the tenor thereof, apply as if it formed a part of the enactment which provides for the making of the order."[1]

The inconclusive results obtained by this method led me to pick a few volumes of the Statutes at random, to collect the instances in each of the power to make rules, to separate those which were to have effect as if enacted in the Act from those about whose effect nothing was said, and then to compare them from the point of view of the importance or triviality of their subject matter. In 1870 nine statutes delegated rule-making power, and in seven of them the rules were to be deemed to be within the powers conferred by the Act and to be of the same force as if enacted in the Act — little doubt here about their force. It is not difficult to see why a code of rules providing against the spread of cattle disease in Ireland should be protected against vexatious actions by irritated farmers,[2] or a special proclamation putting into force repressive measures against violence should be immune from attack on the ground of a procedural defect.[3] And considerations of expert knowledge presumably led to the continuance by statute of certain prerogative rights over the coinage.[4] But the same legislative sledge hammer is employed to defend rules of court[5] and departmental regulations fixing forms and modes of procedure.[6] The gloom does not lift on an examination of those two cases where the section is not found; for although one seems trivial, the arrangement of the internal affairs of the Mint,[7] the other, delegation to the Postmaster-General to make regulations prescribing times of posting and the size of parcels, and prohibiting the sending of in-

[1] Factory and Workshop Act, 1901. 1 Ed. 7, c. 22, sec. 126 (4).

[2] Cattle Disease (Ireland) Amendment Act, 1870. 33 & 34 Vict., c. 36, sec. 2.

[3] Peace Preservation (Ireland) Act, 1870. 33 Vict., c. 9, sec. 21.

[4] Coinage Act, 1870. 33 Vict., c. 10, secs. 11 and 12; see also Naturalisation Act, 1870. 33 Vict., c. 14, sec. 11 (4).

[5] Matrimonial Causes (Ireland) Act, 1870. 33 & 34 Vict., c. 110, sec. 18; Irish Land Act, 1870. 33 & 34 Vict., c. 46, sec. 31.

[6] Tramways Act, 1870. 33 & 34 Vict., c. 78, sec. 64.

[7] Coinage Act, 1870. 33 Vict., c. 10, sec. 13.

decent articles through the post,[1] touches individual liberty closely. The one gleam of light comes from the Coinage Act, where internal regulations have no statutory force, but rules fixing the design or dimensions of coins, defining bronze legal tender, regulating the trial of the pyx, have; but even this fitful gleam is darkened by considerations of ancient prerogative.

In 1880, as it so happens, there are only two new rule-making powers granted, to the High Court to make rules regulating their practice and procedure in reference to cases stated under the Taxes Management Act [2] (which fall to the Rules Committee under the Judicature Act), and to the Lord Lieutenant in Ireland to regulate forms and procedure under the Births Registration Act (but his rules are to have effect as if enacted in the Act).[3]

In 1890 there is a certain similarity to be observed in the rules which are to have effect as if enacted in the Act. They deal with matters of substance where Parliament might have decided to deal with them itself, but instead was content to give general instructions and leave the details to be worked out by a department. Parliament was at last persuaded by the principle of the compulsory load line, but considered that it lacked the knowledge to decide where it should be put and how it should be marked;[4] and it was because of lack of aptitude that it refused to prescribe the trivial but vital features of lunacy administration,[5] or of the winding up of a company.[6] But there is no provision that the rules shall be deemed within the powers of the Act, and it is therefore possible that the section may be only a declaration of the obvious. The rules whose effect is not defined all deal with minor aspects of procedure [7] — except section 275 of the Lunacy Act, which plays havoc with the generalisation, providing as it does that the visiting committee may make general rules and regulations as to the management of asylums.

---

[1] Post Office Act, 1870. 33 & 34 Vict., c. 79, secs. 9 and 20.

[2] Taxes Management Act, 1880. 43 & 44 Vict., c. 19, sec. 59 (2) (e).

[3] Births and Deaths Registration Act (Ireland), 1880. 43 & 44 Vict., c. 13, sec. 34.

[4] Merchant Shipping Act, 1890. 53 Vict., c. 9, sec. 2 (2).

[5] Lunacy Act, 1890. 53 Vict., c. 5, sec. 338.

[6] Companies Act, 1890. 53 & 54 Vict., c. 63, sec. 26.

[7] Police (Scotland) Act, 1890. 53 & 54 Vict., c. 67, sec. 7 (8); Elections (Scotland) (Corrupt and Illegal Practices) Act, 1890. 53 & 54 Vict., c. 55, sec. 47; Companies (Winding-up) Act, 1890. 53 & 54 Vict., c. 63, sec. 13; Lunacy Act, 1890. 53 Vict., c. 5, sec. 161.

Four other years were investigated, 1900, 1906, 1910, and 1920. A power to make rules was delegated on seventeen occasions during the first three, and yet on no one of these occasions are the rules to have effect as if enacted in the Act. They differ widely in importance. A department is to make rules for the purpose of carrying out the recommendations contained in the General Summary of the Report of the Irish Education Commissioners [1] as to dangerous railway operations,[2] the duties of the public trustee,[3] and filling in one of the earliest skeleton Acts, the Census of Production Act, 1906,[4] as to the exemption from tax of certain cars [5] and the supply and maintenance of rescue appliances and ambulances in mining operations.[6] On the other hand, many of the rules are procedural merely, governing appeals to referees of valuation,[7] costs on the confirmation of new justices' licenses to sell liquor,[8] or the fees payable on an application for cottages and allotments.[9] The general scope of power is very wide,[10] but in no case was the provision in question to be found. Indeed it seems to have been neglected after the first rush of enthusiasm, and only to have been revived for general use after the War. But a cursory comparison of the rule-making powers of 1870 with those, say, of 1910 will show how difficult it is to attempt even a guess at the intended meaning of the section; for why declare in 1870 that the rules of the Privy Council in Ireland regulating procedure on the sale of lands to tenants shall be "deemed to be within the powers conferred by this Act, and shall be of the same force as if enacted in this Act,"[11] and yet in 1910 leave undefined the effect of rules dealing with similar subject matter? [12]

[1] Intermediate Education (Ireland) Act, 1900. 63 & 64 Vict., c. 43, sec. 1 (1).
[2] Railway Employment (Prevention of Accidents) Act, 1900. 63 & 64 Vict., c. 27, sec. 1.   [3] Public Trustee Act, 1906. 6 Ed. 7, c. 55, sec. 14 (1).
[4] Census of Production Act, 1906. 6 Ed. 7, c. 49, sec. 8.
[5] Finance Act, 1910. 10 Ed. 7, c. 8, sec. 86 (7).
[6] Mine Accidents (Rescue and Aid) Act, 1910. 10 Ed. 7, and 1 Geo. 5, c. 15, sec. 1 (1).   [7] Finance Act, 1910. 10 Ed. 7, c. 8, sec. 33 (5).
[8] Licensing (Consolidation) Act, 1910. 10 Ed. 7, and 1 Geo. 5, c. 24, sec. 13 (4).
[9] Labourers (Ireland) Act, 1906. 6 Ed. 7, c. 37, sec. 31.
[10] See also Notice of Accidents Act, 1906. 3 Ed. 7, c. 53, sec. 4; Merchant Shipping Act, 1906. 6 Ed. 7, c. 48, sec. 10 (2) (c), sec. 10 (3) (c), sec. 17, sec. 40; Moneylenders Act, 1900. 63 & 64 Vict., c. 51, sec. 3 (1).
[11] Irish Land Act, 1870. 33 & 34 Vict., c. 46, sec. 41.
[12] Mine Accidents (Rescue and Aid) Act, 1910. 10 Ed. 7, and 1 Geo. 5, c. 24, sec. 2 (7).

The year 1920 was a bumper one for departmental rule-making. Parliament and the nation had become accustomed during the War to executive regulation, and when Parliament entered upon its task of making up the arrears of four years and inaugurated the work of rationalisation, legislation of necessity was cast in a skeleton form. During the following decade most important statutes make some delegation of legislative power. The 1920 volume of the Statutes contains not only the Seeds Act, by which the Minister was empowered to prescribe the seeds to which the Act was to apply,[1] but also the Air Navigation Act and the Roads Act, and it was of these three Acts in particular that C. T. Carr was speaking when he said that when Parliament legislates at high pressure, and when there is hardly time to think how an Act is going to work out, it is natural to delegate wide general powers of making rules and regulations for carrying the Act into effect.[2] Out of nineteen statutes which delegate a power to make rules, however, only seven declare that the rules are to have effect as if enacted in the Act. Two of them are concerned with the troubles in Ireland, a situation peculiarly adapted for ousting the jurisdiction of the regular courts, and one providing a strong argument in favour of a conclusion that the section means exactly what it says: where an uncompensated injury has been done in any area the Lord Lieutenant may deduct, and provide for the manner of deduction of, grants payable to the council of the area;[3] and to provide for the restoration of order he is empowered to make regulations under D.O.R.A. which were to go one step further than D.O.R.A. in that the regulations were to have effect as if enacted in the Act.[4] The Emergency Powers Act, passed to deal with possible labour troubles in England, was to the same effect.[5] The Gas Regulation Act represented an effort to reorganise the price and the quality of gas without forcing each undertaker to come to Parliament for a special Act: here the Board of Trade was to stand in the place of Parliament itself and grant power to charge for thermal units, recast the prices in the light of new conditions, and prescribe the permissible proportion of carbon monoxide. The provisions of every order issued under the Act were to have effect as if enacted in the Act,

[1] Seeds Act, 1920. 10 & 11 Geo. 5, c. 64, sec. 7 (1) (c).
[2] Delegated Legislation, p. 17.
[3] Criminal Injuries (Ireland) Act, 1920. 10 & 11 Geo. 5, c. 66, sec. 2.
[4] Restoration of Order in Ireland Act, 1920. 10 & 11 Geo. 5, c. 66, sec. 2.
[5] Emergency Powers Act, 1920. 10 & 11 Geo. 5, c. 55, sec. 2.

and Parliament confirmed the interpretation of their own intentions when they provided by section 10 that any far-reaching scheme must be approved by resolution of both Houses before coming into effect.[1] But once again the inference falls just short of certainty, for by section 16 mere rules of procedure are thus dignified. The Unemployment Insurance Act, however, is so plain a piece of skeleton legislation, sketching out as it does a general framework and leaving to the Ministry of Labour the fulfilment of Parliament's intention in building up the machinery for payment of contributions and for appeals, and in legislating for special cases,[2] and the Savings Banks Act so clear a case of implicit trust in the financial experts of the Treasury,[3] that the doubts raised by section 16 of the Gas Regulation Act are almost offset. But why is the code to be issued under the Air Navigation Act,[4] the provisions to regulate the establishment of the Road Fund,[5] or to apply in effect the state health insurance scheme to disabled soldiers [6] — why are all these rules together with those under the Census Act and the Seeds Act deprived of statutory force, if the section indeed has that effect? With the possible exception of the emergency act they are no less worthy.

Nevertheless, it is generally supposed that the section has, and is intended to have, an operation more significant than that of declaring the Common Law. Lord Hewart's attitude is one of fearful doubt: "This provision is apparently thought to give the rule or order the status of an Act of Parliament, the validity of which cannot in any circumstances be questioned." [7] C. K. Allen, however, is of the opinion that the jurisdiction of the courts is thereby ousted,[8] and Lord Banbury's comment on the refusal of the House of Lords to adopt an amendment of a clause to this effect in the Land Drainage Bill was, "So we are going to give force to certain arrangements by people of whom we know nothing as if the arrangement were enacted in an Act of Parliament." [9]

[1] Gas Regulation Act, 1920. 10 & 11 Geo. 5, c. 28, secs. 1 and 2.

[2] Unemployment Insurance Act, 1920, 10 & 11 Geo. 5, c. 30, secs. 6, 13 (4), 17 (4), and 35 (1) and (4).

[3] Savings Banks Act, 1920. 10 & 11 Geo. 5, c. 12, sec. 1.

[4] Air Navigation Act, 1920. 10 & 11 Geo. 5, c. 80, sec. 3.

[5] Roads Act, 1920. 10 & 11 Geo. 5, c. 72, sec. 3.

[6] National Health Insurance Act, 1920. 10 & 11 Geo. 5, c. 10, sec. 13 (1).

[7] The New Despotism, p. 66.

[8] Allen, Law in the Making, p. 324. Mr. Allen, however, has changed his opinion since *Yaffe's Case*; see Bureaucracy Triumphant, Chapter IV, *passim*.

[9] 77 Lords Deb. (5th Series), p. 850, May 19, 1930.

II

A Brief Survey of the Principal Statutes under Which Rules Are to Have Effect as if Enacted in the Act

Assuming, then, that the section does indeed give an especial sanctity to rules made under it (as is justifiable in view of the feeling of the courts in general that the section means something, and of the fact that the answer of the statutes themselves is inconclusive), what authorities have been permitted to make such rules? Almost all types of authority, from the Council of the Pharmaceutical Society in Ireland to the Privy Council in England. I have already pointed out that the section is by no means new. Discounting instances which occur in consolidating Acts, and making due allowance for those instances which I must have missed, there are well over 150 statutes in which this power is delegated during the period 1850–1931, and less than fifty of these were passed after 1900. Far the earliest to be generally entrusted with the full powers of Parliament were the judges. Between 1850 and 1860 there are fifteen statutes to this effect. The well-known Act of 1850, which empowered the judges to make alterations in the mode of pleading,[1] was originally passed for a duration of five years (it was then in the nature of an experiment), but was continued after the expiration of the period. In the same year the power was also granted without a time limit to certain judges of the Chancery to make rules regulating the stating of special cases,[2] to the King's Bench in Ireland to regulate proceedings in ejectment and replevin,[3] and to the Vice Chancellor of Lancaster to regulate the procedure of his Chancery Court.[4] In 1852 (for this was the great period of procedural reform) the Common Law Procedure Act took the first important step of handing over the making of rules and writs to the judges,[5] and by similar statute the Chancery judges were permitted to remodel their own procedure.[6] The benefits of

[1] Alterations in Pleadings Act, 1850. 13 & 14 Vict., c. 16, sec. 1; continued in 18 & 19 Vict., c. 26.

[2] Court of Chancery Act, 1850. 13 & 14 Vict., c. 35, sec. 31.

[3] Process and Practice (Ireland) Act, 1850. 13 & 14 Vict., c. 18, secs. 12 and 16.

[4] Court of Chancery (County Palatine of Lancaster) Act, 1850. 13 & 14 Vict., c. 43, sec. 1.

[5] Common Law Procedure Act, 1852. 15 & 16 Vict., c. 76, sec. 233.

[6] Improvement of the Jurisdiction of Equity Act, 1852. 15 & 16 Vict., c. 86, sec. 63.

the new principle were then extended to courts of limited jurisdiction, the Stannary Courts, the Landed Estates Courts in Ireland,[1] and to particular aspects of the business of the Superior
Courts at Westminster.[2] But, as I have already stated, the Judicature Act which set up a new body, the Rules Committee, to
regulate matters of practice under the new régime did not give
statutory force to its rules — possibly because a power so tremendous, substantive law being still to some extent secreted in the inter-
stices of procedure, seemed to demand control.[3] After the root-and-
branch reorganisation of 1873 and the establishment of the Rules
Committee, there was little scope for new grants of power; but in
at least two cases the Committee was directed to make rules of
statutory force to cover a limited field, the proceedings of the courts
of revising barristers,[4] and the costs and forms of the Provincial
and Consistory Courts.[5]

In like manner the Lord Chancellor, with his historic control
over the funds of the Chancery and over lunacy and bankruptcy,
had exercised similar wide powers of rule-making,[6] and with the
recognition of a new form of property, and new methods of transferring real estate, had been called in to form a register,[7] a function
peculiarly within the ambit of an officer combining in himself the
law and the administration. It was natural, then, in each case for
Parliament to rely to a considerable extent on his discretion. His
duties and so his powers continued, but of the judges this was not
strictly true.

The end of such grants of power to the judiciary having been
accomplished, and the powers being in the main to meet a transitory need, no more is heard about them. But to the other departments of government new social values brought new duties. At

[1] Jurisdiction of Stannary Court Amendment Act, 1855. 18 & 19 Vict.,
c. 32, sec. 23; Sale and Transfer of Land Act (Ireland), 1858. 21 & 22 Vict.,
c. 72, sec. 30.

[2] Crown Suits Act, 1855. 18 & 19 Vict., c. 90, sec. 3; Estates (Ireland)
Act, 1856. 19 & 20 Vict., c. 120, sec. 30.

[3] Judicature Act, 1873. 36 & 37 Vict., c. 66, sec. 74.

[4] Parliamentary Registration Act, 1878. 41 & 42 Vict., c. 26, sec. 39.

[5] Clergy Discipline Act, 1892. 55 & 56 Vict., c. 32, sec. 9 (1).

[6] Lunacy Acts Amendment Act, 1889. 52 & 53 Vict., c. 41, sec. 88; Bankruptcy Act, 1883. 46 & 47 Vict., c. 52, sec. 127; Court of Chancery Funds
Act, 1872. 35 & 36 Vict., c. 44, secs. 18 and 19.

[7] Registration of Trade Marks Act, 1875. 38 & 39 Vict., c. 91, sec. 7; Land
Title and Transfer Act, 1875. 38 & 39 Vict., c. 87, secs. 106, 111, and 121.

first these were cast upon the rudimentary group of departments
which were grouped round the Privy Council, and the rules were
issued in the name of the Council; for this reason, among others,
more rules with statutory force issue from this source than from
any other. The characteristic functions of the executive are to
deal with emergencies at home and to conduct foreign affairs, and
these functions are not less noticeable today than they were in the
days before specialisation had set in. Where the emergency involves the existence of the State, the powers granted are wide;
indeed they could be exercised under the prerogative,[1] and in this
case the effect of a statute is to limit rather than to enlarge it.[2]
Acts passed during and immediately after the menace of the
Franco-Prussian War empowered the Council in an emergency to
call out the militia, to take possession of the railroads, and to
prohibit the export of any articles which "His Majesty shall judge
capable of being . . . made useful in increasing the quantity of
military or naval stores . . . or any sort of victual which may be
used as food." [3] Any court which wished to interfere would find
it difficult in face of the generality of words used, and neither in
those Acts, nor in the series of Defence of the Realm Acts issued
in 1914 and 1915, were the rules to have effect as if enacted in the
Act. But the judges having shown some disposition to interfere
with the working of D.O.R.A. despite its generality,[4] the section
was in 1920 inserted in the Restoration of Order in Ireland Act to
meet the existing troubles there, and in the Emergency Powers
Act to meet possible crises at home in the future.[5] It was now clear
that there was to be no interference by the judiciary in the face of
an emergency.

The most ancient emergency power of the Council which rests
on statute, to check diseases and especially those of animals, was

---

[1] See the Proclamation of August 4, 1914.

[2] A-G v. De Keyser's Royal Hotel, [1920] A.C. 508.

[3] Militia Act, 1875. 38 & 39 Vict., c. 69, sec. 44; Army Regulation Act,
1871. 34 & 35 Vict., c. 86, sec. 16; Customs Laws Consolidation Act, 1876.
39 & 40 Vict., c. 36, sec. 138.

[4] See dissent of Lord Shaw in R. v. Halliday, [1917] A.C. 260; Newcastle
Breweries Ltd. v. R., [1920] 1 K.B. 854 (but disapproved in Hudson's Bay
Company v. Maclay, (1920) 36 T.L.R. 475); Chester v. Bateson, [1920]
1 K.B. 829.

[5] Restoration of Order in Ireland Act, 1920. 10 & 11 Geo. 5, c. 31, and see
per Lawrence, C. J., in ex parte Brady, (1921) 37 T.L.R. 854; Emergency
Powers Act, 1920. 10 & 11 Geo. 5, c. 55.

even in 1848 exercised through rules endowed with all the finality of an Act of Parliament.[1] Of this fact there can be no question; for, despite a provision to that effect in the Act, doubts later arose as to the position of these rules, and in 1866 their statutory force was confirmed ab initio.[2] The scope of the rules under the Act of 1848 was not very wide (they regulated such things as the removal of sheep from infected areas), but in 1869 the Council was permitted to make any orders "whatsoever . . . which the Privy Council think it expedient to make for the better execution of the Act,"[3] and the consolidating Act in 1878 shows that orders which touched closely the property of the individual, orders declaring a place to be infected within the meaning of the Act, and orders commanding the slaughter of a herd were beyond question.[4] Most of this Act is contained in the Act of 1894 and is still part of the law of England, although it is now administered by the Ministry of Agriculture; but the Council is still the appropriate body to prohibit the entry of disease into the Kingdom (an ancient head of jurisdiction),[5] and accordingly it was the Council which in 1919 was empowered to exclude from entry goods likely to be infected with anthrax by an order not subject to review.[6] Both types of power, it must be mentioned, were also exercised by the Privy Council in Ireland;[7] these also were intended to be within the sole discretion of the executive, Parliament going in two statutes so far as to make clear its meaning beyond doubt by the use of the "conclusive evidence clause" (of which later).

Perhaps the most important part of the Privy Council's activities is its conduct of foreign affairs. Now the Crown has not only a prerogative right to legislate for the colonies, it has also exclusive control over the power of war and peace — and consequently over the treaty-making power. But in most cases those same colonies

---

[1] Contagious Diseases of Animals Act, 1848. 11 & 12 Vict., c. 107, sec. 4.

[2] 29 & 30 Vict., c. 15, sec. 4.

[3] Contagious Diseases of Animals Act, 1869. 32 & 33 Vict., c. 70, sec. 75.

[4] Id., 1878. 41 & 42 Vict., c. 74, secs. 10, 15, and 58 (2).

[5] See 26 Geo. 2, c. 6, sec. 1, and R. v. Harris, (1791) 4 T.R. 202; also an Act of 6 Geo. 4, c. 78, sec. 2.

[6] Anthrax Prevention Act, 1919. 9 & 10 Geo. 5, c. 23, sec. 1 (2).

[7] Contagious Diseases (Ireland) Act, 1866. 29 & 30 Vict., c. 4, sec. 2; Cattle Disease (Ireland) Act, 1870. 33 & 34 Vict., c. 36, sec. 12; Criminal Law and Procedure (Ireland) Act, 1887. 50 & 51 Vict., c. 20, sec. 12; Peace Preservation (Ireland) Act, 1870. 33 & 34 Vict., c. 9, sec. 21; Protection of Person and Property (Ireland) Act, 1881. 44 Vict., c. 4, sec. 1 (1).

have a representative legislature of their own, and where that is the case they stand in legal theory in the same position as other rule-making authorities to whom Parliament has delegated legislative power. Any Act they pass must conform to the Colonial Laws Validity Act, and is liable to be held ultra vires by the courts of the colony or the Judicial Committee of the Privy Council. An extension of the legislative power of any colony can only be made by Parliament or at its command,[1] and to prevent difficulties aris-ing extension by the Council must be shown to have the same force as extension by Parliament. So far as I am aware, such execu-tive extension has not often been made. The Colonial Prisoners Removal Act directed the Council to empower the legislature of any British possession to pass Imperial extradition laws, and pre-sumably in view of the fact that the Order in Council in effect makes an amendment to the enabling Act of the colony, it was to rank with a statute of the Imperial Parliament and have effect as if enacted in the Act.[2] But it is the peculiar nature of the treaty-making power which has been responsible for most instances of the use of the section. The Crown may bind itself internationally without so much as consulting Parliament, but if it wishes the provisions of the treaty to bind British subjects and their private rights, it must at least have the express authority of Parliament for so doing;[3] for the Crown may not legislate without the consent of Parliament. It is, then, most important to show clearly that, where the provisions of a treaty are to be put into English law by the executive (and it is the executive which has dealt with the treaty throughout), the Council stands in the place of Parliament. Full dress Acts of Parliament, for instance, were usually passed to carry into effect international fishing treaties, and their provisions were set out in full in the Schedule;[4] but where more detailed orders were thought necessary to carry into effect the scheduled provisions of the Behring Sea Award, Parliament had to lay stress upon the capacity in which the Council was issuing the orders.[5] After the World War the congestion of domestic business in Par-

[1] This statement must be taken with some reservations in the case of the self-governing dominions.

[2] Colonial Prisoners Removal Act, 1884. 47 & 48 Vict., c. 31, sec. 12.

[3] The Parlement Belge, (1879) 4 P.D. 129; Walker v. Baird, [1892] A.C. 491 semble.

[4] E. g. Sea Fisheries Act, 1883. 46 & 47 Vict., c. 22, sec. 23; Seal Fishery (N. Pacific) Act, 1893. 56 & 57 Vict., c. 23.

[5] Behring Sea Award Act, 1894. 57 Vict., c. 2, sec. 3 (1).

liament, and the complexity of the peace treaties, was such that the executive was constituted, as it were, a Parliament ad certam rem, and it was provided in the Treaties of Peace Act, 1920, that "His Majesty may make such appointments, establish such offices, make such Orders-in-Council, and do such things as appear to be necessary for carrying out the said Treaties and for giving effect to any of the provisions of the said Treaties." [1] Here the power to make orders for giving effect to treaty provisions was of necessity, as I see it, the power of Parliament itself.

The Council is also concerned with the machinery of government. It is at once formally the most important, and in practice the least differentiated, organ of the executive, and thus is best fitted for marshalling and remarshalling the departments which perform the duties of actual administration, or supervising the practical side of the administration of justice and the machinery of voting. And where the orders issued under this head by the Council have a statutory finality, the reason is not hard to find. Once a change has been effected it is most inconvenient — just as in the case of an extensive housing scheme, although this factor carried no weight with the Court of Appeal in *Yaffe's Case* — to have the new arrangements upset on the petition of one possibly unworthy citizen for some trivial defect in procedure. So that the Council has in the past been permitted to lay down in its discretion rules fixing the divisions of the High Court and their vacations,[2] the circuits and the place and date of assizes,[3] and to make special provision for the detention of special classes of offenders pending trial at the Central Criminal Court.[4] With respect to voting, the Council was early empowered to alter the place of polling already fixed by statute,[5] and when in 1918 the proposal to establish a system of proportional representation was passed into law, it was the Council which was directed to prescribe the method of voting and the transferring and counting of votes — an unenviable task.[6] In this matter, too, the Privy Council in Ireland had roughly the

[1] Treaties of Peace Act, 1920. 10 Geo. 5, c. 6, sec. 1 (1). See in particular 11 & 12 Geo. 5, c. 11, and 14 Geo. 5, c. 7.

[2] Judicature Act, 1873. 36 & 37 Vict., c. 66, secs. 27 and 32.

[3] Judicature Act (Amendment) Act, 1875. 38 & 39 Vict., c. 77, sec. 23.

[4] Trial of Offenses Act, 1856. 19 & 20 Vict., c. 16, sec. 14; Jurisdiction in Homicides Act, 1862. 25 & 26 Vict., c. 65, sec. 18.

[5] Elections Act, 1853. 16 & 17 Vict., c. 68, sec. 7.

[6] Representation of the People Act, 1918. 7 & 8 Geo. 5, c. 64, sec. 20 (3).

same functions and performed them under the same conditions.[1] But these were changes of small importance in comparison with the sweeping reorganisation of the departments undertaken at the close of the War. The haphazard assignment of duties among the various authorities which had resulted from the habit of either creating temporary ad hoc bodies and later handing over their duties to that department whose work was most closely allied to theirs, or of charging a committee of the Privy Council, perhaps even a secretary of state, with the new duties, had become intolerable — how intolerable was not realised until war-time experience showed the necessity and the benefits of efficient coördination. A Royal Commission on the Machinery of Government was appointed with Lord Haldane as chairman; the Commission reported in 1918, and soon after the end of the War the Government proceeded to carry some of its proposals into effect. As an instance take the Ministry of Health, one of the first fruits of reorganisation. The Act creating it expressly transfers to the new Ministry the duties of the Local Government Board, the Insurance Commissioners, and certain health powers of the Board of Education, but subsection 2 of section 3 provides that it shall be lawful for His Majesty by Order in Council to transfer to the Minister the health powers of the Minister of Pensions, the lunacy and mental deficiency powers of the Secretary of State, and finally "any other powers and duties in England and Wales of any Government department which appear to His Majesty to relate to matters affecting or incidental to the health of the people." [2] No statutory effect, however, was expressly given to orders made under the Act of 1919; indeed they had no force until approved by resolutions in both Houses (sec. 8 [2]). There is some doubt about the legal effect of such an order. On the one hand it would seem that in passing their resolutions the Houses are only exercising powers of their own delegation and so do not put the order beyond the reach of the courts. On the other hand it might well be argued that in interfering with such an order the Court

---

[1] Elections (Ireland) Act, 1850. 13 & 14 Vict., c. 68, sec. 22; Assizes (Ireland) Act, 1850. 13 & 14 Vict., c. 85, sec. 2; Chairmen's Jurisdiction Act, 1876. 39 & 40 Vict., c. 71, secs. 2 and 3; Supreme Court of Judicature (Ireland) Act, 1877. 40 & 41 Vict., c. 57, secs. 30 and 32; Supreme Court of Judicature (Ireland) (Amendment) Act, 1887. 50 Vict., c. 6, sec. 2.

[2] Ministry of Health Act, 1919. 9 & 10 Geo. 5, c. 21, sec. 3 (1), (2); see also Ministry of Transport Act, 1919. 9 & 10 Geo. 5, c. 50, secs. 2 and 28 (1).

would be interfering with the business of Parliament. The second point of view carries great practical weight (Parliament would not have approved if the order did not express its own intention), but the reasoning of Younger, L. J., in *R. v. Electricity Commissioners*,[1] that in declaring an order ultra vires before Parliament has had time to give it their necessary approval is not a hindrance but a help to a body not apt to canvass nice questions of law, could without difficulty be applied here. In any case there is small likelihood of a challenge.

The remaining rules with statutory finality issued by the Council dealt with matters which have since been entrusted to the various departments, weights and measures, dockyards, shipping, and a few others,[2] and need not be discussed here.

At the other end of the social scale of rule-making authorities stand semi-public bodies and commissioners. I have already made casual comment upon the semi-public bodies in connection with *Cleeland's Case*, and that case shows the possible danger involved in setting the rules of a monopolistic organisation like the Pharmaceutical Society of Ireland upon a par with an Act of Parliament. Different considerations arise in the case of the only other private body which has ever possessed this extreme power, the Bank of England. The Bank, transacting as it does the financial business of the government, is intimately involved with the governmental process, and although it is no part of the system, and so has no representative who may be questioned in Parliament, it is subject to just as much control by Parliament as is a group of commissioners. Parliament might at any time determine the existence of such a group, and in the case of the Bank transfer its business elsewhere — although that is not very likely to happen. It is not, however, very extraordinary to find the Bank permitted to make final rules relative to conversion of, and proof of title to, government stock, Parliament itself being hardly fitted to discuss the details of a financial transaction, whereas the Bank is intimately acquainted with such matters.[3]

In the adolescent period of modern English government any

---

[1] [1924] 1 K.B. 171, p. 212.

[2] E. g. Weights and Measures Act, 1878. 41 & 42 Vict., c. 49, secs. 5, 8, 41, 47, and 63; Dockyard Regulation Act, 1865. 28 & 29 Vict., c. 125, secs. 3, 5, 6, and 7; Sea Fisheries Act, 1868. 31 & 32 Vict., c. 45, sec. 23; Midwives Act, 1918. 8 & 9 Geo. 5, c. 43, sec. 1; Naval Savings Bank Act, 1866. 29 & 30 Vict., c. 43, sec. 5.

[3] National Debt Act, 1870. 33 & 34 Vict., c. 71, sec. 39; Stock Certificate

new duties undertaken by Parliament were entrusted in general either to the Privy Council or to a body of commissioners created ad hoc; it was particularly where the new duties were confined to a relatively narrow and well-defined field, and were not expected to be permanent, that a commission was set up. I have discovered ten of these commissions which were at some time and for some purpose, small or great, empowered to issue rules of statutory effect; and in rules I do not include orders half judicial and half legislative, such as the Enclosure Commissioners made when they confirmed a valuer's award,[1] or regulated the holding of a particular allotment in common created by them for the parties.[2] The widest powers of rule making were exercised by the commissioners appointed in the middle of the nineteenth century to reorganise the two universities and the public schools. Under the Government of Oxford Act, 1854, college statutes were to be drawn up by the Commissioners, and after approval by the Privy Council they were to have full effect.[3] The same procedure was followed in the case of the public schools,[4] but that Parliament was more concerned about the statutes of the university is shown by the passage of a special Act six years later to create machinery for the approbation of an ordinance drawn up by the Oxford University Commissioners.[5] But even this field was narrow, and indeed in all cases, except that of the Insurance Commissioners of 1911, the commissioners may not do much more than regulate their own proceedings, the manner of application, forms and fees,[6] or perhaps the requisite proofs of a claim, or the returns to be made.[7] One interesting instance escapes classification and so deserves special mention. In the Private Legislation Procedure (Scotland) Act, 1899, which enabled most of Scots private bill legislation to be done by Provisional Order, the Chairman of Committees in the House of Lords and the Chairman of Ways and Means in the Commons have certain important duties, among them that of making general orders to

Act, 1863. 26 & 27 Vict., c. 28, sec. 10; India Stock Act, 1863. 26 & 27 Vict., c. 73, sec. 9.

[1] Enclosure Act, 1845. 8 & 9 Vict., c. 118, sec. 105.

[2] Enclosure Act, 1801. 41 Geo. 3, c. 109, sec. 13.

[3] Government of Oxford Act, 1854. 17 & 18 Vict., c. 81, sec. 35.

[4] Public Schools Act, 1868. 31 & 32 Vict., c. 118, sec. 9.

[5] Oxford University Act, 1860. 23 & 24 Vict., c. 23.

[6] E. g. Improvement of Land Act, 1864. 27 & 28 Vict., c. 114, sec. 90; Public Works Loans Act, 1875. 38 & 39 Vict., c. 89, sec. 41.

[7] Government Annuities Act, 1929. 19 & 20 Geo. 5, c. 29, sec. 52.

regulate the rather complicated proceedings under the Act, and by subsection 3 of section 15 subject to disallowance by resolution of both Houses "every general order purporting to be made in pursuance of the Act shall be deemed to have been duly made and within the powers of the Act, and shall have effect as if enacted in this Act." [1] The powers of the Insurance Commissioners caused some concern to Dicey,[2] but in the matter of rule making they are not of great importance; although they might by order make special provision as to seasonal trades, inmates of charitable homes, and certificated teachers (but only along lines carefully sketched out by Parliament), the *regulations* do not cover anything more exciting than the constitution and powers of district insurance committees, or the arrangements with medical practitioners for the administration of medical benefit.[3]

It would be tedious to travel at length through all the final rules which may be issued by the other departments. It is enough to record, first, that the great majority are procedural, and second, that the Board of Trade and the Secretary of State have the highest score to their credit — just what might have been expected from departments of such importance and such long standing. The widest powers yet granted, however, are found in an Act administered by the Minister of Health, the Poor Law Act of 1927, by which the Minister is directed to make rules declaring in effect to what extent, and for what period, upon what conditions, at what time and place, and in what manner outdoor relief may be granted,[4] and in an earlier Act belonging to the same department, under which regulations are issuable to govern the constitution of approved benefit societies, conditions of membership therein, and other similar subjects.[5]

Thus far nothing startling has emerged from a rapid review of those statutes in which rules are declared to have effect as if enacted in the Act, and apart from the emergency powers of the Council, where freedom from control is the immediate object, and its control of foreign affairs, in which a rule must for the reasons stated look as like a statute as possible, there are few occasions of

---

[1] 62 & 63 Vict., c. 48, sec. 15.

[2] Law and Opinion, Introduction to Ed. 2, p. xl.

[3] National Insurance Act, 1911. 1 & 2 Geo. 5, c. 55, secs. 15, 59 and 65.

[4] Poor Law Act, 1927. 17 & 18 Geo. 5, c. 14, sec. 73 (1) (read with sec. 211 [2]).

[5] National Health Insurance Act, 1924. 14 & 15 Geo. 5, c. 38, sec. 93 (1).

importance in which the jurisdiction of the courts suffers curtailment. The instances given by Lord Hewart [1] cannot, apart from the section of the Poor Law Act paraphrased above, cause any alarm; the truth is that read by itself a section which purports to give finality to any rules has a terrifying air about it, but an examination of the permissible scope of the regulations — and surely that is the vital point — dispels all fears. The three examples to which he refers [2] deal with procedural regulations, viz. the payment of fees, the publication of notices, and the holding of inquiries. And what chance is there, particularly in the light of the dicta in the *Swansea Case* or the *Arlidge Case*, that any person would wish to challenge them? And if the Rules Committee can be trusted to refrain from oppressive rules, why not the Electricity Commissioners, the Board of Trade, and the Minister of Labour?

III

Conclusive Evidence Clause

There is only one class of case in which the judiciary have admitted that their jurisdiction to review legislative rules and orders is excluded: where there is a provision in the Act like that in Schedule III, 2, of the Housing Act of 1925, "the confirmation by the Minister shall be conclusive evidence that the requirements of this Act have been complied with and that the order has been duly made and is within the powers of this Act." Such a provision is of comparatively rare occurrence, and is the strongest expression of its intention which Parliament has ever made — except in two isolated instances, section 5 of the Extradition Act of 1870, under which an Order in Council putting the Act in force with respect to the nationals of treaty powers is "conclusive evidence that the arrangement therein referred to complies with the requisites of this Act, and that the Act applies in the case of the foreign state mentioned in the order, *and the validity of the order shall not be questioned in any legal proceedings whatever*," and section 3 of the Parliament Act, 1911, which declares that "any certificate of the Speaker of the House of Commons given under this Act shall be conclusive for all purposes *and shall not be questioned in any court of law*."

[1] The New Despotism, pp. 68–69.
[2] Electricity Supply Act, 1919. 9 & 10 Geo. 5, c. 100, sec. 34; Gas Regulation Act, 1920. 10 & 11 Geo. 5, c. 28, sec. 16; Unemployment Insurance Act, 1920. 10 & 11 Geo. 5, c. 30, sec. 35 (4).

The Extradition Act worried C. K. Allen,[1] but the provision does no more than make clear the undoubted prerogative right of the Crown with respect to aliens,[2] and prevent a court from inquiring into the question of whether a treaty was in fact made, a prohibition no more startling than that attaching to the question of the existence or sovereign status of foreign powers.[3] Of the Parliament Act Dicey said that "this enactment, if strictly construed, would protect any Speaker who, either from partisanship or to promote some personal interest of his own, signed a certificate which was notoriously false, from being liable to punishment by any court of law whatever"; [4] it would, but the infinitesimal risk involved is more than counterbalanced by the advantage accruing from it. What if it had been left open for a member of the House of Lords to canvass the question in court of whether a bill was a money bill or not? The efficient working of the Parliament Act hinges on the Speaker, and if his discretion is to be hampered and his decision to be delayed, the blocking action of the Lords designed to be removed by that Act could be reëstablished by indirect means. Besides, the provision does not do much more than reiterate a Common Law principle, that the courts will not interfere in the business of Parliament, — a principle, incidentally, which has recently suffered some shocks.[5]

The oft-quoted case of *Ex parte Ringer* [6] is the only direct authority for the proposition that where an Act contains such a provision the Court cannot interfere; but Scrutton, L. J., rested his decision in *Yaffe's Case* principally on the argument that if Parliament had wished to exclude the courts from reviewing the confirmation order before him, they would not have said as they did in section 40 (5), that the order when made shall have effect as if enacted in the Act, but would have used the stronger words applied by them in the Schedule to a compulsory purchase order. There is, however, an Irish case to the contrary; [7] the Waterford Bridge Act, 1906, empowered the Corporation to make by-laws as to the time and mode of vessels passing through the bridge, but made no

---

[1] Law in the Making, p. 324.

[2] *Ex parte Venicoff*, [1920] 3 K.B. 72.

[3] Luther *v.* Sagor, [1921] 3 K.B. 532; Duff Development Company *v.* Kelantan Government, [1924] A.C. 797.

[4] Law of the Constitution, Introduction to Ed. 8, p. xxxviii.

[5] R. *v.* Electricity Commissioners, [1924] 1 K.B. 171.

[6] (1909) 27 T.L.R. 718.

[7] Corporation of Waterford *v.* Murphy, [1920] 2 I.R. 165.

provision for fees. The Corporation passed a by-law, charging fees for opening it at inconvenient hours, which the Court held ultra vires. Section 10 was then relied on. This section provided that "a printed copy of such by-laws . . . shall be conclusive evidence of the validity of such by-laws"; but the Court, employing the technique employed so fruitfully a few years later in *Yaffe's Case,* fastened on the word "such" and concluded that "such by-laws" could only mean by-laws that might be made under the earlier part of the section — with regard to the time and mode of passage. The Court thought that *Lockwood's Case* was not in point, and with that I heartily agree; but no reliance seems to have been placed on the strong words of the statute itself, words far stronger than those considered in the case which the Court discussed. The decision amounts in effect to a holding that a rule or by-law can never be withdrawn from review by the courts, except perhaps by a provision so blatant as to be positively indecent.

"In passing such a clause Parliament, it may be thought, was really stultifying itself because having inserted express provisions in the Act for the protection of persons liable to have their property taken . . . it has by means of the 'conclusive evidence' clause rendered such provisions nugatory." [1] "Such a section was a standing invitation to the Board to exceed its powers." [2] These are the comments of Lord Hewart and the editors of a recent case book on the case of *ex parte Ringer.* But it is worth while to consider the situation to which the clause was there applied, and at which presumably Lord Hewart directs his objections; for all his instances except one [3] deal with an order permitting the compulsory purchase of land. The Board of Agriculture was empowered to purchase land compulsorily for allotments; it was directed to have regard to certain wishes of owners. The applicant applied for certiorari alleging that the direction had not been observed in his case. The Court decided that the "conclusive evidence clause" barred all review. Now what would be the result of granting certiorari in such a case? It would then be the legal duty of the Board to restore the land. In the meantime the Council might have gone

[1] The New Despotism, p. 73.

[2] Keir and Lawson, Cases in Constitutional Law, p. 144.

[3] London Traffic Act, 1924. 14 & 15 Geo. 5, c. 34, sec. 10 (6), where the requirements, compliance with which is conclusively proved by the order, are that the advisory committee be consulted, and the Secretary of State be apprised of any regulations which will impose new duties on the police!

ahead with the allotment scheme. It might even happen that, a year after proceedings were over and done with, a litigious farmer would discover that he had certain rights unnoticed at the time of taking. Worse than that, suppose years later the allotments were given up and the Council wished to dispose of the land, to the Government, for instance, as a site for a post-office; must the title be held defective because a court decides ex post facto that the Board did not take all the steps which the statute in the opinion of the Court required? Much depends on settling the title to land once and for all, and where the procedure to be followed in compulsory taking is as complicated as that of the Lands Clauses Acts, a provision of this nature seems wise. A court, after all, found itself able to introduce complexity into the comparatively simple procedure for making an improvement scheme,[1] with the result that slum clearance in Derby and Liverpool was held up on the application of worthless slum-owners. But even delay is not so disastrous as a peremptory order of a court when the scheme is well under way, ordering the aggrieved party to be put back into possession or compensated at an extravagant rate for the "wrong" done him.[2] It is true that with such a clause as this the procedural directions laid down in the statute are not enforceable by the courts; but if the Board had wilfully neglected them — to suppose a situation comic in its improbability — there is little doubt that questions would have been asked in Parliament, and in any case it is not reasonable to suppose that officials would treat the Act as so much waste paper merely because of the absence of the man with the club. Questions of government cannot be settled by drawing analogies from the behaviour of a pickpocket when the policeman is off his beat.

There are very few instances of the use of this section in statutes

[1] R. v. Minister of Health, ex parte Davis, [1929] 1 K.B. 619; ex parte Yaffe, [1930] 2 K.B. 90.

[2] The Report of the Ministry of Agriculture on the Agricultural Marketing Act, 1931, has this comment (p. 17) on the "conclusive evidence clause" in sec. 1 (8): "The effect of this provision is that once a scheme has been approved it shall not be liable to be nullified on the ground of a technical flaw either in the scheme itself or in the procedure followed prior to its approval. The confusion which would arise if a scheme were suddenly to be ruled illegal after it had been in operation for any length of time can readily be appreciated: in fact it would be impracticable to set up a Board with extensive powers of holding property, incurring liabilities, and, perhaps, of trading, if the courts could hold at any time that the scheme and, indeed, the very existence of the Board had been a nullity from the start."

relating to England, and still fewer which cover legislative orders as opposed to those which are quasi-judicial, orders establishing a charge to secure a loan or confirming a valuation list, for example.[1] Of a general legislative order I have found only one instance — not counting those which deal with trivial rules of procedure [2] — besides those quoted and explained above, the Explosive Substances Act of 1875, where orders granting permissions to build factories for explosives and orders approving rules to be observed in their manufacture may not be questioned,[3] perhaps for no particular reason, perhaps because the handling of explosives is preeminently a matter for the unfettered discretion of experts.

In the case of local orders there are — if repetitions in consolidating acts are excluded — no more than seven occasions on which the section has been used. Five are concerned with the compulsory acquisition of land,[4] the other two with the confirmation of schemes, the Light Railways Act of 1896 [5] and the Agricultural Marketing Act of 1931.[6] There is no reason why the section should appear in the Light Railways Act and yet be absent from almost all the other statutes where it rests with a department to confirm a scheme; it may be there in view of section 9 (3), which provides that if the Board thinks that "by reason of the magnitude of the scheme or for any special reason the proposals ought to be submitted to Parliament they shall not confirm it," and may be meant to affirm that, in any other case but that, the Board stands in the place of Parliament. That is certainly the reason for its appearance in the Agricultural Marketing Act. The bill came up in the middle of the period of regression from excessive delegation; the clause was in the bill when it originated, and appears in the Act, but there was added in committee a provision that no scheme should go into force without a resolution of approval by each House, — surely a

[1] E. g. Improvement of Land Act, 1864. 27 & 28 Vict., c. 114, sec. 55; Housing Act, 1925. 15 Geo. 5, c. 14, sec. 32 (2); Valuation of Property (Metropolis) Act, 1869. 32 & 33 Vict., c. 67, sec. 45.

[2] Tramways Act, 1870. 33 & 34 Vict., c. 78, sec. 64; Public Works Loans Act, 1875. 38 & 39 Vict., c. 89, sec. 41.

[3] Explosive Substances Act, 1875. 38 Vict., c. 17, sec. 83.

[4] Local Government Act, 1894. 56 & 57 Vict., c. 73, secs. 9 (7) (c) and 42; Small Holdings and Allotments Act, 1907. 7 Ed. 7, c. 54, sec. 26 (3); Education Act, 1921. 11 & 12 Geo. 5, c. 51, Sched. V (2); Housing Act, 1925. 15 Geo. 5, c. 14, Sched. III, 2; Salmon and Freshwater Fisheries Act, 1923. 13 & 14 Geo. 5, c. 16, sec. 16.

[5] Light Railways Act, 1896. 59 & 60 Vict., c. 48, sec. 10.

[6] Agricultural Marketing Act, 1931. 21 & 22 Geo. 5, c. 42, sec. 1 (8).

sufficient safeguard, — and that even after the scheme came into force it should remain open to registered producers to reject the scheme by means of a poll.[1] The legislative history of this Act gives some hope that Parliament will be anxious to exercise the control, if there is to be control, and not leave it to fortuitous interference by the courts.

But this division of the inquiry is no more illuminating in its results than my efforts to discover the rationale of the use of the "have effect as if enacted in the Act clause." For the Irish Acts are hopelessly inconclusive; it is not difficult to see the need for putting repressive measures beyond the reach of the courts,[2] but why — or what is the meaning of — this section in connection with an order to hold special revising sessions, or an order extending the jurisdiction of certain local courts?[3] And why should an order confirming an Irish housing scheme be protected by this section, when English schemes are only to have effect as if enacted in the Act?[4] Even that part of the subject which in the eyes of the judges in *Yaffe's Case* was beyond question turns out to be as irrational and mysterious as that about which they expressed doubt.

IV

SKELETON LEGISLATION

Certain powers of the departments, particularly of the Board of Trade and the Secretary of State, raise quite another question, that of skeleton legislation. Where the Board of Trade is empowered to draw up a final list of safety appliances that must be carried in a ship, or to regulate a dangerous practice of fishermen,[5] or the Secretary of State to make special safety orders to fit the conditions

[1] Agricultural Marketing Act, 1931. 21 & 22 Geo. 5, c. 42, secs. 1 (8) and 3 (1) and (2).

[2] Peace Preservation (Ireland) Act, 1870. 33 & 34 Vict., c. 9, sec. 21; Protection of Persons and Property Act (Ireland), 1881, 44 Vict., c. 4, sec. 1 (1).

[3] Registration (Ireland) Act, 1873. 36 & 37 Vict., c. 30, sec. 4; Local Bankruptcy (Ireland) Act, 1888. 51 & 52 Vict., c. 44, sec. 18. See also Marshalsea (Dublin) Act, 1874. 37 & 38 Vict., c. 21, sec. 4; Town Improvement Act (Ireland), 1854. 17 & 18 Vict., c. 103, sec. 15.

[4] Labourers (Ireland) Act, 1906. 6 Ed. 7, c. 37, sec. 6 (4).

[5] Merchant Shipping (Life Saving Appliances) Act, 1888. 51 & 52 Vict., c. 24, sec. 3 (1); Merchant Shipping (Fishing Boats) Act, 1887. 50 Vict., c. 4, sec. 10 (1).

of special mines or factories,[1] the insertion of a section purporting to bar review by the courts only reinforces the reluctance of the judges to interfere with technical regulations. But Parliament has gone further than this and empowered a department to make a code, a Cremation Code, an Air Code, a Highway Code;[2] it was on this principle that England was governed from 1914 to 1918 under the redoubtable Defence of the Realm Acts, and lived in the spring and summer of 1926 under the executive regulations authorised by the Emergency Powers Act. It might be thought that here the limit was reached, but the Cotton Cloth Factories Acts go to the extent of permitting the Secretary of State "to make regulations for the purpose of giving effect to such of the recommendations contained in the Report (of a departmental committee) . . . as he may deem necessary for the protection of health in cotton cloth factories," [3] a power paralleled only by an Act of 1900 which permitted the Irish Education Department to do much the same thing.[4]

It was round the latest Cotton Cloth Factories Act that an epic battle was fought in the House of Lords during 1929. The objections to such a bill were obvious, especially in a House where growing Socialism was not regarded with favor, and at a time when Lords and Commons alike were setting their faces resolutely against the supposed menace of the bureaucracy; the department was to pass into law the recommendations of its own committee, and no reports of the recommendations had at the time of the debate been placed in the hands of the Lords. By the terms of the bill an absolute discretion was left in the Secretary of State to choose which recommendations he should embody in the order; it was this feature which caused Lord Carson to break out with the bitter comment, "But that a Secretary of State should take up a departmental report and say, 'All this is now to be law as I wish to lay it down in regulations and according to my selection,' and put it into language that will suit himself. Why not abolish Parliament

[1] Coal Mines Regulation Act, 1887. 50 & 51 Vict., c. 58, sec. 51 (1); Factory and Workshop Act, 1901. 1 Ed. 7, c. 22, sec. 126.

[2] Cremation Act, 1902. 2 Ed. 7, c. 8, sec. 7; Air Navigation Act, 1919. 9 Geo. 5, c. 3, sec. 1; Motor Car Act, 1903. 3 Ed. 7, c. 36, secs. 2 and 7; Road Traffic Act, 1930. 20 & 21 Geo. 5, c. 43, sec. 45.

[3] Cotton Cloth Factories Act, 1897. 60 & 61 Vict., c. 58, sec. 1; Cotton Cloth Factories Act, 1911. 1 & 2 Geo. 5, c. 21, sec. 1 (1); Cotton Cloth Factories Act, 1929. 19 & 20 Geo. 5, c. 15, sec. 1.

[4] Intermediate Education (Ireland) Act, 1900. 63 & 64 Vict., c. 43, sec. 1 (1).

altogether?"¹ Lord Desborough did his best to explain that there
could be no objection to the committee, for it was agreed on by
both employers and labour, and that the provisions of the bill were
too technical to be understood by anyone except an expert, but he
retreated from the position of the two earlier Acts in consenting
to omit the section which gave statutory finality to the rules when
made, and in submitting an amendment which provided that the
rules were to lie before Parliament in draft before going into operation. Even so, Lord Banbury was not pacified; for him the amendment was "as regards the House of Commons not worth the paper
it is written upon."² He may have been right, but the problem
before the House was peculiar, and there was no alternative. Any
debate upon the technicalities of a bill of this nature would have
been farcical, and it may well be that in the circumstances any
objection at all was academic; for the committee was agreed to by
both employers and employees, and they were the only persons
conceivably to be affected. If any Lord took the trouble to glance
at the orders later issued by the Secretary of State under the Act,
he doubtless congratulated himself that he had not been forced to
reveal his ignorance on matters of ventilation, the diameter of
steam pipes, and hygrometer readings.³ Sir John Marriott read
them, we know, for he used the volume of the Rules to illustrate
an anti-bureaucratic argument — without, however, referring to
their subject matter or to the two earlier statutes upon the same
facts.⁴

Parliament here resigned in favor of the executive, a thing which
it has never otherwise done, except to meet an emergency. The
two outstanding examples of executive action in the face of a
crisis — if we except the two Acts of 1931, the National Economy
Act and the Abnormal Importations Act, in which there was no
power to make regulations but only to issue orders of defined scope
— are the Defence of the Realm Acts and the Emergency Powers
Act.

The Defence of the Realm Acts were passed to meet the crisis
of the World War. The consolidating Act of 1914 ⁵ reads more like
the preamble to a nineteenth-century statute than a legislative

¹ 72 Lords Deb. (5th Series), p. 936, February 14, 1929.
² 72 Lords Deb. (5th Series), p. 1191, February 28, 1929.
³ 1929. S.R. & O., p. 442.
⁴ Prologue to The Crisis of English Liberty (1930), p. 10.
⁵ 5 Geo. 5, c. 8, sec. 1.

grant of power; it provides that "His Majesty has power during the continuance of the present war to issue regulations for securing the public safety and the defence of the realm," permits trial by court-martial, and specifies particular but all-inclusive purposes for which regulations may be made, the last clause of subsection 1 reading, "or otherwise to prevent assistance being given to the enemy or the successful prosecution of the war being endangered." Regulations were issued under it by Order in Council, and in time further regulations under them. Even in the early days of the War the regulations went pretty far. By the consolidated regulations of November 28, 1914, areas might be cleared of their inhabitants, roads stopped up, and suspected persons removed. Article 48 made any person "who does any act preparatory to the commission of any act prohibited by the regulations" guilty of an offence against them, and by Article 49 it was the duty of any person "who knows that some other person is acting in contravention of any provision of these regulations to inform the competent naval or military authority of the fact," and if he failed to do so he was guilty of an offence against the regulations. By the end of the War there were regulations under the Act which amended the Dogs' Act, prohibited dogshows, and forbade the sale or gift of cocaine or opium to an actress; [1] and it is common knowledge that even now there are restrictions, upon the sale of chocolate for instance, which derive their force from this war-time Act. In 1920 the Act was called upon to do duty in another field, civil war in Ireland, and the Restoration of Order in Ireland Act made assurance doubly sure by clapping on to the powers of D.O.R.A. the provision that the rules should have effect as if enacted in the Act. [2]

The Emergency Powers Act — "a solution . . . for the difficulty . . . of reconciling the sovereignty of Parliament with the need for swift executive action in a case of emergency" [3] — was designed to deal with serious labour troubles, which even in 1920 loomed on the horizon. On the proclamation of a state of emergency — each proclamation to last for one month only — the executive was empowered to make regulations for securing the essentials of life to the community; the regulations were to be laid before Parliament, and their continuance after the expiration of seven days was con-

[1] Regulations 2 S, 9 DD., 40 B, quoted in The Rule of D O R A, 1 J.S.C.L. (3rd Series), 1919, Part I, p. 37.

[2] 1920. 10 & 11 Geo. 5, c. 31, sec. 1.

[3] Keir and Lawson, Cases in Constitutional Law (1928), p. 353.

ditional upon a resolution of approval by both Houses. When made they had effect as if enacted in the Act, and were not subject to the Rules Publication Act.[1] In 1926 the long-feared storm broke; the Act was put into force and regulations were issued under it. How effective the Act is cannot be estimated from the outcome of that crisis, — for there was no attempt to deprive the community of the essentials of life, — but my only concern here is with the regulations issued under it. Orders in Council empowered the executive to take possession of land, food, forage, materials, and stores, to regulate the supply and distribution of food, to organise road transport, to direct traffic on the highways, and to supervise shipping and the clearance and loading of ships. Restrictions on personal liberty were imposed; by Article 22 (2) the Secretary of State was permitted to prohibit the holding of a meeting "where there appears reason to apprehend that the assembling of persons for the purpose of holding it will conduce to a breach of the peace," and by Article 33 (2) any police constable could arrest without warrant any person "who so acts as to endanger the public safety or who is guilty or suspected of being guilty of an offence against the regulations."[2] Orders restricting the sale and consumption of essentials were issued under the regulations: the amount of coal to be supplied and used for domestic consumption, the manufacture of gas, or industry was limited,[3] and every person within metropolitan London with milk at his disposal was required to stand ready to put it at the disposal of the London Milk Pool Committee.[4]

Few will maintain that it is a pleasant feeling to be dragooned into observing restraints to which they never gave even Rousseau's implied consent, and which they cannot challenge in the courts without difficulty; but no one will deny that the weakness of a democracy most appears in times of crisis, and that few people will be found to set a political theory before a full stomach. What is a crisis is an interesting question. The Emergency Powers Act is a novel piece of legislation, for it grants war powers to deal with an internal economic enemy. The two Acts of 1931 are even more novel.[5] They may not have been significant of anything except a desire to play to the international gallery. If they were more than

---

[1] Emergency Powers Act, 1920. 10 & 11 Geo. 5, c. 55, sec. 1.
[2] Emergency Regulations, No. 2 Code, May 29, 1926.
[3] Coal (Emergency) Directions, May 1, 1926.
[4] Milk Distribution (Emergency) Order, May 3, 1926.
[5] The National Economy Act and the Abnormal Importations Act.

that, there is every expectation that with the decline of her prosperity England will find it more and more necessary to take drastic measures to avert catastrophe — and the method of executive legislation avoids, as Mr. MacDonald found, a great deal of acrimonious discussion.

These regulations were issued to meet crises. What of the codes promulgated with other ends in view? While the majority of rule-making powers are not of sufficient scope to fill the volumes of Statutory Rules and Orders with codes, and while there has not been during the last ten years any perceptible increase in the actual number of rules, it is probable that in the future Parliament will be forced to rely increasingly on delegation; and even now there are plenty of examples of this code-making power. There can be no doubt of their extent (the County Court Rules of 1903 cover 500 pages; the regulations of 1930 under the National Health Insurance Act, 1924, cover 200) nor of their importance (the Cremation Order, 1903, regulated what was then a novel practice). Sometimes — and this is particularly true of codes of procedure — the authority is content to transplant rules issued by Parliament on an analogous occasion; the general orders, for instance, made by the two Chairmen of Committees acting jointly with the Secretary of State for Scotland under the Private Legislation Procedure (Scotland) Act are nothing more than a restatement of the Standing Orders of the two Houses which govern private bills.[1] But sometimes — as in the Cremation Order — the department breaks new ground. There the department provided not only for the maintenance and inspection of crematoria, but it had to face the problem created by this legalisation of a method of disposal of corpses which might prove a godsend to criminals; accordingly the rules contained an elaborate exposition of the certificates which must be obtained and the post-mortems which must be held, and a form of searching questions to be answered was appended.[2]

A consideration of the Irish Prison Order of 1902 or the Public Assistance Order of 1930 opens up wide vistas; how simple the words of grant in the Act from which depend these miniature statutes! The 1930 order repeals all previous orders: it has 180 articles and lengthy schedules; it prescribes rules for the treatment of inmates of workhouses, of casuals, and pauper lunatics. The Prison Order runs the gamut of prison life in forty-eight pages of

[1] Order of May 28, 1900.
[2] Regulations of March 31, 1903.

print: the behaviour of prisoners, offences and their punishment, diet, the conduct of prison officers. The National Health Insurance Regulations of 1930 have less dramatic appeal, but in them provision is made for special cases, for exempt persons' dental benefit and medical benefit, while the position of approved benefit societies is defined with a particularity which could not be entered into in the Parliament of today. It is legislation of this nature which has at last made clear how great a change has come about beneath the surface of the legal concepts of the English Constitution.

The conservative element in Parliament is never tired of calling upon Parliament to reassert its supremacy. But the most cursory examination of a volume of Statutory Rules and Orders shows that complete control could never be reasserted today if Parliament sat all the year round from morning till night. Lord Hewart is more reasonable when he asks Parliament at least to be conscious of what it is doing when it delegates the power to make rules. There are two aspects of the question which Parliament would do well to bear always in mind, the scope of the power and the legal effect of the rules when made. Remembering that there are many occasions in which for Parliament to prescribe details is for it to meddle with things its does not understand, members have been on the whole willing to lay little emphasis on the scope of the power granted, but to insist strongly on controls.

Control is either by the courts or by Parliament itself. The control of the courts is in any case sporadic, and proceeds by the devious path of the legal mysteries. The courts further purport to deal only with questions of power, not questions of policy; but since their decisions rest mainly on statutory interpretation, and ambiguous words derive their force not from any innate virtue of their own but from what the interpreter puts into them, these decisions are in effect judgments of a court upon what in their opinion should be the scope of executive discretion. Only the accident of the point being raised in a controversy makes it justiciable before a body of men more accustomed to unravel the niceties of a charter party than to build up a system of government. If executive legislation is objectionable on the ground that the control of Parliament through criticism of the Minister is illusory, the action of the judiciary in substituting its own opinion, formed after hearing an hour or two of argument, for the opinion of a department fully conscious of the problem with which the power in question was granted to deal is still more so. Granted that there must be checks and balances, why should our system of government be conceived of as a pyramid with the courts at the apex, where even the enactments of a legally supreme Parliament may be "construed," and the actions of the Civil Service, the best informed and most forward looking body of persons in England today, regulated from the point of view of an outside jurisdiction?

Nevertheless, restoration of control means to most restoration of control by the courts. So that during the period of regression the section giving to rules the same effect as if they were enacted in the Act disappears; "prima facie" is substituted for "conclusive" in the conclusive evidence clause; [1] and confirmed orders by a department instead of being placed beyond the reach of the courts — they are as much legislation as a private bill is legislation — are brought before the court by a form of procedure expressly designed for that purpose.[2] Some enthusiasts are disposed to consider all matters suitable for judicial review; nothing could be more clearly legislative than an order of the Minister regrouping catchment areas, or adding to and subtracting from the areas listed in a schedule, and yet it was seriously suggested that an appeal from it should lie to a High Court judge assisted by technical officials.[3] Here was a question of policy eminently suitable for the consideration of a committee of Parliament, but right out of the field of analytical court proceedings.[4]

Parliament is the natural body to control the exercise of powers which it has granted. But it cannot be said at present that Parliament's approval of rules goes any further than the approval of their general policy. There might be little objection even to an ultra vires rule so approved, if there was any degree of certainty that it had been examined by a committee and let through. But not all rules have to be laid before the Houses, and where this requirement is made by the enabling Act, the practical difficulties in the way of procuring that someone shall have taken notice of them are insuperable.[5] Almost one quarter of the 600 members

[1] See 77 Lords Deb. (5th Series), p. 932, May 20, 1930 Land Drainage Bill; Road Traffic Act, 1930. 20 & 21 Geo. 5, c. 43, sec. 90 (8).

[2] See Housing Act, 1930. 20 & 21 Geo. 5, c. 39, sec. 11 (3); Public Works Facilities Act, 1930. 20 & 21 Geo. 5, c. 50, Sched. I, Part III, 2.

[3] 77 Lords Deb. (5th Series), p. 762. May 19, 1930. Lord Bayford.

[4] I. G. Gibbon, The Appellate Jurisdiction of Government Departments, 7 J.P.A. 269 (1929).

[5] See Lord Banbury in 72 Lords Deb. (5th Series), p. 1191, and 75 Lords Deb. (5th Series), p. 1391.

of the House of Commons are lawyers, but what is everybody's business is nobody's business, and the parliamentary duties of these lawyers only begin when the serious business of the day, the care of their practice, is over.

Parliament has in recent years adopted a new procedure of approval by resolution. This is applied to some rules which adapt or modify an Act,[1] to some which are of substantial importance and are likely to restrict the liberty of the citizen, — such as the Highway Code, regulations under the Emergency Powers Act, and orders regulating the price and export of coal,[2] — and to schemes of the same nature, such as reorganisation orders by the Electricity Commissioners, orders of the Board of Trade under the Gas Regulation Act, and the formation of marketing bodies by the Minister of Agriculture.[3] This procedure only applies where it is mandatory by the Act delegating the power, but it became very popular in 1930 and was made obligatory on nine occasions. There are, however, practical difficulties involved in it: if the resolution is non-political, little interest will be taken in it; if it raises deep questions of policy, there may be a tendency to fight old battles over again; while the limits within which it can be employed must of necessity be narrow where the time of Parliament is limited. But intelligently used, the procedure is capable of reconciling control with the demands on Parliament's time.

This piecemeal method of dealing with the problem is hardly satisfactory. It does little to restore public confidence and nothing towards introducing uniformity into this section of English law. I do not suggest that all types of rules, procedural and substantive in their varying degrees, should be treated in exactly the same manner; that would be to ignore the very real differences in their importance. But the recent innovations have all been introduced by way of amendment in debate and without any reference to building up a consistent legislative practice, and I do suggest that

[1] E. g. Mental Treatment Act, 1930. 20 & 21 Geo. 5, c. 23, sec. 15 (2); Road Traffic Act, 1930. 20 & 21 Geo. 5, c. 43, sec. 10 (4).

[2] Road Traffic Act, 1930. 20 & 21 Geo. 5, c. 43, sec. 45 (2); Emergency Powers Act, 1920. 10 & 11 Geo. 5, c. 55, sec. 2 (2); Mining Industry Act, 1920. 10 & 11 Geo. 5, c. 50, sec. 3 (2). See also Census Act, 1920. 10 & 11 Geo. 5, c. 41, sec. 3 (2); Housing (Financial Provisions) Act, 1924. 14 & 15 Geo. 5, c. 35, sec. 6.

[3] Electricity Supply Act, 1919. 9 & 10 Geo. 5, c. 100, sec. 7; Gas Regulation Act, 1920. 10 & 11 Geo. 5, c. 28, sec. 10; Agricultural Marketing Act, 1931. 21 & 22 Geo. 5, c. 42, sec. 1.

Parliament should have before it some ideal at which it aims, and some recognition of its prior legislative habits. With a growing consistency in methods of control Sir John Marriott's suggestion of a Sessional Joint Committee would be enabled to function with some ease.[1] Mr. Baldwin thought existing methods of control enough, objected to discouraging individual enterprise, suggested that the committee would be inadequate to deal with technical rules. These are not the real difficulties; of individual enterprise there is none, not all rules are technical, and there is no reason why the committee should not be empowered to hear the evidence of the department on those that are. Who would be willing to undertake the onerous duty of sitting on the committee? Could it deal with "ultra vires?" To the exclusion of the courts or not? Would Parliament stand behind the committee? These are the troublesome questions. But given the present demand for increased control, and the chaos which has resulted from treating each piece of procedure as if it were an isolated instance, and from the acrobatics of the courts in seeking to keep executive legislation where they wish it to be, the time is ripe for undertaking any experiment which may conduce to more rational methods of control and a greater public confidence.[2]

[1] 226 Com. Deb. (5th Series), p. 24, March 24, 1929.
[2] This very short statement of the problem of control assumes as its background Carr's discussion in Delegated Legislation, chap. 4, with particular reference to those aspects of it there discussed which do not depend on the vigilance of Parliament or the courts.

CHAPTER IV

PRIVATE BILL LEGISLATION BY A DEPARTMENT

THE most interesting topic in the sphere of delegated legislation is procedure by scheme. Procedure by scheme is a polite term for private bill legislation by a department. Sometimes the department draws up the scheme itself; sometimes it originates from another quarter, usually a local authority, and then the department is charged with the duty of investigation, and may by its order give full effect to the proposals submitted. But just as the constitutional doctrine of the supremacy of Parliament has obscured the true nature of skeleton legislation, so also it has always been thought that in granting special powers to a railway or reorganising a bishopric the department was acting in a "mere administrative capacity" — whatever that may mean. But the theory of the law, that as long as the subordinate body acts within its powers it is in effect Parliament, is a fiction directly Parliament divests itself of the last leading-string and ceases to require that the orders be laid before it — a step taken in the Housing Act, 1909. And yet, however wide the powers granted by Parliament, the portmanteau phrase "delegated legislation" is believed to cover all sins, for Parliament, it is said, is the source of the power and tomorrow may recall it. The very words of the Acts are eloquent of the outworn theory; all that section 40 (5) of the Housing Act, 1925, said was, "The order of the Minister when made shall have effect as if enacted in the Act." On the face of it the Minister issued a final confirming order and nothing more; in fact he was doing what historically the Select Committee had always done, reporting in favor of the bill. But he was doing more even than that: his report to himself had all the force that could be given to it by a third reading in the House of origin, a duplication of the procedure in the other House, and the Royal Assent. To a local authority there is nothing new or startling in the scheme powers of the Minister. In all matters of local legislation the Minister to the local authority is Parliament, in the same sense as to the average citizen the policeman is the law: a private bill must be accompanied by a report on it from the department concerned, and a

Provisional Order comes into Parliament under its sole auspices. But the clamour raised against the hold of the departments over local affairs [1] — and indeed an authority cannot pass a by-law or move for a private bill without their sanction — is surpassed by the irritation occasioned by the expense, the delays, and the risk of blocking motions incidental to an application to Parliament for new powers.[2] It is not from the local authority that objections to scheme procedure come.

The power to issue confirming orders differs in several ways from the power to make rules. Some of the differences are of course the same as those to be observed between a public general Act and a private Act — that the initiative lies elsewhere than with the confirming authority, that the procedure is markedly judicial, and that the objections of aggrieved persons are more tenderly regarded. But they run deeper than that. Skeleton legislation has in the past, except for emergency regulations and rules of court, been confined to the settlement of details, the establishment of a register or the administration of the poor law.[3] There Parliament is not displaced from an immemorial function; it still lays down rules to bring into existence the new condition of affairs which it has in mind, but leaves a small portion of the field uncovered. But where a scheme is drawn up, submitted to the Minister, considered at a local inquiry, given further consideration in Whitehall, and finally approved, the order creates something out of nothing; a new condition arises at the bidding of the department, working, it is true, along lines laid down by the enabling Act, but with a scope which leaves the vital questions, those of policy and expediency, for the department to settle in its own discretion. The projects undertaken by scheme procedure cannot for sheer constructive scope be parallelled by any products of the rule-making power; the reorganisation of the mining industry, slum clearance, and a new system of compulsory marketing have all been withdrawn from the ambit of a committee.

Scheme procedure is not, however, quite the same as private bill legislation; the application is not for powers over and above those granted by the general law — for the enabling Act is a public

[1] See First Report of Royal Commission on Local Government (1925), p. 175.

[2] E. D. Simon, A City Council from Within (1926), p. 109.

[3] Patents Act, 1883. 46 & 47 Vict., c. 57, sec. 101 (1) (a); Poor Law Act, 1927. 17 & 18 Geo. 5, c. 14, secs. 73 (1) and 211 (2).

general Act. But before those general powers can be exercised by any person whatever the department must be satisfied of the expediency of granting them in the particular case, and so performs much the same function as a committee of Parliament sitting on a private bill. The decision is not irrefragable; in the background hover the courts, nearer since *Yaffe's Case* than before it, but even they are in theory concerned with power, not policy.

This, then, is the process whose final step, the issue of a confirming order, is rendered deceptively negligible by the fact that the order is not printed in the volumes of Statutory Rules and Orders, being considered as an executive rather than a legislative act.

Again, the history of the scheme procedure is vastly more illuminating than that of the power to make rules. It is not only an instance of how the process of generalisation, the very life of the Common Law, imperceptibly goes on in the field of legislation, special grants of a power to clear slums giving way to a general Act; [1] it is an example of the gradual relaxation of parliamentary control. I have shown that there is little rhyme or reason in the grants of statutory finality to rules; until recent years there was no sign of consistency in the requirement that the rules should be laid before Parliament. What is more, there was no process intermediate between legislation by Parliament itself and the making of rules by a department; the delegation once embarked upon was absolute. That was natural enough for a Parliament which permitted autonomous bodies to regulate the relations of their own members to the body itself and the relations of the members inter se, which had not yet carried over into the sphere of general legislation the practice of delegating the exhaustive consideration of a private bill to a committee. It is only when one examines the long history of private bill legislation from the day when a bill came before the whole House, through the establishment of committees, the invention of the Provisional Order, the provision that in certain cases the order though technically provisional need not be embodied in a bill and submitted to Parliament to take effect, to the

[1] Read the Liverpool Sanitary Amendment Act, 1864 (27 & 28 Vict., c. lxxiii), in the light of the Housing Act, 1890. See on this matter Williams, Private Bill Legislation (1927), p. 111. Cf. also the development of the Company Acts, the history of the change over from legislative to judicial divorce, and the process whereby private Health Acts gave way to adoptive general and later to mandatory general Acts.

full-fledged procedure by scheme, that one stands a little astonished
at the different development which was going on simultaneously
in the two parallel lines of cases. Reasons for the difference are
not hard to find. Parliament was unwilling to delegate the power
of general legislation, — the raison d'être for its existence and in
most cases involving a new departure of principle, — and so at
first left only matters of no ultimate consequence to be so regulated. It was enough to provide that these rules lie on the table,
in early days in draft for as long as three months, but later for a
much shorter period and after they had taken effect. By the middle
of the nineteenth century, zero hour for the new system of government, private bills had long ceased to be brought before the whole
House; the tradition of delegation was well started. Once started,
a rationalisation upon the work done by the committees, investigation of the expediency to the public of special privileges applied
for by a private interest, showed no cause why the investigation
should not be done elsewhere, first as preliminary to parliamentary
proceedings, then as exclusive of them. Parliament was, then, not
unwilling to loose its hold on a part of its business which it did not
treat as true legislation, and the path of future delegation being
plain, went early ahead with it. After the War, owing to the importance of the problem now dealt with by rules and schemes alike,
Parliament awoke to the essential similarity of the two parallel
processes, and there was added to the two methods by which general Acts may be created and the several methods for private Acts
the procedure by Special Order — evolved, it is said, by an accident in the Electricity Supply Bill, and unnoticed until the Act
went into force.[1]

The history and the intermediate stages of the scheme procedure
throw the first clear light on the meaning which Parliament — or
at any rate the various draftsmen concerned — put on the words
"shall have effect as if enacted in this Act" in this connection.[2]
This is particularly true of the Housing Acts. Under the 1890
Housing Act the order confirming a scheme had in general no

[1] Sir Ernest Moon, Royal Commission on Local Government, Minutes of
Evidence, p. 342, par. 5184.

[2] A note by the editors on Education Act 1902, sec. 21 (3) in (1903) 1 L.G.R.
90, reads, "The provision in subsection 3, that a scheme when approved is to
have effect as if enacted in this Act, will prevent the raising of any question as
to whether a scheme made and approved is, as regards procedure in conformity
with the Act, is or is not intra vires. See *Lockwood's Case*, [1894] A.C. 347."

authority until scheduled to a bill and passed through Parliament.[1] But even there it was provided that where the demolition order had been made and carried out, or where there was an unhealthy area, but the area was too small to be treated by Provisional Order and there was no opposition, a scheme might take effect on the order of the Local Government Board and have effect as if enacted in the Act.[2] The Act of 1903 further removed the necessity for confirmation by Parliament where the land could be purchased under voluntary agreement or where, although the proposal was to apply for compulsory powers, no compulsion was in fact necessary, all parties being satisfied.[3] By the Act of 1909 in no case is there to be any confirmation by Parliament,[4] and the provisions of that Act were reproduced in the Act of 1925.[5] Can there be any doubt that where there is a process of evolution from Provisional Order procedure to an order of the Board declared to have effect as if enacted in the Act, first in the trivial case of an area too small to be worth the expense of obtaining a confirmation bill, then in all schemes however large if there are no persons aggrieved, until finally the department has the final say in all schemes and under all circumstances — can there be any doubt that Parliament has been slowly substituting the discretion of the Minister for the discretion of a committee, and by a declaration that the order is to have effect as if enacted in the Act and an omission of the usual provision that the orders be laid before it, intends to make it clear that not only was the Minister standing in the same position as Parliament, but that his orders have all the force of an Act of Parliament? Why, then, did *Yaffe's Case* go off as it did? That legislative history was considered in the argument we know. Scrutton, L. J., dealt with the point in his judgment, and admitted that the scheme procedure was a substitute for legislation by Provisional Order in an earlier Act and was intended to have the same effect. In the early part of his judgment he decided for other reasons that the section was tautologous. He then noticed the argument from history, and reasoned that, Parliament having meant by it to declare expressly the effect of an order only if intra vires, the fact of the Minister being in the same relation to his order as Parliament in the prior Act to a provisional order was quite irrele-

---

[1] 53 & 54 Vict., c. 70, sec. 8 (6).   [2] Id., sec. 39 (1) (*a*) (*b*).
[3] Housing Act, 1903. 3 Ed. 7, c. 39, sec. 5 (2).
[4] Housing Act, 1909. 9 Ed. 7, c. 44, sec. 24 (1) (2).
[5] Housing Act, 1925. 15 Geo. 5, c. 14, sec. 40.

vant: an ultra vires Provisional Order cannot be challenged in the courts only because of the curative magic that lies in the action of Parliament upon it. The uncontrolled position of the department, then, was only an added reason for the Court to interfere. Given Scrutton, L. J.'s., method of treatment, his conclusion is sound. But did he fully appreciate the meaning of the argument put to him? It was directed to clearing up the meaning of those very words which he had declared tautologous; even if the Court was not convinced, the contention was, by the dictionary meaning of the terms, the surrender of all control by Parliament and the placing of the Minister in the same position as the legislature made them free of ambiguity. No doubt a court as determined as the Court of Appeal could have successfully met the argument, but it is unfortunate that neither that court nor the House of Lords gave it the attention it deserved.

In a very early instance of scheme procedure — where the scheme to be confirmed is an agreement for joint working between two railways, and a proposal to sell surplus lands previously acquired under compulsory powers (but is no different in principle from a housing scheme) — it is provided that the certificate of the Board of Trade granting the necessary permission "shall be as absolutely valid and conclusive to all intents as if the contents thereof . . . had been expressly enacted by Parliament; and the validity of the certificate shall not be impeached on account of any alleged informality in any court or elsewhere." The sidenote reads "Operation of Certificate as a Special Act." [1] On objection, however, by a railway or canal company the procedure must be by private bill.[2] The words are very strong indeed, and I do not mean to say that they cover our case; but the Act of 1864 does show that it was not unthinkable even then to substitute a department for Parliament in the work of private bill legislation, even in connection with a railway, the especial preserve of Parliament. To take a later example, both courts in *R.* v. *Light Railway Commissioners* recognised the effect of the scheme procedure under the Light Railways Act, 1896:[3] Shearman, J., explains the difficulties sought to be remedied by substituting the new procedure for Provisional Orders,[4] and Phillimore, L. J., says

---

[1] Railway Companies (Powers) Act, 1864. 27 & 28 Vict., c. 120, sec. 17; to the same effect Railway Construction Facilities Act, 1864. 27 & 28 Vict., c. 121, sec. 19.   [2] Railway Construction Facilities Act, sec. 8.

[3] Light Railways Act, 1896. 59 & 60 Vict., c. 48, sec. 10.

[4] *R.* v. Light Railway Commissioners, [1915] 1 K.B. 162, p. 169.

that "by the application for an order authorising a light railway something equivalent to a railway bill promoted in Parliament is intended." [1] The Ministry of Transport Act, 1919, empowered the Minister to issue orders reorganising the railroads, provided the estimated expenditure on each order did not amount to more than a million pounds; above that figure orders had to be approved by resolution of both Houses, or the resolution might direct the matter to proceed by private bill. The orders of the Minister were to have effect as if enacted in the Act.[2] These were the basic orders, and it is not conceivable, particularly not in view of this express provision, that Parliament intended the basic order to have any less effect than one of the same nature but involving a larger sum, merely because the latter was subjected to consideration by a committee in both Houses.[3]

Many of the Acts authorising procedure by scheme have several shades of control, and show on their face that they trace their descent from procedure by private bill. A Provisional Order is only a particular type of private bill; a preliminary investigation is held by the department in order to make clear to applicants and petitioners the weakness or strength of their case, and is a way of shutting off at the start applications which have little chance of being successful before a committee. The bill (which must be endorsed by the department from which it emanates) is in theory a public general bill, but on arrival in Parliament is given the same treatment as a private bill. If it is unopposed it goes to the Unopposed Committee, if it is opposed it goes to a select committee; and by "opposed" is meant that a petition has been presented against it while it is pending in Parliament. A Provisional Order, then, despite the local inquiry held by an official and the part which a department plays in giving its approval, is more like a private bill than a scheme. Nevertheless, where the undertaking involves a large sum of money or excessive interference with private rights, the applicant is informed by the department that

---

[1] Id., [1915] 3 K.B. 536, at 544.

[2] Ministry of Transport Act, 1919. 9 & 10 Geo. 5, c. 50, sec. 3 (1) (d).

[3] The same point is brought out by an Act of 1881; the Board of Trade was empowered to grant rights of clam and bait fishery by Provisional Order, but where the order dealt only with an area of five acres or amended a previous order, on confirmation by Order in Council it took effect as if enacted in the Act. See Fisheries (Clam and Bait Beds) Act, 1881, 44 Vict., c. 11, sec. 4; also Fisheries Act, 1877. 40 & 41 Vict., c. 42, sec. 7.

he must conduct his own case in Parliament without the benefit of the prima facie virtue which is his where he comes into Parliament under the official wing. If, for instance, he applies for health powers under an Act which permits procedure by Provisional Order, — and that is the only case in which it is permissible, — and the powers asked for are in excess of the provisions granted by the general law, he must go to Parliament direct. The Act itself will either lay down the circumstances in which a Provisional Order is inadmissible, where there are objections, for instance,[1] or will leave it to the discretion of the department.[2] An order, however, is the creation of a department, and takes effect without confirmation by Parliament, and there are occasions when the Minister is empowered to proceed by order, but may in his discretion or must on petition proceed by Provisional Order. By the Public Health Amendment Act of 1885 the Local Government Board were empowered to create a port sanitary authority by order, but upon objection made by any riparian authority they were relegated to Provisional Order, and under the Public Health Act of 1848 the Privy Council was empowered to put the Act, an adoptive one, in force upon petition by the inhabitants of any area A, but where the Act was to be put in force by the same petition in area B also the General Board of Health had to submit a Provisional Order to Parliament for confirmation.[3] This process of evolution, whose effects can be traced in the shades of control, is even more strikingly displayed where an Act is later amended to relax the procedural requirements. On objection to the granting of a certificate under the Railway Companies Powers Act, 1864, proceedings before the Board of Trade were to cease and further proceedings to be by way of private bill, but an Act of 1870 for private bill substituted Provisional Order.[4] An even nicer instance of the same process, the evolution from Provisional Order to order,

[1] Local Government Act, 1926. 16 & 17 Geo. 5, c. 38, sec. 2; Railway Companies Powers Act, 1864. 27 & 28 Vict., c. 120, sec. 8.

[2] See Private Legislation Procedure (Scotland) Act, 1899. 62 & 63 Vict., c. 47, sec. 2 (2); and with respect to Special Orders, Ministry of Transport Act, 1919. 9 & 10 Geo. 5, c. 50, sec. 29 (3).

[3] Public Health Amendment Act, 1885. 48 & 49 Vict., c. 35, sec. 3; Public Health Act, 1848. 11 & 12 Vict., c. 63, sec. 10. See also Drainage (Ireland) Act, 1880. 43 & 44, Vict., c. 27, sec. 2; Merchant Shipping Act Amendment Act, 1862. 25 & 26 Vict., c. 63, sec. 40.

[4] Railway (Powers and Construction) Act, 1870. 33 & 34 Vict., c. 19, sec. 3.

is a section of the Electricity Supply Act of 1919 which provides that anything which under the Electric Lighting Acts of 1882 may be effected by Provisional Order may now be effected by Special Order made by the Commissioners and confirmed by the Board of Trade.[1] Special Orders here emerge for the first time. They stand intermediate between orders and Provisional Orders, a Special Order being drawn up by a department but taking effect only on resolution of both Houses; they are not, as might be thought, a link in the evolutionary chain, but a later invention to take care of schemes in which the need for dispatch must be reconciled with the need for control over projects which cannot be taken care of by private bill (for their purpose is to insure uniformity rather than diversity in carrying out the wishes of the individual or the authority) or by public general Act (for they are primarily local and adoptive, if "adoptive" can be applied to something which is not yet in existence).[2]

What, it may be asked, is the reason for procedure by scheme? If Parliament is the source of new rights, and given committees of investigation to sit on the granting of privileges in excess of the general law, why not rest content with private bills? There are many reasons. For one thing, a great deal of modern legislation refuses to fit into either of the traditional classes of bills. As long as the central government did not interfere beyond keeping the peace at home and abroad, and could shut its eyes to the existence of more or less autonomous governments in various fields, railway companies, local boards of health, guardians of the poor, or turnpike trustees, its sphere of action was in practice limited; general legislation was directed against specific abuses, and if an autonomous government found itself in need of new powers it had to petition Parliament to grant the privilege. But as soon as the function of government began to be thought of as constructive rather than repressive, and as soon as all England became knit together as a result of specialisation in industry, it became necessary to introduce uniformity into methods of local government, to pursue a consistent and social policy. These positive ends could

[1] Electricity Supply Act, 1919. 9 & 10 Geo. 5, c. 100, sec. 26.

[2] E. g. Gas Regulation Act, 1920. 10 & 11 Geo. 5, c. 28, sec. 10; Agricultural Marketing Act, 1931. 21 & 22 Geo. 5, c. 42, sec. 1 (8). Special Order procedure is not, however, confined to orders confirming schemes. It now extends also to rules which modify an Act of Parliament (Mental Treatment Act, 1930, sec. 15 [2]), to rules and executive orders of great importance (Emergency Powers Act, 1920. sec. 2 [2]; Safeguarding of Industries Act, 1921, sec. 2 [4]).

not be attained by the Procrustes' bed of a public Act, while a private bill, being voluntary and subject only to the consideration of committees of shifting personnel, gave too wide a scope to local or special interest. And how deal with a plan of coöperative marketing or a reorganisation of the transport utilities? Not by general Act; England is not yet ready for more than an adoptive socialism, and even if she were, the problems of the particular area or group of companies are too diverse to come within portmanteau commands. A private Act, on the other hand, lacks the very thing desired from Parliament, a power to coerce the few opponents who can, if left to themselves, feather their nest at the expense of those who have surrendered in favour of each other their legal right to compete. Procedure by Provisional Order was meant to combine the virtues of both public and private bills, to combine uniformity with diversity, utopian policy with investigation of facts as they were. But more often than not the result was only a duplication of expense; an opponent who failed at the local inquiry would present a petition against the confirmation of the bill pending in Parliament, and thenceforth it would have to proceed, as it still does, in the manner appointed for a private bill.

Again, in passing a private Act Parliament still thinks of itself as benignly granting a privilege and is chary of its favours. There is no harm in thus regarding a grant of incorporation to a rubber company, but where a local authority, now almost a dependency of the central government and an appendage to the Ministry of Health, comes to ask for permission to carry into effect a public adoptive Act designed to relieve unemployment, it is ridiculous that it should have to sue humbly and pay enormous fees for the grant of a power to do something which Parliament has morally obliged it to do. And yet clearly that power could not be granted by a general Act to all local authorities without investigation of local conditions.

The shortest path to understanding the factors which have been responsible for increasing devolution in private legislation is to sketch procedure by Provisional Order and private bill, and point out the difficulties inherent in both. I shall consider both mainly from the point of view of local legislation, because a bill promoted by a local authority is admittedly semi-public, and the tendency today is to regard most activities as "affected with a public interest."

The functions performed by Parliament in passing a private Act

are partly legislative, partly judicial: legislative because in form
the bill passes through the same stages as a public bill and will be
rejected if Parliament thinks it harmful to the public,[1] judicial in
that not only does the hearing before a committee proceed on
substantially the same lines as the proceedings in a court of law,
counsel appearing on both sides, producing evidence, and conduct-
ing examination and cross-examination, but fees must be paid, and,
if the parties abandon the bill and no other parties undertake its
support, the bill is lost however sensible the House may be of its
value.[2] Before the bill reaches a committee the promoters must
show that they have satisfied the stringent requirements of Standing Orders with respect to notices, advertisements, and deposit of
plans. But the bill cannot be set down for consideration at all unless the requirements have been complied with by the several dates
appointed; if, for instance, the advertisements have not appeared
in the London Gazette before November 27 the promoters will
have to wait another year before they can present their bill. When
the Examiners are satisfied that compliance with Standing Orders
has been proved, the bill is assigned to one of the Houses. After
two readings, the first purely formal, the second formal unless a
member has been induced to raise a motion with regard to it, the
bill is assigned to a committee. There any person wishing to oppose it must show that there is something in the bill itself which
tends to injure him — and a ratepayer has in Parliament no locus
standi to oppose a bill promoted by a local authority — and the
hearing then proceeds in a whirl of expert witnesses and expensive
counsel. The Committee reports to the House, and a third reading
is then had, when there is still an opportunity for the petitioners
to suborn a member to vote its rejection. But that is not all.
Despite its exhaustive consideration in the House of origin — if
local legislation, before the Select Committee on Local Legislation
in the Commons, which requires copious statistics and a detailed
report from the Ministry of Health and the Home Office [3] — the

[1] E. g. the rejection of the Birkenhead Provisional Order in 1920 by a Parliamentary Committee for lack of substantial support by the ratepayers in the
areas proposed to be incorporated. First Report of Royal Commission on
Local Government (1925), p. 158, par. 347.

[2] See May, Parliamentary Practice, 13th ed. (1924), p. 671.

[3] This Committee was appointed specially at each session and sat about
fifty days each year. It was discontinued in 1931 "in the interests of expedi-
tion and economy"; and bills were sent instead to ordinary committees with
a special reference to personnel. See 9 J.P.A. 489, October, 1931.

bill must forthwith go to the other House and there pass through the same stages before it is ready for the Royal Assent.[1]

It is with reference to local legislation that the present procedure by private bill is most open to attack. No doubt the local authorities are the "laboratories of social ideas for the nation";[2] Williams, in arguing that Parliament should retain control of private legislation, derives much of the Public Health Act of 1848 and the Housing Act of 1890 from local Acts.[3] But the laboratory has had to pay a heavy price for the privilege of that happy compliment. Although much of the heavy cost involved — it was estimated by a member in the House of Commons that an unopposed bill costs from £600 to £700 and an opposed bill about £2,000 — is the result of the penchant of local authorities for retaining only the most expensive counsel, that is almost inevitable under the present system where so much depends on counsel making an impression. And counsel are not responsible for all the expenditure. The mass of printing, notices, advertisements, statements, are probably necessary to give due warning to persons likely to be affected, but what can be said of a procedure which is so intricate that even the preliminaries must be entrusted to a parliamentary agent, and so unpliable that in cases of congestion bills must start again de novo the next December and new fees be paid? And before the bill ever gets to a hearing a local authority must send its officials up to London to dawdle about the corridors of the Houses of Parliament until its bill comes up.

The most forceful criticism, however, can be levelled against the core of the whole process, the hearing before the Committee. It is here that questions of general expediency are considered and the clauses gone through one by one, but not as before a body of practical legislators. The proceedings are modelled closely on those in a court of law; instead of clerks to local authorities being asked to state the case for and against, counsel who derive all their information from those clerks must elicit it by examination of witnesses before a committee who may know little or nothing about local government in general, or the actual organisation of the district which they are considering. When the case is closed the Committee deliberate and announce their decision, but give no reasons

[1] See Williams, Private Bill Legislation (1927), pp. 28–83.
[2] See 231 Com. Deb. (5th Series), p. 2128, Mr. Aneurin Bevan, November 13, 1929.
[3] Private Bill Legislation, p. 111.

for it. It may be that before a jury impartiality can only be assured if the jury is permitted to draw its conclusions only from the evidence produced in court. But the elaborate façade of judicial ignorance is somewhat out of place before a legislative body which should be engaged in constructive work and have its eyes wide open. Compare with this a local inquiry conducted by an inspector of the Ministry of Health who has read up the history of the case before him, has visited the area concerned and talked with the local officials, and is ready to hear anybody and everybody — even a ratepayer — before he comes to a conclusion and writes his report for Whitehall. Williams, however, regards the departments as a baneful influence; he deals at length with an occasion where the Home Office so vigorously opposed two clauses in a private bill that although they were allowed by the Local Legislation Committee they had to be omitted on account of threats by that department to have the bill defeated at the third reading; so he is unwilling to have their sphere enlarged.[1]

A good deal of local legislation, however, is already dealt with by Provisional Order. A department, after holding a public local inquiry under an Act which permits new powers to be acquired in this manner, makes an order, but this order as yet binds nobody. The essence of the procedure is that to be passed into law the order must be scheduled, probably with other orders, to a bill by the department responsible for it, and then be submitted to a Parliament as a public general bill. Before scheduling the order to a bill the department sees that all the requirements of the enabling Act as to notices, inquiries, and lapses of time have been complied with by the applicants, and then sets the stamp of its approval upon it. The bill must reach Parliament before Whitsuntide, and after the first reading it is referred to the Examiners of Private Bills, before whom compliance with the Standing Orders applicable must be proved. If any petitions against the bill are received it is referred to a select committee (and this in the House of Commons opens up all the orders scheduled to the bill), and is treated as if it were a private bill. If unopposed, it goes to the Unopposed Bills Committee. This Committee has to consider not only whether anything new is being asked for but whether the order is intra vires, and in this they are aided by a representative from the department re-

---

[1] For other criticisms see 231 Com. Deb. (5th Series), p. 2125; Williams, Private Bill Legislation, pp. 110–119; E. D. Simon, A City Council From Within, p. 109.

sponsible, who sees the counsel to the Speaker before the Committee sits, and if the bill is common form tells him so.[1] After the bill is reported it is read a third time.

Procedure by Provisional Order, then, does not differ greatly from procedure by private bill; practically the only difference is that the department takes the place of Parliament in the initial stages in protecting interested parties. The preliminary local inquiry may clear some objections out of the way, so that by the time the order is scheduled to a bill it is unopposed, and no parliamentary counsel need be retained; on the other hand, if the opponents stand firm there is an added expense, for besides the cost of appearing before a committee there is the cost of the local inquiry. The procedure, however, must have proved fairly satisfactory in noncontentious matters. It is the normal method used for the compulsory acquisition of land,[2] when it usually takes the form of an order permitting the Lands Clauses Act to be put into operation. It is not confined to this use; new jurisdictional areas,[3] new undertakings by a body with limited powers of the same nature as those expressly authorised by Parliament,[4] and alterations in the constitution of local government bodies [5] have thereby been effected, and after 1899 all save exceptional cases of Scotch private legislation were thus dealt with.[6] But even here the most serious disadvantage of private bill procedure, the delay, is still present. Application to the department must be made in September, October, or November, and the order must be ready to be scheduled to a bill by Whitsuntide or else the applicant will have to wait another year: even if application is made in September, the powers desired cannot be granted until the end of the following summer. As long as the procedure is confined to cases where some far-reaching change is contemplated cooling time is all to the good,

[1] Sir Ernest Moon, Royal Commission on Local Government, Minutes of Evidence, p. 345, par. 5240, 5241.

[2] E. g. Public Health (Scotland) Act, 1867. 30 & 31 Vict., c. 101, sec. 90; Drainage of Land Act, 1861. 24 & 25 Vict., c. 133, sec. 21; Port of London Act, 1908. 8 Ed. 7, c. 68, sec. 6.

[3] E. g. Merchant Shipping Act Amendment Act, 1862. 25 & 26 Vict., c. 63, sec. 40; Brine Pumping (Compensation for Subsidence) Act, 1891. 54 & 55 Vict., c. 40, sec. 3.

[4] E. g. Light Railways (Ireland) Act, 1889. 52 & 53 Vict., c. 66, sec. 5; Fishery Harbours Act, 1915. 5 & 6 Geo. 5, c. 48, sec. 2 (3).

[5] E. g. Local Government Act, 1888. 51 & 52 Vict., c. 41, sec. 10; Burgh Police (Scotland) Act, 1892. 55 & 56 Vict., c. 55, sec. 44.

[6] Private Legislation Procedure (Scotland) Act, 1899. 62 & 63 Vict., c. 47.

but it is still the most common even for matters of administrative detail, and is plainly out of place where quick action is required, as for instance where a local authority desires to relieve unemployment by a highway project and needs powers of compulsory purchase.

The procedure was criticised from both points of view by the Royal Commission on Local Government. They thought that the present provisions for the acquisition of land for highway purposes by a local authority were inadequate both on the ground of delay (a necessary concomitant of the procedure under discussion) and because of the incorporation therein of certain sections of the Lands Clauses Act of 1845, — again a very usual feature of the procedure for compulsory acquisition, — which imposed stringent conditions on entry after purchase. The Commission was not averse to taking away more powers from Parliament; they recommended the procedure by order of Schedule III, 2, of the Housing Act, 1925,[1] and they were unanimously agreed that reorganisation of local government areas should be effected by order of the Minister. Indeed the only matter on which they were unable to agree was whether or not the orders should be liable to annulment by an address to the Crown.[2] That, then, was their opinion upon the use of Provisional Orders in non-contentious matters.

On the other hand, they advised a partial return to procedure by private bill upon proposals for the constitution or extension of county boroughs, and this step back, unusual in the period of extension of delegation, was taken in an Act of 1926.[3] The old section 54 of the Local Government Act of 1888 allowed any town council desiring the change to do one of two things — either represent that a Provisional Order should be made giving effect to the proposals, or promote a private bill. Town councils usually proceeded by Provisional Order, for they felt that local matters should be dealt with locally and of course hoped to save expense. But they found that for various reasons they were not able to dispense with counsel or expert witnesses at the inquiry, and that more often than not the order was opposed in Parliament, thereby doubling instead of halving the cost. Between 1888 and 1922, seventy-

---

[1] Royal Commission on Local Government, Final Report (1929), p. 48, par. 163, 164.

[2] Royal Commission on Local Government, Second Report (1928), p. 18.

[3] Local Government (County Boroughs and Adjustments) Act, 1926. 16 & 17 Geo. 5, c. 38.

two Provisional Orders were made for the extension of county boroughs and forty-four of them were opposed in Parliament, while of twenty-three made for the constitution of county boroughs fourteen were thus opposed; and the estimated cost of uniting the Three Towns into Plymouth in 1914 fell not far short of £20,000.[1] Even the local inquiry was objected to in the evidence of certain local government associations, — and this despite the fact that not only are aggrieved ratepayers given an opportunity to be heard at the inquiry, but the place of hearing is convenient for them, — on the ground that the department unduly favoured the absorption of smaller municipalities. The most telling evidence against the procedure, however, was to the effect, first, that there was a substantial discrepancy between the decisions of the Ministry and the decisions of parliamentary committees, the committees taking a wider view of the issues; and, second, that, although the order was provisional only, the case was already weighted in favour of the proposal, that although the Minister had recently said that in introducing the bill he did not go further than to indicate that there was a prima facie case in favour of the proposal upon which it was for Parliament to make a decision, in practice parliamentary committees did not regard the Minister's introduction of the bill as a purely formal act.[2] The Commission recognised the lack of confidence felt by the local authorities, and therefore recommended that in future all proposals for the constitution of county boroughs (as to which objection is almost certain) should be made by private bill, and proposals for their extension should only be by Provisional Order where no objections were made.

The troublesome delays caused by the mandatory provisions as to dates in both procedure by private bill and Provisional Order — necessary indeed to insure that the Committees get through their work before the end of the session — are avoided where a permanent body has charge of the scheme. The Circular of the Minister of Health on the Public Works Facilities Act of 1930 [3] is directed to showing how that Act speeds up the acquisition of new powers by a local authority in the relief of unemployment, by substituting

[1] Royal Commission on Local Government, First Report (1925), pp. 164 169.

[2] Royal Commission on Local Government, First Report (1925), p. 177, par. 494, 488.

[3] Circular 1141, August 22, 1930. 28 L.G.R., Part II, p. 648.

an order for a Provisional Order where land is to be compulsorily acquired, and an order for a private bill where the new powers applied for are those which the authority must have to carry out projects which certain public Acts morally bind it to undertake, and yet gives adequate protection by insisting on compliance with the Standing Orders of Parliament as to the deposit of estimates and plans, and the giving of notice to persons likely to be affected. This Act goes further than most in relaxing the usual requirement of a local inquiry, except where an objection is made to the scheme; but this is explained by the urgency of the problem which has to be faced.

Procedure by scheme is an effort to develop to its full what is best in procedure by Provisional Order. In form the advance made in scheme procedure is not startling. In the case of a Provisional Order also the Minister was charged with seeing that the proposals were expedient, and that all due notices had been given and requirements performed; there also he settled the scheme by his order. The difference is only that the order, instead of being provisional, now has final effect. But see what a change has in fact come to pass. The investigation by an inspector at a local inquiry is now the only investigation which will ever be made, the only forum for objections. Duplication of costs is impossible, blackmail by petitioners is restricted to one stage, a decision by the department reached upon consideration of the report cannot now be reversed except by appeal to the same department. At most the order will be liable to annulment upon resolution, but such a resolution is made before the full House, and is more likely to raise ticklish questions of politics than a calm consideration of the order itself; in any case such a resolution is very rarely made. But the outstanding virtue of this procedure lies in the local inquiry, a virtue shared, of course, by Provisional Order procedure, but for reasons already given not always effective there. It is undoubtedly an important step forward that the issue should be judged by an expert who has read himself into the history and the underlying assumptions of the borough which is asking for new rights, but even more important that, where the rights desired are to be exercised in a particular area, the expert should go there, see and hear for himself, and subject himself to those intangible currents and cross-currents of feeling that give life to information. All this is lacking to a committee of Parliament as it sits in Westminster and hears the words spoken in support and the words of reply.

The proceedings are intensely practical. When an inquiry is to be held the department assigns someone to take charge of it. He may be an official of the department, like the inspectors who took care of proposals to constitute new county boroughs, or the statute may sometimes require that a person not in the employ of any government department be appointed.[1] In any case he will be appointed for his peculiar fitness to deal with the situation in hand. The Swansea School dispute, involving difficult questions of law, was entrusted to Hamilton, K. C. (as he then was); the Arlidge controversy, where the issue was the sanitary condition of the complainant's house, was given to a housing inspector from the Local Government Board. Engineering inspectors of the Ministry of Health held the inquiry under the old procedure for constituting a county borough, — for it is the sufficiency of drainage water and other sanitary services that is there the first consideration, — and the now famous Liverpool Housing Scheme was investigated by an architect.[2]

The best available description of the local inquiry, and what the "inspector" does both before and after it, is contained in the summary of the evidence given by two engineering inspectors of the Ministry of Health before the Royal Commission on Local Government.[3]

A memorandum of facts is prepared by the department for the inspector, and the inspector, after giving about three weeks notice of the inquiry, sends out requests for statistics to the local authority. He goes down to the locality some days before the inquiry, has the benefit of conversation with the local officials concerned, the Medical Officer upon a clearance scheme, or the heads of the various local departments where the area is to be reorganised, and views for himself the slum property or the district in question. This tour of inspection, by which the inspector can form his own impressions of the situation, not only saves hours at the inquiry by enabling him to exclude irrelevant or false testimony, but gives him a background against which he can view the relevant evidence produced on either side. Indeed it has been described as the most important part of the whole procedure of local inquiry.

The procedure at the local inquiry depends partly upon the

[1] As in Port of London Act, 1908. 8 Ed. 7, c. 68, sec. 6 (2).
[2] See Board of Education v. Rice, [1911] A.C. 179, p. 180; Local Government Board v. Arlidge, [1915] A.C. 126; ex parte Yaffe, [1930] 2 K.B. 127.
[3] Royal Commission on Local Government, First Report (1925), p. 146 ff.

statute under which it is held. All the information relevant to the new scheme has been previously open to inspection by persons interested, and they can therefore come to the inquiry with a statement of all the grievances which they wish to present. Sometimes the statute requires objections to be in writing, but an objector may always present his case orally as well, either in person or through his solicitor or counsel. Counsel are heard, there is examination and cross-examination — less academic a proceeding here, where the inspector himself is by now fairly certain of the basic facts and the fundamental issues; after that the inspector is ready to hear persons more remotely affected. The inquiry may be adjourned from day to day, and its length will depend on the difficulty or the contentious nature of the case.

The inspector then returns to London to write his report. This report, which may be anything from fifty to three hundred pages, is a statement and analysis of the facts; in it the inspector gives what recommendations he wishes, but he is of course to some extent guided by his knowledge of the character of the decisions of Parliament and the Minister on past proposals of the sort. The report is then submitted to the Minister for his decision.

It is at this point that the most serious objections are raised by those who are opposed to the methods of departmental decision. Their criticisms are directed chiefly at quasi-judicial decisions, as to which I express no opinion; but when the editors of a book of cases on constitutional law refer to *ex parte Ringer* to illustrate their strictures on the ouster of the jurisdiction of the courts to review quasi-judicial decisions by a department,[1] and C. K. Allen refers to the "administrative procedure" in *Yaffe's Case* as "arbitrary throughout,"[2] it is difficult to resist the inference that they are confusing cases where the Minister's decisions are truly judicial — whether, for instance, this particular house measures up to a sanitary standard imposed by the Act — with cases where they are primarily legislative. In confirming a scheme, as in *Yaffe's Case* and *ex parte Ringer*, the Minister certainly reaches a decision, — Parliament in passing a new Act reaches a decision, — but it is only that sort of decision which is reached by a committee sitting on a private bill. *R. v. Electricity Commissioners*,[3] in extending the scope of prohibition to an extent unsupported by

---

[1] Keir & Lawson, Cases in Constitutional Law (1928), p. 143.
[2] Bureaucracy Triumphant (1931), p. 78.
[3] [1924] 1 K.B. 171.

any of the numerous citations relied on by the Court, is responsible for the mischief, and since that case is not likely to be disturbed it is perhaps unwise to quarrel with those who base their strictures upon the new law which it created. Nevertheless it seems odd to ask that the Minister should give reasons for his decision in confirming a scheme, when the Committee need give none for its decision in passing or rejecting a bill — although it is worth remarking that the Ministry of Health in 1921 adopted a practice of giving reasons for its decision upon a proposal to constitute or extend a county borough. Those who complain that the report of the inspector to the department is kept secret surely forget that only by secrecy can the inspector give his frank impressions and yet be secure from libel actions, and that only in this way can the responsibility of the Minister to Parliament be maintained. For directly it is possible to pin the decision upon one particular civil servant rather than upon the Minister, the last shaky leg of that constitutional theory collapses. Even during the period of regression the House of Lords stood firm in refusing to allow an amendment to the Housing (No. 2) Bill that, where the Minister confirms a scheme with a modification not recommended in the report, he should lay the report before Parliament with the reasons for his modification; for "it is a rule which has long been maintained that these reports of officers to the administrative departments should not be disclosed in any way." [1] Again, it is often said that the Minister is in effect permitted to decide contrary to the evidence presented in the report; and yet with respect to the constitution of county boroughs by Provisional Order the objection of local authorities was exactly the opposite: that the Minister tends to take the advice of the inspector.[2] And this is how the Commission summarised the evidence of two inspectors: "While the recommendations of the inspectors are not necessarily accepted by the Minister we were told by Colonel Norton that he thought that his *recommendations* had been accepted in nine cases out of ten; and Mr. Hetherington said that he thought that *every recommendation* which he had made on a proposal for the extension of a Borough had been accepted." [3]

The reason I have dealt thus at length with procedure by private

[1] 78 Lords Deb. (5th Series), p. 656, Lord Parmoor, July 21, 1930.

[2] Royal Commission on Local Government, First Report (1925), p. 176, par. 487.

[3] Id., par. 426. The italics are mine.

bill, Provisional Order, and order, and made comparisons between them, is not because of any real importance of the scheme procedure either in the past or in the present, but because it is the legislative method of the future — probably in the modified form of Special Order. If Parliament is to remain the source of all new rights, and if, as seems probable, we are entering on a period of governmental regulation more extensive than ever before, Parliament cannot hope, from mere pressure of business, to effect reorganisation in any other way than by executive order. The emphasis today is upon resemblances rather than differences; nevertheless there are differences in all situations and all activities which, while susceptible of treatment under a wide general policy, must be taken into account if the policy is to be put into practice — and no one would suggest that Parliament deal with all types of subtly different situations within the covers of one general Act. I have also tried to show that it is the rational method for constructive legislation, resting as it does on the principle of investigation by experts. Above all it is the method of conciliation. Much more is likely to be accomplished by establishing a new machinery of industrial coöperation or local interaction, and leaving its adoption to the initiative of the trades or areas desiring it, than by any ruthless war cry of "socialism in our time." The procedure, however, is by no means new, nor must it be supposed from what has gone before that it is used mostly in local legislation. The most striking instances do indeed deal directly or indirectly with local government, the division of boroughs into wards, the adjustment of the privileges of an authority which has become extinct,[1] the acquisition of land for local purposes,[2] schemes for slum clearance and town planning,[3] but the procedure has been used for the reorganisation of educational charities,[4] to confirm creditors' schemes and agreements among railway companies,[5] to aid new

[1] Municipal Corporations Act, 1882. 45 & 46 Vict., c. 50, secs. 30 and 213.

[2] Local Government Act, 1894. 56 & 57 Vict., c. 73, sec. 9; Public Health (Scotland) Act, 1897. 60 & 61 Vict., c. 38, sec. 145.

[3] Housing Act, 1903. 3 Ed. 7, c. 39, sec. 5 (2); Housing Act, 1909. 9 Ed. 7, c. 44, sec. 24 (1) (2); Housing Act, 1925. 15 Geo. 5, c. 14, sec. 40; Housing Act, 1909. 9 Ed. 7, c. 44, sec. 54; Town Planning Act, 1925. 15 Geo. 5, c. 16, sec. 2.

[4] Endowed Schools Act, 1869. 32 & 33 Vict., c. 56, secs. 35–39; Educational Endowments (Scotland) Act, 1882. 45 & 46 Vict., c. 59, secs. 21–32; Educational Endowments (Ireland) Act, 1885. 48 & 49 Vict., c. 78, sec. 27.

[5] Liquidation Act, 1868. 31 & 32 Vict., c. 68, sec. 10; Railway Companies Powers Act, 1864. 27 & 28 Vict., c. 120, secs. 4–17.

construction by existing railways, or to afford a cheap method of
constructing new railways.[1] The setting up of administrative
machinery by a department [2] or the settling by it of its own pension schemes [3] — these are trivial matters; but to allow a department to provide for insurance against unemployment in any industry by means of a special scheme [4] is to allow the Minister to
give statutory effect to his own scheme by his own confirmation, an
effect paralleled, it is true, by the power to make special rules for
special cases under the Factory Act and the Coal Mines Acts,[5] but
more startling here because the child of the private bill, whose
nature it is to proceed from the initiative of the individual person
or corporation, here denies its parentage and is affiliated to the
public general bill. Only after the World War is this procedure by
scheme moulded to the task for which it seems destined, the application of adoptive socialistic measures to the groups or areas willing to try the experiment. The Electricity Supply Act permits the
Commissioners to divide England into districts and establish electricity authorities in them; the Mining Act provides for cases
where the majority of owners in a district wish to amalgamate but
are unable to bring in the small minority whose coöperation is
essential for success; the Agricultural Marketing Act enables trading boards to be set up by order.[6] Therein the underlying principles of public and private Acts are reconciled.

Procedure by scheme, then, although it has, I believe, a great
future, has had a relatively undistinguished past. As in the case
of Provisional Order, the details of the procedure are laid down in
the Act in which the power is granted, but it is interesting to compare the cumbrous methods of an Educational Endowments Act,
obviously designed to be no less cumbrous than procedure by

[1] Railway Construction Facilities Act, 1864. 27 & 28 Vict., c. 121, secs. 6–
17; Light Railways Act, 1896. 59 & 60 Vict., c. 48, secs. 7–9; Tramways
Construction (Ireland) Act, 1861. 24 & 25 Vict., c. 102, sec. 9.

[2] War Pensions Act, 1921. 11 & 12 Geo. 5, c. 49, sec. 1; Education Act,
1902. 2 Ed. 7, c. 42, sec. 17.

[3] Education (Scotland) Act, 1908. 8 Ed. 7, c. 63, sec. 14 (4).

[4] Unemployment Insurance Act, 1920. 10 & 11 Geo. 5, c. 30, sec. 18.

[5] Factory Act, 1901. 1 Ed. 7, c. 22, sec. 126 (2); Coal Mines Regulation
Act, 1887. 50 & 51 Vict., c. 58, sec. 51 (1).

[6] Electricity Supply Act, 1919. 9 & 10 Geo. 5, c. 100, sec. 7; Mining Industry Act, 1926. 16 & 17 Geo. 5, c. 28, secs. 1–7; Coal Mines Act, 1930.
20 & 21 Geo. 5, c. 34, sec. 1; Agricultural Marketing Act, 1931. 21 & 22
Geo. 5, c. 42, sec. 1. Cf. also Public Works Facilities Act, 1930. 20 & 21
Geo. 5, c. 50, secs. 1 and 2.

private bill, with the methods of the Housing Act of 1925, whose
sole object was dispatch. In the Scots Act of 1882 [1] there is room
for objection at any one of six stages, first at the public local inquiry held by the Commissioners before ever they make the draft
scheme, second during the two months immediately following its
publication, when a second inquiry may be demanded; thereafter
objections in writing will still be received: another opportunity is
given after the submission of the scheme by the Commissioners to
the Scotch Education Department; between the date of the publication of the scheme by the department and the date when the
department may give its approval its legal validity may be questioned in the courts; and finally it is still open to any person aggrieved to induce either House to pass a resolution praying that
it be annulled. Besides these abundant safeguards there are time
requirements carefully directed to slowing up the passage of the
scheme: two months must elapse between the publication of the
draft scheme by the Commissioners and its submission to the department and between the receipt of the scheme by the department and its confirmation; and if a petition against its going into
force is then presented to the department, the scheme must lie for
two months before Parliament. But under the Housing Act of
1925 the local authority draws up the scheme on representation
by the Medical Officer and submits it to the Minister: the Minister may refuse at his discretion to proceed, but if he decides to
go ahead he sees that the elementary requirements of notice have
been complied with, demands such evidence in support of the
scheme as he sees fit, and then sends a person to hold a public local
inquiry to ascertain the correctness of the official representations
that the area concerned is unhealthy, that the scheme is adequate
to deal with the situation, and to hear all objectors. Upon receipt
of the report drawn up by the person who presided at the inquiry,
the Minister may confirm the scheme with or without modification, and the confirming order — the scheme, that is — has effect
as if enacted in the Act.[2] When the improvement scheme goes into
force, all orders for the compulsory purchase of land or buildings
contained in the scheme are made by the local authority and confirmed by the Minister, and these orders are expressly excluded
from review by any court.[3] Neither improvement scheme nor

---

[1] Educational Endowments (Scotland) Act, 1882. 45 & 46 Vict., c. 59,
secs. 21–32.   [2] Housing Act, 1925. 15 Geo. 5, c. 14, secs. 35–40.
[3] Housing Act, 1925. 15 Geo. 5, c. 14, Sched. III, 2.

compulsory purchase order is required to be laid before Parliament.

Simple as the procedure was under the Housing Acts, it satisfied neither social reformers nor constitutional theorists. It was objectionable to the theorists from the absence of control either by Parliament or, as it seemed, by the courts, to the reformers because, under the interpretation placed upon the Act of 1925 by the courts, a scheme had to be more precise than was practicable before the Minister could legally confirm it. That was the quarrel before the case of *ex parte Yaffe* in 1930. *Davis' Case* had gone far enough in quashing the Derby scheme for lack of particularity before the Minister had confirmed it, a decision questionable not only as placing an unreasonably restrictive interpretation upon the Act, but because it deprived the Minister of his power to cure a defect by modification. But when in *Yaffe's Case* both the Divisional Court and the Court of Appeal made the requirements even more stringent, and the Court of Appeal and the House of Lords showed themselves willing to intervene even after confirmation by the Minister,[1] Parliament repealed the section which had given rise to such difficulties and passed the Housing Act of 1930. Indeed it was high time; for the two years preceding the new Act slum clearance work had been practically at a standstill owing to the Derby and the Liverpool judgments.[2] Commenting on the new Act which did away with the necessity for a scheme, the Labour Minister of Health, a social reformer, thus expressed himself: "I said in the House of Commons that if it were not so serious the old procedure for slum clearance would have been comic. To go through the stage after stage which was necessary before you really began to clear a slum must have discouraged many a housing reformer. I think we have got down to the bone now in this matter of procedure, and we have simplified it as far as we could. We have taken steps to insure as far as we can that there shall not be in future any of the litigation which we have suffered recently on the question of slum clearance."[3]

The "steps taken" to which the Minister referred resulted in the emergence of a device, not entirely new but, so far as I am

---

[1] The House of Lords, however, held the scheme intra vires. *Ex parte Yaffe*, [1931] A.C. 494.

[2] Henderson and Maddock, Introduction to the Housing Acts, 1925–1930 (1931), p. 10.

[3] Quoted in Hill, The Complete Law of Housing (1931), p. xlvii.

aware, new in England,[1] which may do much to reconcile control
with speed and stability in legislation by scheme. Section 11 (3)
of the Act of 1930 provides that the validity of a clearance order
or compulsory purchase order may be brought up before the High
Court within six weeks after it is made and the Court "if satisfied
that . . . the order is not within the powers of this Act, or that the
interests of the applicant have been substantially prejudiced
by any requirements of the Act not having been complied with,
may quash the order," and that subject to that subsection "an
order shall not, either before or after its confirmation, be questioned by prohibition or certiorari or in any legal proceedings
whatsoever." Thereby is ruled out any possibility of the recurrence
of a situation like that in *Davis' Case* or *Yaffe's Case*. Private
persons must ascertain their rights before the guillotine falls. After
the six weeks of grace an order has full statutory force and the
authority may go ahead without fear. It is important to notice
that in order to avail himself of a procedural defect — one of
Mr. Yaffe's grounds of attack — the applicant must have been
"substantially prejudiced" by it; this Mr. Yaffe was not, for he
had an abundant opportunity of examining those plans which he
complained were not sent to the Minister, and of raising the matter
at the inquiry. The wording of the subsection has been criticised
on the ground that the requirement of "substantial prejudice"
can never come into operation as a limitation on the power of the
court to interfere; for if any requirements of the Act have not been
complied with, the order must ipso facto be "beyond the powers
of the Act" and so falls within the first part of the subsection,
where substantial prejudice need not be shown.[2] Does not this
take too rigid a view of the doctrine of ultra vires? At common
law a scheme was ultra vires if it either undertook to regulate more
than the Act permitted, or, while dealing only with the proper
subject matter, failed to follow the letter of the procedural requirements. The subsection makes a distinction between these two
distinct types of ultra vires, and lays it down that where the latter
type is relied on the applicant must show that he was injured by it.
However that may be, the section is found in other Acts passed in
1930, the Public Works Facilities Act and the Land Drainage Act,

---

[1] See Educational Endowments (Scotland) Act, 1882. 45 & 46 Vict., c. 59,
sec. 30; id., 1928. 18 & 19 Geo. 5, c. 30, sec. 25; and its anomalous form in
Endowed Schools Act, 1869. 32 & 33 Vict., c. 56, sec. 39.

[2] Hill, The Complete Law of Housing (1931), p. 193.

for instance.[1] The Public Works Facilities Act allows a local authority to acquire by ministerial order new powers for the relief of unemployment, the Land Drainage Act empowers the Minister to establish drainage boards, and these boards may vary navigation rights and levy navigation tolls, also by order. Since in each case individual rights are likely to be considerably affected, since also intolerable uncertainty would result if the relief projects of the authorities or the orders of the drainage board could be attacked on the ground that authority and board were, as to the matters they had purported to regulate, legally nonexistent, the problem was how to protect the individual without hampering the body or the authority. This section afforded a neat solution.

Another notable contribution to the methods of private legislation was made in 1919 — by accident, it is said. The Electricity Supply Bill as introduced into Parliament embodied the usual procedure by Provisional Order, but during the course of the inquiry before the Standing Committee of the House of Commons to which it was referred the procedure became transformed during the protracted sittings without the alteration having been discovered by the officials of the House.[2] The Act, as it emerged, directed the Electricity Commissioners to settle schemes for the setting up of new electricity authorities and to submit them to the Board of Trade for its confirmation, but provided by subsection 2 of section 7 that "any such order . . . shall not come into operation unless and until it has been approved . . . by a resolution passed by each House, and when so approved shall have effect as if enacted in this Act." This procedure (now called procedure by Special Order), which combines the manifest advantages of a local inquiry and settlement of the scheme by experts with the no less manifest advantage of insuring parliamentary approval, was at first defective in that no person aggrieved could object in Parliament except by raising a debate on the resolution. But Standing Orders have now remedied the situation. Standing Order of the House of Lords No. 191 directs all Special Orders — and this term covers rules as well as schemes — to be referred to the Special

---

[1] Land Drainage Act, 1930. 20 & 21 Geo. 5, c. 44, Sched. II, Part III, 2; Public Works Facilities Act, 1930. 20 & 21 Geo. 5, c. 50, Sched. I, Part III, 2; Poor Law Act, 1930. 20 Geo. 5, c. 17, sec. 142; Housing (Scotland) Act, 1930. 20 & 21, Geo. 5, c. 40, sec. 11 (3).

[2] Sir Ernest Moon, Royal Commission on Local Government, Minutes of Evidence, p. 342, par. 5184.

Order Committee. If they decide that it is like a private bill they allow petitions to be presented and in the light of the petitions consider whether there ought to be further inquiry by a select committee. If they decide it is like a public bill they must consider whether its provisions raise important questions of policy or principle, and how far it is founded on precedent; if need be, there is further inquiry made before the House proceeds to a decision upon the resolution.[1] Although the procedure traces its origin from Provisional Order, it is now a common method of control in all types of delegated legislation; rules modifying the provisions of an Act of Parliament,[2] a change in the speed limit, the Highway Code,[3] and orders raising the rate of import duty under an Act of 1921 [4] have thus been brought up for review by Parliament before going into effect, while regulations under the sweeping provisions of the Emergency Powers Act [5] and orders issued to remove a difficulty under the Local Government Act, 1929,[6] could only continue after a certain period on resolution of approval. Indeed the instances of its use as a method of private legislation are comparatively rare, chiefly because it is still the fashion to require local authorities and other semi-public bodies to proceed by private bill. The above-mentioned schemes under the Electricity Supply Act, the more far-reaching schemes of railway reorganisation, and the constitution of marketing boards about fill the list.[7]

Procedure by Special Order raises two nice questions of judicial control. First, may the order be quashed before Parliament has passed upon it? Second, does the resolution of approval bar review by the courts?

What is the nature of the order before Parliament has had anything to do with it? If it is a mere suggestion which Parliament can follow or not as it choose, it is plain that certiorari cannot issue,

[1] Williams, Private Bill Legislation, p. 120.

[2] Road Traffic Act, 1930. 20 & 21 Geo. 5, c. 43, sec. 91 (3) (4); Mental Treatment Act, 1930. 20 & 21 Geo. 5, c. 23, sec. 15 (2); Water Undertakings (Modification of Charges) Act, 1921. 11 & 12 Geo. 5, c. 44, sec. 2 (2).

[3] Road Traffic Act, 1930. secs. 45 (2) and 10 (4).

[4] Safeguarding of Industries Act, 1921. 11 & 12 Geo. 5, c. 47, sec. 2 (4).

[5] Emergency Powers Act, 1920. 10 & 11 Geo. 5, c. 55, sec. 2 (2).

[6] Local Government Act, 1929. 19 Geo. 5, c. 17, sec. 130.

[7] Electricity Supply Act, 1919. 9 & 10 Geo. 5, c. 100, sec. 7; Ministry of Transport Act, 1919. 9 & 10 Geo. 5, c. 50, sec. 3 (1) (d); Agricultural Marketing Act, 1931. 21 & 22 Geo. 5, c. 42, sec. 1 (8). See also Gas Regulation Act, 1920. 10 & 11 Geo. 5, c. 28, sec. 10 (2) (b).

and this for two reasons. Certiorari necessarily involves the existence of a decision to quash; the decision need not have been given
by a court in the strict sense, nor in a matter judicial rather than
legislative, but it must be a decision proceeding from a body under
a duty to act judicially. And if Parliament is still free to amend or
modify as it choose, then any action by the courts involves an
interference with the business of Parliament. The question came
up in *R*. v. *Electricity Commissioners*,[1] where the Court granted
prohibition to restrain the Commissioners from holding a local
inquiry on a draft scheme that was ultra vires. The procedure
there was by Special Order; the Commissioners were to draw up
a draft scheme, hold a local inquiry upon it, and submit it to the
Board of Trade for approval (with or without modification), but
the order was not to come into operation unless approved by a
resolution of each House. It was argued that the Commissioners
gave no decision but only advice, and that Parliament had reserved to itself all control over the schemes. The Court thought
otherwise, pointed out that it was the scheme of the Commissioner
which eventually took effect, and that in deciding the question of
ultra vires a court would be helping rather than hindering Parliament. Since the procedure was entirely novel there were no direct
precedents, and the cases dealing with prohibition and certiorari
with respect to Provisional Orders were too chaotic to be of much
use.[2] But here, as in *Yaffe's Case* a few years later, the Court was
content to interpret the words in the statute and quote precedents
without inquiring what actually happens to a Special Order before
it passes into law. A Provisional Order decides nothing until Parliament has passed the bill to which it is scheduled. When the bill
reaches Parliament it is subject to petition, and if petitioned against
will be referred to a select committee; there it may be amended to
such an extent that the department which made it would not recognise its own child. Even unopposed orders are examined to see if
they are intra vires.[3] As for a Special Order, although it rests far
more in the power of the department than a Provisional Order,
Standing Order No. 191 referred to above shows how far short of a
"decision" such an order falls — when it must be groomed by the

[1] [1924] 1 K.B. 171.
[2] See Sir Lynden Macassey, Law Making by Government Departments,
5 J.S.C.L. (3rd Series), Part I, p. 73 (1923).
[3] Sir Ernest Moon, Royal Commission on Local Government, Minutes of
Evidence, p. 345, par. 5241.

Special Orders Committee, one of whose duties is to report to the House "where the Committee have any doubt whether the Order is intra vires."

On the other hand a Special Order is as much the child of the department as a ministerial order, and it is possible, if we disregard the historical origin of the Special Order, to consider the Special Orders Committee as a safeguard merely, and not as an integral part of the passage of the order, while intervention by the courts has this double advantage, that they are more fitted to decide the question of ultra vires, and besides may be invoked at an earlier stage. *R.* v. *Electricity Commissioners* is in any case the outcome of the jealous feelings which the judiciary entertain towards executive bodies, and illustrates how desire and considerations of convenience outweigh the continuity of precedent.

When a private bill or a Provisional Order has passed into law it cannot be challenged: Parliament has enacted it, right or wrong. What about a Special Order after approval by resolution of both Houses? Sir Lynden Macassey thought in 1923 that it was beyond question.[1] But he rested upon the express words of the statutes known to him which related to Special Orders in the nature of private bills "that they should have effect as if enacted in the Act"[2] — words which have been shorn of much of their force since *Yaffe's Case*. There is nothing in the definition of a Special Order to require finality after approval; Standing Order No. 191 defines it as "any Order in Council, departmental order, rules, regulations, schemes . . . to be laid in draft before the House and requiring an affirmative resolution of the House before becoming effective." It is true that the four statutes in which schemes are made by Special Order all contain a provision directed to securing finality. But suppose a provision of the Highway Code to contain ultra vires matter and to have been passed by resolution. The Road Traffic Act says nothing about the Code being then of statutory effect.[3] It would seem that approval by resolution should not, on the reasoning of *R.* v. *Electricity Commissioners*, exclude the jurisdiction of the court: although Parliament has given its approval, the order is not a statute. For one thing it lacks the Royal Assent; for another thing the two Houses here act only in a subordinate capacity, exercising powers of approval delegated to them

---

[1] Law Making by Government Departments (*supra*), p. 89.

[2] Electricity Supply Act, Ministry of Transport Act, Gas Regulation Act.

[3] Road Traffic Act, 1930. 20 & 21 Geo. 5, c. 43, sec. 45 (2).

by Parliament, and it may be argued that in approving an ultra
vires order the two Houses are themselves acting ultra vires. There
is no magic in a resolution, however clearly it may express the will
of the Houses: a resolution of the House of Commons, then in
exclusive control of money bills, authorising the collection of the
rate of income tax fixed by it but not yet expressed in statutory
form, was in 1913 held incompetent to legalise the collection.[1]
Parliament has been sensible of this difficulty, sensible also of the
disturbing influence of *Yaffe's Case*: for schemes under the Agricultural Marketing Act, 1931, are protected after approval by the
"conclusive evidence" clause [2] and with reference to schemes under
the Public Works Facilities Act, 1930, conferring new powers on
local authorities, it is provided that "a scheme under this section
shall be of no effect unless confirmed by Parliament, and if the
Minister submits a scheme for such confirmation, he shall do so
by introducing into Parliament a Bill to confirm the scheme; and
the Bill after introduction shall be deemed to have passed through
all its stages up to and including Committee and shall be ordered
to be considered in either House as if reported from a Committee,
and when the Bill has been read a third time and passed in the
first House of Parliament the like proceedings shall be taken in the
second House of Parliament." [3] A scheme under the latter Act
not only has the effect of an act, it is itself an Act of Parliament,
duly receiving the Royal Assent.

[1] Bowles *v*. Bank of England, [1913] 1 Ch. 57.
[2] Agricultural Marketing Act, 1931. 21 & 22 Geo. 5, c. 42, sec. 1 (8).
[3] Public Works Facilities Act, 1930. 20 & 21 Geo. 5, c. 50, sec. 1 (9).

CHAPTER V

THE POWER TO MODIFY AN ACT OF PARLIAMENT

THE delegation to a department of the power to modify an Act of Parliament has suffered many an attack at the hands of the critics of twentieth-century English government, but none so furious or so one-sided as that launched by Lord Hewart. The subject is taken up under the kindred but more controversial "power to remove difficulties," which itself is noticed only in so far as it raised a storm of protest in both Houses during the spring of 1929.[1] There is no mention of the kind of circumstances that make this clause a practical necessity, of its past history, or of action taken under a similar clause in other Acts. A grant of power to the Minister of Health to "make such order for removing the difficulty as he may judge necessary for that purpose, and any such order may modify the provisions of this Act" has dramatic appeal; it opens up vistas of government by Whitehall, and of the Minister calmly reversing the local government policy of Parliament by a stroke of the official pen. But during the first two months of the operation of the Act, just that period in which the power would most naturally be exercised, only one such order was issued, and this dealt with nothing more exciting than the water rate of Bootle. Lord Hewart could not, of course, have foreseen what would be done or not done under it, and he might plausibly argue that here at any rate public opinion has made itself felt, but it is surely not too much to expect him to refer to orders issued under a similar section of the Rating Act, 1925[2] — of which mention will be made later.

Lord Hewart, however, is not the only offender in this matter. The debate of January 29, 1929, in the House of Commons is full of airy generalities that counsel would hesitate to produce in court but are quick to voice in the Commons. Mr. Gerald Hurst declared, and quite rightly, that "the Bill . . . seeks to give effect to a power of suspension and dispensation,"[3] and as if he was thereby

[1] The New Despotism, pp. 52–57.
[2] 15 & 16 Geo. 5, c. 90, sec. 67 (1).
[3] 224 Com. Deb. (5th Series), p. 970, January 29, 1929.

clinching the argument Sir Henry Slesser reminded the House that the clause was like Henry VIII's Statute of Declarations. If this was the temper of two distinguished lawyers there is some excuse for the dictum by another gentleman that if the Minister is given a loophole to amend the Act so painfully debated "we might as well shut up the House of Commons," [1] and for Miss Lawrence's cry from the heart, "Then [the clause] gives the Minister power to override the guarantee. Is that true? It seems to me too dreadful to be true." [2] What Minister would have the courage under a "temporary and transitory provision" to "amend or repeal an Act of Parliament or any portion of an Act of Parliament" [3] was not explained; as for Mr. Hurst, the Bill of Rights declared not the law of God but the pardonable prejudices of 1688, while Sir Henry Slesser's reference to the Statute of Declarations leaves out of account nearly four hundred years of history — years which have seen the gradual necessary subordination of the individual to the common will in the change from a rural to an industrial England, from simplicity to infinite complexity. At any rate there is some difference between a grant of power that "anything enacted by King Henry VIII or by Order-in-Council shall have the force of law" [4] and a discretionary power to remove difficulties that are only too likely to arise when the whole structure of local government is reorganised in sweeping terms by Act of Parliament.

The Minister of Health pointed out that there was nothing new about the clause, and produced a list of precedents beginning in 1888, but they were thrust aside as "bad precedents," [5] and he was reminded that the argument from precedent is dangerous, "for each precedent may go a little further than the last." [6] Nevertheless the Minister had made his point; the British subject has not because of this clause slept less soundly of nights since 1888.

Sir Leslie Scott's temperate suggestion, to keep the clause, but

[1] 224 Com. Deb. (5th Series), p. 989, January 29, 1929.

[2] 224 Com. Deb. (5th Series), p. 554, January 25, 1929.

[3] 224 Com. Deb. (5th Series), p. 989, Mr. Rye, January 29, 1929.

[4] London Times, February 16, 1929, quoted in The New Despotism, p. 57; but see Carr, Delegated Legislation, chap. 6.

[5] By Mr. Greenwood. Of Mr. Chamberlain's speech Sir John Marriott says in his prologue to The Crisis of English Liberty (p. 12): "The Minister sought indeed to justify his original clause by reference to many precedents, but the references merely proved that the vigilance of Parliament has been less conspicuous than the arrogance of the Departments."

[6] By Sir Leslie Scott (p. 984).

allow some form of appeal on the question whether there was a difficulty, or whether the method adopted by the Minister was necessary or expedient, passed more or less unnoticed. It is open, however, to several practical objections, among them the triviality of the questions likely to be presented and the difficulty of bringing the matter before the courts with sufficient dispatch, that is when account is taken of their rooted antipathy to any proceeding which smacks of giving an advisory opinion. Further, how is a lawyer any better judge of a difficulty in administration than a civil servant? That, it might be said, is not the question; it is a matter of "checks and balances." True; but granted that the principle upon which that doctrine rests is fundamentally sound, there is little reason in this year of grace for continuing to emphasise unduly the threefold nature of government. Wisdom and discernment are not the exclusive privilege of the courts, and where the problem is in essence one of policy Parliament should be slow to entrust its solution to a man who is better versed perhaps in the constitutional learning of the seventeenth century than in the present-day practice of government, and is apt also to forget that even Dicey in his exposition of the Rule of Law recognized the impossibility of understanding the English Constitution apart from its extra-legal conventions.

The clause passed the House of Commons and came up to the Lords in the form set out above; for the amendments promised by the Government turned out to be no more than verbal, "make any appointment or do any other thing" being clearly covered by the words "make such order for removing the difficulty as he may judge necessary." Upon the part of the clause which had drawn so strong a protest from the Commons there was no discussion, and the Lords were content to deal with realities and establish a parliamentary control that was consistent with dispatch by providing that the order should go into force as soon as made, but making its continued validity after the expiration of three months conditional on the passing of an affirmative resolution by each House. The Lord Chancellor declared himself ready to give instances of the exercise of this power under the Rating Act of 1925 if he did not think "that probably the general necessity for some such power as this was a matter which was fully recognised in this House." [1] Earl Russell, a doughty opponent of bureaucracy, thus expressed himself: "My Lords, few members of your Lordships'

[1] 73 Lords Deb. (5th Series), p. 382, March 8, 1929.

House ... feel more strongly than I do about the danger of bureaucratic government and the danger of government by ministerial orders, and therefore I looked at this clause with suspicion.
I am bound also to say that I did not go quite as far as some of
my friends because *one has to go by common sense in these matters*.[1]
When I looked at the Bill and saw the complexity of it and the
number of things to be adjusted, I asked myself what I would feel
if I were Minister of Health and had to administer it. I am bound
to admit that one would want some sort of Stuart dispensing
power. It is not unreasonable to take some power of this kind to
deal with difficulties not foreseen at the time." [2]

And that was the end — except for the anticlimax that up till
December 1930 only one order had been issued under section 130.

The power to remove difficulties is, however, as I pointed out
above, merely a special application of the power to modify; and
the power to modify is closely related to the power of dispensation
and suspension, which by no means perished forever on the passage
of the Bill of Rights — though as a prerogative right it did. It
will readily be recognised that there are two main classes of occasion on which the power to modify might conceivably be granted:
where the passing of a new Act makes meaningless or inapplicable
a number of older Acts, general or local, and where the very nature
of the new Act makes it advisable to grant power to amend the
Act itself in order to meet circumstances so unusual or trivial that
Parliament does not consider it worth while to legislate specially
for them. It is to this second class that the power to remove difficulties belongs, and it is an extreme instance of the class; for
whereas in the usual case the special circumstances justifying
exercise of the power to modify are pretty closely defined by the
Act,[3] here the right of exercise accrues "if any difficulty arises ...
in bringing into operation this Act" or the like (and the Minister
is sole judge of what is a difficulty), and to meet it he may "by
order do anything which appears to him necessary or expedient ...
for bringing ... this Act into operation." [4] The first class of circumstances is not for the moment important; that is normally a
question of verbal revision, and nothing more.

[1] The italics are mine.

[2] 73 Lords Deb. (5th Series), p. 610, March 14, 1929.

[3] See Factory and Workshop Act, 1901. 1 Ed. 7, c. 22, sec. 3 (2); Police
Act, 1910, 10 Ed. 7 & 1 Geo. 5, c. 13, sec. 1 (2).

[4] See Unemployment Insurance Act, 1920, 10 & 11 Geo. 5, c. 30, sec. 45;
National Insurance Act, 1911. 1 & 2 Geo. 5, c. 55, sec. 78.

Immense as the power to remove difficulties may be, its use has more often than not been confined within narrow bounds: in the early instances, section 108 of the Local Government Act, 1888, and section 80 (1) of the Local Government Act, 1894,[1] the only difficulty which might be so removed was one[2] arising upon the first election of certain new local officials and their first meeting. Here, the reorganisation to be effected being narrow in scope, the power granted was necessarily narrow. But the reasons which prompted the insertion of such a clause in these Acts are no different from those operating in later Acts where the power is wider. In each case a new and complicated machinery is to be set up for the first time; Parliament has said the word, but it remains to the department to carry out the command. This the department can only do by issuing instructions to the officials of the local units concerned. A new elective system, for instance, requires the preparation of new lists and the Act is due to come into force on a certain day; what if the local Act of the municipality makes no provision for the expenditure of money for such purposes, or the compiling of the lists proves in certain cases so troublesome that they cannot be in by the day appointed in the principal Act? Without such a power in the department the municipality must inevitably break the law, or at least be deprived of the new privileges for a time. Or suppose an irregularity in the procedure, so that a writ of certiorari might issue at the relation of some truculent ratepayer: whatever may be said of such a situation in normal times, it would be sheer madness to penalise a slip among unfamiliar technicalities and demand that the whole business be done over again according to the letter of the Act. It is to such absurdities that strict legalism would lead.

The larger the scheme to be put into force the more potent the argument for granting this curative power. Sir John Anderson, however, believes that this clause was designed to apply solely to machinery, but gave no power to modify any substantial provision of the Act itself, and quotes section 78 of the National Insurance Act, which provides for its use in reference to the constitution of the body of insurance commissioners and no more.[3] This theory

[1] 50 & 51 Vict., c. 41, sec. 108; 56 & 57 Vict., c. 73, sec. 80 (1).

[2] Other instances of the same type are: Education (Scotland) Act, 1918. 8 & 9 Geo. 5, c. 48, Sched. II, 15 (5); Metropolitan Water Act, 1902. 2 Ed. 7, c. 41, sec. 51 (1) (2); Local Government Act (Ireland), 1919. 9 & 10 Geo. 5, c. 19, sec. 10 (2); Poor Law Act, 1927. 17 & 18 Geo. 5, c. 14, sec. 13.

[3] Bureaucracy, 7 J.P.A. 9 (1929).

gives a good account of the Acts of 1888 and 1894 (they plainly went no further), but whatever the purpose of the framers of the clause in the Act of 1911, later statutes have expressly applied it to the substance, and, as I submit, with justification.

It may not be a very serious matter if the elections of, say, Henley Parish are delayed or declared null and void, but where a new social policy is launched on the country much depends on a favourable impression being created at the outset. "You could come to Parliament for an amending Act," say the legalists — yes, and thereby reopen for debate what must by its very nature have been controversial stuff, quite apart from popular disgust at the dilatory methods of government, and the unfairness of depriving some area or class of the privileges which their fellows are by now enjoying. So that in the Acts establishing the dole and the new contributory pensions, and those reorganising the system of rating and local government, Parliament had no constitutional qualms about empowering the departments to remove difficulties.[1] Parliament does not thereby make reflections upon its own lack of foresight; lawyers who are pretty good at the game of "suppose" cannot foresee every combination of circumstance, even in so limited a field as that of real property, and there are many matters about which, if foreseen, Parliament would not wish to bother itself. These are the exceptional cases of which Mr. Chamberlain gave an instance in the debate on the power to remove difficulties — an area in the North of England where the duty of maintaining the highways and bridges devolves upon the inhabitants of a lordship, and rates can be levied for the purpose.[2] Likewise Parliament made no express provision for supplementary or special schemes of unemployment insurance, or the application of the Rating Act to exceptional areas.

It is easy to understand a lawyer's horror at this section, for there is nowhere any provision for control by the courts; easy also to understand a layman standing aghast at the generality of the words used. No one can deny that there is some risk involved in so wholesale a delegation, but so far there has been no suggestion of hardship to individuals or of usurpation of the parliamentary

[1] National Insurance Act, 1911. 1 & 2 Geo. 5, c. 55, sec. 78; Unemployment Insurance Act, 1920. 10 & 11 Geo. 5, c. 30, sec. 45; Widows Orphans and Old Age Contributory Pensions Act, 1925. 15 & 16 Geo. 5, c. 70, sec. 36; Rating and Valuation Act, 1925. 15 & 16 Geo. 5, c. 90, sec. 67 (1); Local Government Act, 1929. 19 Geo. 5, c. 17, sec. 130.

[2] 224 Com. Deb. (5th Series), p. 979, January 29, 1929.

power. The generality of the words used is not in itself important; the proper question is what has in fact been done under those words. For if a department went ahead under this power and created a new criminal offence or a new obligation to pay money, there might be just cause for complaint. It was therefore with some curiosity that I went to the volumes of Statutory Rules and Orders to see what wickedness had sheltered behind section 67 of the Rating Act, of which Mr. Ramsay Muir has said that Parliament passed it "apparently without realising the importance of what it was doing." [1] I was almost disappointed to find that the orders were uniformly uninteresting. Two orders extending the time within which rating authorities must submit their schemes for preserving certain exemptions and privileges and for fixing the ratable value of property; [2] another providing that in cases of difficulty a rating officer might be transferred to some authority other than that contemplated in the Act; [3] the order of March 16, 1929, extending the time for approval of the first draft valuation list by assessment committees; a few local orders, among them one settling the percentage reduction of the Pickering Rates and another dealing with the Bootle water rate and directing that for this purpose Bootle shall be deemed within the Liverpool rating area — that was all. What a deal of time and trouble could have been saved if Mr. Hurst and Sir Henry Slesser had inquired, as Lord Hailsham did, of the practice of the Ministry of Health in this matter!

After all the power is not very different in principle from that granted in early days to colonial legislatures of altering the principal Act subject to confirmation by Order in Council, [4] or the power of the Privy Council itself under the Regimental Debts Act, 1893, "to make different provisions to meet different cases or different circumstances." [5] Furthermore, it is strictly limited in duration, under the Rating Act to four years from date of coming into effect, under the Local Government Act to a year and a half. Neither English cities nor the incidence of events are yet sufficiently standardised to be brought safely into the fold of parliamentary

[1] How Britain is Governed, p. 62.

[2] Order of March 22, 1927, No. 261; Order of July 21, 1927, No. 674.

[3] Order of February 18, 1927, No. 80.

[4] See Coin Offences (Colonies) Act, 1853. 16 & 17 Vict., c. 48, sec. 4; Merchant Shipping Act, 1854. 17 & 18 Vict., c. 104, sec. 547.

[5] 56 Vict., c. 5, sec. 13 (1).

formula. Till that happy day the departments will presumably continue to insist on the insertion of some such section as this, and lawyers to register their gallant protest in defence of another lost cause.

There are many statutes in which the power to modify is granted for purposes quite other than those of the power to remove difficulties. Those who object to section 130 of the Local Government Act cannot see how even an emergency can justify the exercise of arbitrary discretion by an official; its supporters might prove less enthusiastic in less clear a case. For the arguments in favour of section 130 will not carry them all the way to, say, section 24 of the Judicature Amendment Act, 1875. Why should the Rules Committee have been permitted to modify prior Acts of Parliament "to such extent as may be necessary in order to adapt existing rules of practice and procedure?" Or what satisfactory reason can be given for allowing the Metropolitan Board of Works with the consent of His Majesty in Council "to alter . . . the rules for the regulation of the thickness of walls contained in the first Schedule?"[1] To answer that these are "matters of mere administrative detail" is not enough; Parliament thought them of sufficient importance to lay down a rule of general application, and many objectors say that to permit modification of such commands is for Parliament to stultify itself. In truth the possible answers are so varied and depend so much upon the subject matter of the legislation and the sort of abuses or difficulties to be met by it that it is more practicable to point out specific instances and with a little explanation let them speak for themselves, without forgetting, however, that behind all delegation of legislative power lies the desire to reconcile democracy with dispatch, the interested but always illuminating innovations of the amateur with the disinterested research of the expert.

The most striking difference between the passing of a new enactment and the emergence of a new principle in the Common Law is the difference in continuity. The Common Law is like an amoeba, and reacts to changes in environment by putting out pseudopodia. The legislature — to use another figure — adds a new patch to the clothes of national life; but the patch must be sewed into the old fabric before it can benefit the wearer. There can hardly be a change in one institution without some effect on others, and in the vast majority of cases Parliament has provided in a schedule or

[1] Metropolitan Building Act, 1855. 18 & 19 Vict., c. 122, sec. 55.

otherwise for those others. But any attempt by Parliament to provide in the principal Act for necessary modifications in the local Acts would fill the Statute Book with details of purely local importance; to require the authority to come to Westminster for an amending Act would arouse effective opposition to any new legislation; to do nothing would abandon the authority to the whimsical interpretations of the courts. The obvious method is to direct the department to go ahead with the principal Act, and where it finds inconsistent provisions of a local Act standing in the way to permit modification so far as may seem to the department necessary to make the provisions of the local Act conform with the provisions of the principal Act.[1] A similar situation, but even more simple, is presented upon the abolition of a governmental unit and the transfer of its powers elsewhere. During the War the Ministry of Pensions, and after the War the Scottish Board of Health and the Ministry of Health, were set up to exercise powers which before had been divided up among a great many separate departments. Parliament did all that was important — decided that the time had come to concentrate interdependent activities under one management, and passed the Acts declaring that they were now so concentrated. It was left to the Council to bring up to date by order the enactments defining these activities.[2] It is difficult to condemn the grant of so limited a power, for there is little discretion in the department. All that needs to be done is to strike out the now obsolete provision of the Act and substitute the new, probably lifted straight from the statute itself. It is a matter of legislative bookkeeping.

Closely akin to this is the practice which has resulted from the unwillingness of Parliament to pass two Acts where one would suffice. Why, for instance, legislate specially for the local government of the Scilly Isles when the institutions are not sufficiently different from those in England to justify special consideration, and yet are not exactly on all fours with them? So that section

[1] Cf. Local Government (Ireland) Act, 1898. 61 & 62 Vict., c. 37, sec. 104 (2) (d); Education (Scotland) Act, 1918. 8 & 9 Geo. 5, c. 48, Sched. V; Rating Act, 1925. 15 & 16 Geo. 5, c. 90, sec. 66; Public Health Act, 1925. 15 & 16 Geo. 5, c. 71, sec. 6; Gas Undertakings Act, 1929. 19 & 20 Geo. 5, c. 24, sec. 1 (3).

[2] Ministry of Pensions Act, 1916. 6 & 7 Geo. 5, c. 65, sec. 2 (1); Scottish Board of Health Act, 1919. 9 & 10 Geo. 5, c. 20, sec. 4 (4); Ministry of Health Act, 1919. 9 & 10 Geo. 5, c. 21, sec. 3 (2), (3), (4). See also Forestry (Transfer of Woods) Act, 1923. 13 & 14 Geo. 5, c. 21, Sched.

138 (3) of the Local Government Act 1929 provides that the Minister of Health may apply the Act to the Scilly Isles, "subject to such exceptions, modifications and adaptations, if any, as may be contained in the Order." [1] And when in 1876 it was decided to go one step further along the road of preventive justice and establish day industrial schools in Scotland to deal with difficult children, the principles upon which an industrial school should be run had already been laid down by an Act of 1866; it only remained for Parliament to direct that these principles should also govern a day industrial school, subject to the modifications that were necessitated by the fact that here the control of the children was to be partial only. What modifications were necessary could best be decided by men of experience and carried into effect by executive order.[2] Similarly on the constitution of the Air Force as a separate unit and the transfer to it of naval and military air duties, His Majesty was directed to apply by Order in Council to the Air Force the enactments relating to the Army with the necessary modifications and adaptations.[3] There is, however, at least one objection to this method of legislation by reference, that in order to obviate one difficulty it creates another; for unless the order is more comprehensive than such orders usually are, the law can only be ascertained by a study of the principal Act and the Act referred to, plus the order modifying it. Difficulties of interpretation and opportunity for error are thus immeasurably increased. At any rate this objection is practical, not constitutional; here again the department has little to do but apply the express words of an Act to an analogous situation.

If the grant of modifying power had only been made to deal with situations like that, there could have been no complaint. But where the continuance of an express command of Parliament is made to depend upon the discretion of an official, it is there that the trouble begins. That Parliament has thus conditioned its own command is either forgotten or brushed aside, and in Parliament itself practical considerations are drowned in the rising tide of debate — when the matter has been debated, that is, for the power was until recently granted without question. In 1915 there was a faint foreshadowing of what was to come. In the bill providing

---

[1] Cf. also Local Government Act (Ireland), 1898. 61 & 62 Vict., c. 37, sec. 104 (1).

[2] Elementary Education (Scotland) Act, 1876. 39 & 40 Vict., c. 79, sec. 16.

[3] Air Force Act, 1917. 7 & 8 Geo. 5, c. 51, sec. 8 (4).

that the Judicial Committee might sit in two divisions was a provision empowering the Lord Chancellor and a committee to issue
rules and orders including "such adaptations in the enactments
relating to the Judicial Committee as may be necessary to give
effect to this Act." Lord Muir-Mackenzie suggested that it would
be possible under these words to change the Act of William IV
upon which the present jurisdiction of the Committee rests, and
accordingly the Lord Chancellor consented to delete the offending
words "to prevent the possibility of such a thing, not taking place,
but being reasonably misapprehended." [1] But the interest for us
lies in the following statement of Lord Muir-Mackenzie: "I have
always thought that a rule-making power ought not to go so far
as to allow the modification of existing Acts of Parliament except
in matters of practice and procedure and things of that nature." [2]
Granted that a power to modify must have some limit, why draw
an arbitrary line? Surely it is common sense to treat each situation on its merits; few, for instance, would advocate the grant of
such power even over procedure where the liberty of the subject
was concerned, but fewer still would deny it to a tariff board.
What is a "matter of practice and procedure?" If the application
of the Companies Act to a particular type of land corporation
proposed to be formed under the Agricultural Land (Utilisation)
Bill, 1931,[3] is to be accounted more than a matter of procedure,
then under Lord Muir-Mackenzie's test Mr. Attlee was wrong in
dismissing as "purely obstructive" the objection of the Opposition
to a clause allowing the Minister of Agriculture to make necessary
modifications in his application of that Act. But if the modification must necessarily be one of substance — and surely it must —
then the test would seem unduly narrow; for Parliament must then
sit down and review a miniature Companies Act for this sporadic
growth, at a time when the general principles applicable to such
a corporation are already in the Statute Book.

Be that as it may, there is no lack of precedent for permitting
a department to modify existing Acts of Parliament in matters of
substance.[4] When in 1869 the Treasury is directed to make orders

[1] 20 Lords Deb. (5th Series), p. 556, December 8, 1915.

[2] Id., p. 554.

[3] 247 Com. Deb. (5th Series), p. 1936, February 4, 1931.

[4] This power is occasionally granted even in a local Act. By Article 17 (1)
of the Derby Court of Record Order of January 1, 1928, made under Derby
Corporation Act, 1927 (17 & 18 Geo. 5, c. xcii, sec. 92 [1]), it was ordered that
the Common Law Procedure Act, 1852, the Common Law Procedure Act, 1854,

with the concurrence of the Lord Chancellor for fixing the salaries and conditions of tenure of the court officers, "any enactment inconsistent with such order shall be repealed." [1] By the London Traffic Act, 1924, the regulations of the Minister of Transport, dealing among other things with the routing of traffic and the tearing up of streets for repair, are to override all prior provisions in all Acts, whether general or local.[2] Under the Day Industrial Schools Act (Scotland), 1893, His Majesty has the same powers as he had under the Scotch Education Act of 1876, with these additions: that he may by order provide for the mitigation of punishments in the Act of 1866, and override that Act in certain cases by sending the delinquent to a day industrial school instead of to the industrial school.[3]

The rationale of such delegation, which in these particular cases has the effect not merely of modifying certain provisions in an existing Act but of sweeping them clear away, is that which lies behind most modern delegation, to give full play to the determinations of the expert. It might have been possible, for instance, to define more exactly the powers of the Minister of Transport, and after a careful revision of all London traffic and street legislation to say, "Thus far shalt thou go and no farther." But the tool is most aptly shaped in the face of the task to be done; decision is delayed until the moment of need, and then no local or outworn regulations must stand in the way of the general plan.

The "flexibility" aspect of the power to modify is even more clearly brought out on those occasions where special conditions have made statutory charges inapplicable but where (as in the period of high prices after the World War) there is no reason why there should not be a speedy return to normal.[4] The "expert"

and the Summary Procedure on Bills of Exchange Act, 1855, should cease to extend and apply to the Borough Court of Derby.

[1] Courts of Justice Salaries Act, 1869. 32 & 33 Vict., c. 91, sec. 14.

[2] 14 & 15 Geo. 5, c. 34, sec. 10 (2). See also Juries Act, 1922. 12 & 13 Geo. 5, c. 11, sec. 6 (1) (e).

[3] 56 Vict., c. 12, sec. 3 (9). See also Motor Car (International Circulation) Act, 1909. 9 Ed. 7, c. 37, sec. 1 (b). For instances where a Special Order is directed to modify or amend the provisions of any Special Act see Gas Regulation Act, 1920. 10 & 11 Geo. 5, c. 28, sec. 10 (2) (h); Road Traffic Act, 1930. 20 & 21 Geo. 5, c. 43, sec. 91 (3).

[4] Harbours (Temporary Increase of Charges) Act, 1920. 10 & 11 Geo. 5, c. 21, sec. 1 (1); Water Undertakings (Modification of Charges) Act, 1921. 11 & 12 Geo. 5, c. 44, sec. 1; Special Acts (Extension of Time) Act, 1915. 5 & 6 Geo. 5, c. 72, sec. 1.

aspect is shown when Parliament is seeking to regulate technical matters in which new inventions or new experience result in a perpetual change of standards.

This second class is sufficiently striking to deserve special mention, and for two reasons: first, because here the Act to be modified is normally the Act under which the power is granted, and so from its very inception appears strangely impermanent; second, because the claim of the expert was early recognised and, if there is any meaning in present tendencies, is likely to have still wider scope in the future. The first reason is not worth serious attention, for although the effect of the kindred power to remove difficulties is from this aspect "to give the Minister . . . power to legislate . . . notwithstanding the fact that Parliament has legislated to the contrary in this year," [1] there is no intrinsic difference between modifying the provisions of the enabling Act and modifying those of a prior existing Act. In both cases Parliament is willing to be overridden, and the latter power approaches more nearly if anything to the "abdication" of which Lord Hewart writes; for there Parliament declares that the law as established no longer fits the facts, and leaves new standards to be fixed by the departments without new guidance.

What of the functions of the expert in this matter? Mention has already been made of the heading to certain provisions of the Merchant Shipping Act of 1854, "subject to any alteration to be made by Trinity House," the power of the Secretary of State under section 33 of the Explosives Act of 1875,[2] and in another Act the section enabling the Metropolitan Board of Works "to alter the rules for the regulation of the thickness of walls contained in the first Schedule." [3] Here Parliament from the beginning distrusted its own ignorance; shipping matters, the proper precautions to be observed in dealing with explosives, the technical side of building, are outside the sphere of the amateur. Why, then, it may be asked, lay down any general rule, if at best it is no more than a tentative suggestion to be followed or disregarded by the expert? The explanation lies in the dates when the legislation is passed, 1854, 1855, and 1875. This is the period of transition, when it was still the practice for Parliament to regulate the smallest and most technical details, but when Parliament had already embarked upon extensive delegation; these Acts are an attempted compro-

---

[1] 224 Com. Deb. (5th Series), p. 970, Mr. Hurst, January 29, 1932.
[2] *Supra*, p. 16.   [3] *Supra*, p. 16.

mise between the conflicting movements. Doubtless today such matters would be left wholly to Whitehall, where the expert can state his case in person to departmental experts who are capable of understanding him.

This explanation, however, does not cover all cases where the device is used to meet conditions which may or may not change thereafter. The Congress of the United States did not, when they were forced by events to pass a flexible tariff, delegate the power of fixing duties without more; they drew up, as historically they had always done, a list of rates, but went on to provide that under certain recited circumstances and within fixed limits the list might be modified by a tariff commission. There is no reason in sense for such a duplication of effort, and indeed the English Abnormal Importations Act of 1931 was a mere grant of power to the Board of Trade to levy duties up to a hundred per cent on Class III imports. But the English were not compelled to save the face of the doctrine of the separation of powers, and it must not be forgotten that the 1931 Act was passed as a temporary measure to meet an emergency. In most cases the English practice is more nearly that of the United States. A sage recognition of the ever-changing standards demanded by experience and the advance of science is responsible for a provision that the executive, the experts, may from time to time "alter the tensile strains to which cables are to be subjected," [1] "make new denominations of standards for the measurement of electricity, temperature, pressure, or gravities, as appear to be of use for trade," [2] "define the amount of error to be tolerated in local standards," [3] and annul or modify safety regulations in a shipping Act.[4] Of like nature is the power to alter forms,[5] the fares and duties on hackney carriages,[6] or the close season for wild birds.[7]

The remaining instances deal with exceptional circumstances, and are so closely related to section 67 of the Rating Act, 1925,

[1] Chain Cables and Anchors Act, 1871. 34 & 35 Vict., c. 101, sec. 6.

[2] Weights and Measures Act, 1889. 52 & 53 Vict., c. 21, sec. 6.

[3] Weights and Measures Act, 1878. 41 & 42 Vict., c. 49, sec. 41.

[4] Merchant Shipping Acts Amendment Act, 1862. 25 & 26 Vict., c. 63, sec. 25.

[5] See, among others, Companies Act, 1862. 25 & 26. Vict., c. 89, sec. 71; Representation of the People Act, 1918. 7 & 8 Geo. 5, c. 64, sec. 13 (2).

[6] Dublin Carriage Act, 1853. 16 & 17 Vict., c. 112, sec. 7.

[7] See Birds Preservation Act, 1869. 32 & 33 Vict., c. 17, sec. 3; Wild Fowl Preservation Act, 1876. 39 & 40 Vict., c. 29, sec. 3.

that I should have discussed them under the power to remove difficulties had it not been for the fact that that section is common form, and so is best treated as a separate topic. They do not, however, go quite as far, for here Parliament has defined the exceptional circumstances in which the department may modify the principal Act. I have found but three such instances; but the underlying ratio is again nothing more than a realisation by Parliament that not all specific cases can come under a general form of words, and an unwillingness, when once the plan of attack is set out, to work out its application in detail to the abnormal situation. That is the occasion par excellence for executive discretion. The Police Act of 1910 laid down that no constable should be on duty more than six days in any week, but left it to the Home Office to insert in its orders putting the Act into force such modifications as might be necessary to provide for the case of small police stations in rural districts;[1] and a requirement of general vaccination within a certain period must naturally allow some leeway for those who come from the remote highlands or islands that are often difficult of access.[2] The 1901 Factory Act spoke to the same effect when it allowed the Secretary of State to substitute as regards any particular industrial process a higher requirement of cubic feet of air per person.[3] Modify the provisions in order to fulfill the true meaning of the Act: that is the golden rule.

Before passing to consider the new control imposed on this power in all Acts since 1929, — and there can be no objection to increased control as long as the power itself is not withheld, — it will be convenient to pass in review a few of the orders issued under it.

At the back of each annual volume of Statutory Rules and Orders is printed a chronological table of Acts of Parliament affected by Statutory Rules and Orders during the current year, "by way of amendment, application, extension, restriction, commencement, or repeal." Each of these terms needs a short comment. To take them in inverse order of constitutional importance: "commencement" refers to the well-recognised practice of direct-

---

[1] 10 Ed. 7 & 1 Geo. 5, c. 13, sec. 1 (2).

[2] Vaccination (Scotland) Act, 1863. 26 & 27 Vict., c. 108, sec. 12.

[3] Factory and Workshop Act, 1901. 1 Ed. 7, c. 22, sec. 3 (2). There are, of course, many cases where the department may make special provisions for special circumstances, but I am here concerned only with cases where the power is expressly granted as a power of modification.

ing that the Act shall not come into operation until the issuance of an executive order. It might be thought that all Acts should come into force when passed, or on a date fixed by Parliament, but there are some occasions when that would be most inadvisable. Many Acts, for instance, are passed to carry out in England the provisions of an international convention; and where, even internationally, the binding nature of the convention depends on each of the parties standing by it, it would not be sound sense to pass it into English law before reciprocity was assured.[1] Again, in domestic matters the legislation may be such that a good deal of preparation is necessary before it is practicable to begin enforcement,[2] or that it is only to apply in a particular event,[3] or that it is experimental and to be applied either in whole or in part to some particular district to be ascertained later.[4]

The majority of orders listed in the table are concerned with "application." The Crown has a prerogative right to legislate for British possessions, and might by Order in Council frame new laws for any Crown colony or protectorate that required them; indeed, Malta's new constitution was promulgated in this manner.[5] But where the subject matter has already been treated by Parliament, it is more convenient, and also more practical, to apply the English Act to the possession, and this was the method adopted when in 1925 the position of the Consular Courts in China was defined anew.[6]

"Repeal" falls properly under "amendment"; for the repeal will never touch more than some minor provisions in an Act, and

[1] See Deserting Seamen Act, 1852. 15 & 16 Vict., c. 26, sec. 1; Seal Fishery (Greenland) Act, 1875. 28 Vict., c. 28, sec. 1; Fugitive Offenders Act, 1881. 44 & 45 Vict., c. 69, sec. 12.

[2] See Local Government (Ireland) Act, 1898. 61 & 62 Vict., c. 37, sec. 124 (1); Police Act, 1910. 10 Ed. 7 & 1 Geo. 5, c. 13, sec. 2; Improvement of Live Stock (Licensing of Bulls) Act, 1931. 21 & 22 Geo. 5, c. 43, sec. 13 (1).

[3] Navy and Marines (Wills) Act, 1865. 28 & 29 Vict., c. 72, secs. 8 and 9; Navy and Marines (Property of Deceased) Act, 1865. 28 & 29 Vict., c. 111, sec. 19.

[4] Land Transfer Act, 1897. 60 & 61 Vict., c. 65, sec. 20 (1); Municipal Corporations Act, 1883. 46 & 47 Vict., c. 18, secs. 2 and 3; Local Government (Ireland) Act, 1898. 60 & 61 Vict., c. 7, sec. 124 (1).

[5] Malta Constitution Letters Patent of April 14, 1921.

[6] By Order of 1925, No. 603, the following Acts among others were applied to China: Evidence by Commission Act, 1869; Fugitive Offenders Act, 1881; Lunatics Removal (India) Act, 1851, secs. 5–7; Public Authorities Protection Act, 1893.

then only as incidental to "application." Under an order applying to the Isle of Wight certain provisions of the Local Government Act of 1929, a conflict arose between the order and the express terms of the Isle of Wight Highways Act of 1925, and under the new system one portion of the local Act, a proviso to a subsection, became so hopelessly inapplicable that it was ordered repealed.[1]

The powers of "extension" and "restriction" are coördinate; here again there is no question of altering the express words of the Act, but by departmental order its scope is either widened or narrowed, in much the same way as a standard Act is applied to new territory. But here the application is normally to a closely related subject matter, and the power to extend has usually been granted by the Act, which is thereby extended. The Notice of Accidents Act, for instance, may be extended to any employment which the Board of Trade thinks especially dangerous,[2] the National Insurance Act to any trade in which a substantial amount of work for war is being carried on,[3] the Trade Boards Act to any trade in which in the opinion of the Minister no adequate machinery exists for the regulation of wages.[4] Executive order may add to the list of poisons the sale of which must be entered in the poison book [5] or to the list of prohibited deleterious liquors; [6] and the Minister of Health is empowered "after a public inquiry and after consultation with any local authorities or interests concerned [to] make orders extending the list of noxious or offensive gases" which must be prevented from escaping into the air.[7] This is just another example of the inevitable process of generalisation clearly brought out in other fields by the Municipal Corporations Act of 1882 and the Public Health Act of 1875.

The coördinate power of "restriction" (a polite term for "dispensation") is directed to another end, that of preventing a gen-

[1] Local Government Act (Application to the Isle of Wight) Order, 1930, No. 757.

[2] 1894. 57 & 58 Vict., c. 28, sec. 2 (2).

[3] National Insurance Act, 1916. 6 & 7 Geo. 5, c. 20, sec. 2 (1).

[4] Trade Boards Act, 1918. 8 & 9 Geo. 5, c. 32, sec. 1 (2); and see Order of June 3, 1926, No. 593, made under the Act of 1909.

[5] Sale of Poisons Act, 1868. 31 & 32 Vict., c. 121, sec. 2.

[6] Intoxicating Liquor (Licensing) Act, 1872. 35 & 36 Vict., c. 94, sec. 21.

[7] Public Health (Smoke Abatement) Act, 1926. 16 & 17 Geo. 5, c. 43, sec. 4; and see 1928, S.R. & O., No. 26. For other instances see Explosive Substances Act, 1875. 38 Vict., c. 17, sec. 104; Wild Birds Protection Act, 1894. 57 & 58 Vict., c. 24, sec. 3; and many others.

eral statute from working hardship or nonsense in particular cases. In enforcing the Copyhold Act of 1894 the Board of Agriculture may suspend "any proceeding for compulsory enfranchisement under this Act, where any peculiar circumstances make it impossible, in their opinion, to decide on the prospective value . . . or where special hardship or injustice would unavoidably result from compulsory enfranchisement." [1] It was on that basis that the Secretary of State was to suspend in an emergency the Act which regulates the hours of work in coal mines,[2] and that the Board of Trade can suspend a section requiring a statement of the origin of imported goods if difficulties arise upon its application.[3] In two cases the discretion granted is very wide indeed. An exemption is permissible under the Truck Act, 1896, "if the Secretary of State is satisfied that the Act is unnecessary for the protection of workmen employed in any trade," [4] and under another Act certain strict procedural requirements may be waived "where the chief registrar is of the opinion that the society is not one to which the provisions ought to apply." [5] Apart from their environment, and apart from those traditions of the Civil Service which are every bit as important as the canons of legal interpretation, these provisions might be construed as leave to the department to deal with the Act when and how it wishes. But few other statutes are as sweeping, and even here the discretion is limited by the fact that every provision of every Act is to be read in the light of the general purposes of the Act as a whole. And surely it is not probable that the officials, who are every bit as intelligent and public spirited as the judges, will be guilty of wilful misunderstanding, especially where any action they take is liable to criticism in Parliament. For an angry Minister may mean loss of advancement to the object of his wrath. If the Truck Act might, under a possible inter-

---

[1] 57 & 58 Vict., c. 46, sec. 12 (1).

[2] Coal Mines Regulation Act, 1908. 8 Ed. 7, c. 57, sec. 4.

[3] Merchandise Marks Act, 1926. 16 & 17 Geo. 5, c. 53, sec. 1 (3); and see Orders of May 16, June 28, and August 3, 1927, by which petroleum, uncompounded drugs, and certain classes of seeds were thereunder exempted. On the whole matter see among others Moneylenders Act, 1927. 17 & 18 Geo. 5, c. 21, sec. 11 (1); White Herring Fishery (Scotland) Amendment Act, 1861. 24 & 25 Vict., c. 72, sec. 5; Official Secrets Act, 1911. 1 & 2 Geo. 5, c. 28, sec. 11.

[4] 1896. 59 & 60 Vict., c. 44, sec. 9.

[5] Collecting Societies and Industrial Assurance Companies Act, 1896. 59 & 60 Vict., c. 26, sec. 11.

pretation of the words used, be rendered nugatory, so might the prisons be emptied by the legally unlimited prerogative power of pardon. After all, we do not live by absolutes but by a rule of reasonable probability.

It is again remarkable, in view of the discussion which has raged around the power to modify, that a search of the volumes of Statutory Rules and Orders from 1925 to 1930 should have revealed no modification of more than trifling importance. I deliberately set out here the instances which in my judgment go furthest, and leave the reader to judge whether they are such as to strike at the foundations of parliamentary government.

In very few instances has an alteration been made in an Act of general application. The Housing (Financial Provisions) Act, 1924, contemplated that after the post-war shortage of materials and skilled workmen was over the cost of building would begin to fall, and provided that the Minister might after October 1, 1926, make alterations in the contribution to be paid by the Minister of Health toward the building of houses. By that date prices had fallen substantially, and the contribution was ordered reduced — to the tune of thirty per cent.[1] My other selections are concerned only with modifications necessary on the application of an old Act to new circumstances, modification therefore in the terms of the Act itself, or with the trifling changes required to bring existing legislation into conformity with the new. When the Rating Act of 1925 was applied by order to the Scilly Isles the local government of the district was being carried on under the provisions of a Provisional Order of 1894 which had been duly confirmed by Parliament. Three articles of the Provisional Order were repealed outright by the order, six new provisions were set out in its body, and an appended schedule declared which of the provisions of the principal Act were to apply and which not. Those directed to apply were in some respects modified. In what did the modification consist? In deleting the arrangements made by Parliament for the application of the Act to various types of local authority, here inapplicable, and in fitting the appeal procedure to the judicial system of the islands.[2] Take another instance: under the

[1] Housing (Financial Provisions) Act, 1924. 14 & 15 Geo. 5, c. 35, sec. 5, and Order of 1926, No. 1586. With this order compare Order of January 17, 1902, No. 23, made under Factory and Workshop Act, 1901, sec. 3 (3), and order of February 3, 1902, No. 59, made under sec. 43 of the same Act.

[2] Rating Act, 1925. 15 & 16 Geo. 5, c. 90, sec. 70; and see Isles of Scilly Order of February 11, 1927.

international convention between England and Denmark providing for reciprocity in matters relating to compensation to workmen for injuries by accident the Workmens Compensation Act of 1925 was applied by Order in Council to Danish subjects in England. These were the modifications: that all questions should be settled by an award of the County Court and in no other manner (the Government, that is to say, undertook responsibility by seeing that the claims were determined exclusively by its own agencies), and that no court fee should be payable by any Danish subject.[1] Now it is clear that if in these two instances the department has been allowed to legislate, it is only in the sense that a Vergilian cento is literary composition. All that the department may do is to set the institutions of the Scilly Isles by the side of the Rating Act, the international convention by the side of the Act of 1925, and by a judicious use of scissors and paste to produce a workable code.

There is a greater discretion involved in the application of section 116 of the Factory Act, 1901, to outworkers; but the 1929 Lampshades Particulars Order practically reproduces the exact words of the section.[2] Once again Parliament is faced with the choice between legislating itself for an exceptional area or class of persons and allowing others to deal with trivialities. It is bad enough that an unwieldy body like the House of Commons should insist on going through the clauses of each bill in detail (half the difficulties of modern statutory interpretation arise from this practice of ill-informed amendment), and if the House finds itself between the devil of triviality and the deep sea of delegation it does well to prefer the sea, and not merely from the point of view of the saving of parliamentary time.

There is no need to give more than one instance of the case where existing legislation has to be brought into conformity with the new. On the going into force of the Local Government (Scotland) Act the change of local machinery was such that many old institutions, on which were based legislation not intended to be touched by that Act, disappeared forever from the stage. The persons, for instance, entitled to vote on the question of local option were defined as "persons qualified to vote for the election of parish coun-

[1] Workmen's Compensation Act, 1925. 15 & 16 Geo. 5, c. 84, sec. 37; Order in Council of June 1, 1926.

[2] Factory and Workshop Act, 1901. 1 Ed. 7, c. 22, sec. 116 (5); see also order of July 14, 1902, made under the same subsection.

cillors";[1] after 1929 there were no more parish councillors, but
there were persons whose functions were near enough to those of a
parish councillor to be substituted for them in the Act of 1913.
The extent of the havoc caused in the wording of the Statute Book
by this Act can be appreciated when it is realised that in the Local
Government (Scotland) Order of 1930 no less than twenty-three
sections, contained in thirteen Acts, had to be thus amended for
conformity.[2] Another typical irregularity corrected by order was
the date by which valuation lists must be completed; this had
been fixed by statute in Scotland since 1894, but under the new
system March 15 was no longer a practical possibility, and a later
date, May 31, was fixed by order of the Secretary of State for
Scotland.[3]

There is only one occasion, so far as I am aware, on which the
modifying power has come directly before a court. Section 43 (3)
of the Workmen's Compensation Act, 1925, allowed the Secretary
of State to make an order extending the provisions of the section
to "injuries due to the nature of any employment specified in the
Order not being injuries by accident, either without modification
or subject to such modifications as may be contained in the Order."
An order was issued extending the provisions of section 43 "to
cataract caused by exposure to rays from molten or red-hot metal,"
but imposing a limit upon the period for which compensation
might be claimed; there was no such limit expressed in the section
itself. Counsel attacking the validity of the limit imposed took
the familiar line that an executive extension of the section must
carry with it the full substantive rights of that section, and that
therefore a modification of the extent of compensation was ultra
vires. The court rejected his contention and upheld the order,
modifications and all.[4] Now, this was a very substantial modification, — in effect it remakes the section, — and under ordinary
circumstances it might have given the Court some trouble. But
as it so happened, counsel for the appellant was in a peculiar position, — to win his case he had to establish that an order, issued

---

[1] Temperance (Scotland) Act, 1913. 3 & 4 Geo. 5, c. 33, sec. 15.

[2] Local Government (Scotland) Act, 1929. 19 & 20 Geo. 5, c. 25, sec. 76 (1);
see Local Government (Scotland) Order, 1930, No. 1026; see also Local Government (Educational Authorities, Audit of Accounts) Order (Scotland), 1929.

[3] Local Government (County Districts, Valuation of Railways, etc.) Order
(Scotland), 1929, amending Valuation of Land (Scotland) Acts Amendment
Act, 1894. 57 & 58 Vict., c. 36, sec. 2.

[4] Leonard v. Redbrook Tinplate Co., [1930] 1 K.B. 643.

on the discretion of the Secretary of State to apply the section to a disease to which he was not forced to apply it, was good as to the application but bad as to the conditions imposed, — and had to argue warily; further, certain provisions of the Act of 1925 which under certain circumstances took away a right of compensation granted by earlier Acts were expressly described as "modifications" of those earlier Acts. In that case there could be no doubt of the extent of modification envisaged by Parliament when it used the term.

I have already described the panic into which the legal profession and the two Houses had been driving themselves in the post-war period, and how in 1929 there was a definite reassertion of parliamentary control. Among the first "abuses," as they were called, to meet with more than rhetorical attack was this power to modify an Act of Parliament. Lord Brentford, in proposing his amendment to a clause of the Mental Treatment Bill, viewed the problem from two angles. He asked first why, if an Act of Parliament was to be altered, it should not be altered by Parliament. But as an ex-Home Secretary he was too familiar with the business of administration to rely on so slender an argument, and laid all his emphasis on the need for increased control — to which his amendment was directed. He pointed out that merely to require the rules to be laid on the table of both Houses was an illusory protection, at any rate in the Commons, and Lord Banbury, in supporting him, threw valuable light on how far the practice of government is removed from theory when he said, "The matter can only come on after eleven o'clock, it is very difficult to keep a house, and it is very difficult to find out whether there are any rules lying on the table or not. It took me many years before I knew where to look and see if there were any rules or not." [1] The amendment was levelled at the casual methods prevailing in the House of Commons, and was in the form of a proviso to a section requiring rules to be laid before Parliament when made "that where any such rule modifies or adapts this Act or any other enactment the rules shall not come into force or have any effect unless within the same period of twenty-one days it has been approved by a Resolution passed by both Houses of Parliament." It is of interest not because it is new (for it had its genesis in 1919 with reference to schemes, and had been applied to statutory rules in both the Local Government Acts of 1929), but because it is an avowed withdrawal from sec-

[1] 75 Lords Deb. (5th Series), p. 1387, December 17, 1929.

tion 338 of the Lunacy Act of 1890, which it expressly repealed. There subsection 6 directed that "all rules made under this section shall be laid before Parliament . . . and shall be judicially noticed and have effect as if enacted in this Act"; here a distinction is taken between those rules which modify an Act of Parliament and those which do not.[1] At first sight the amendment appears adequate (there is much to be said for allowing the exercise of this power only under the strictest supervision), but in the course of the same debate Earl Russell voiced an objection which has since proved to be justified, that it is difficult to decide when a rule does modify or adapt. He also had something to say about the demands on the time of Parliament; but if he meant by that anything more than a reference to the fact that members display little interest in the practical working of government, it is difficult to go along with him. Members being agreed — and agreed they certainly are — that the departments should not legislate unchecked, it is the business of the Government to make time.

Two occasions already, one in the Lords, the other in the Commons, have revealed the sort of difficulty with which this procedure will have to contend. When Mr. Tom Johnston moved the approval of the Local Government (Adaptation of Enactments) (Scotland) Order it was to an almost empty House, and his explanation showed the changes made in the Acts to be so trifling that they were not worth the serious attention even of the irritable handful which was present — especially since they had already been considered by the House of Lords.[2] But public confidence is an important element in government, and may sometimes justify the use of a sledge hammer to crack a nut if by that means, not only wrong, but even the appearance of wrong, is avoided.

As Earl Russell foresaw, a difficulty arose when the Mental Treatment Rules came before the House of Lords for approval "so far as they modify or adapt any of the provisions of the Lunacy Act, 1890." In moving the Resolution of approval Lord Sankey was forced to admit that "in a code of Rules of this size it is a matter of extreme difficulty to discriminate between those Rules or portions of Rules which modify or adapt any enactment, and

[1] Mental Treatment Act, 1930. 20 & 21 Geo. 5, c. 23, sec. 15 (2); see also Local Government Act, 1929. 19 Geo. 5, c. 17, sec. 130; id. (Scotland) 19 & 20 Geo. 5, c. 25, sec. 76 (1); Road Traffic Act, 1930. 20 & 21 Geo. 5, c. 43, sec. 10 (4).

[2] 247 Com. Deb. (5th Series), p. 1588, February 2, 1931.

those which merely apply existing enactments to the new conditions resulting from the Mental Treatment Act," and he therefore asked the House to refer to the whole code and to pass the Resolution. He explained that they had been published for forty days under the Rules Publication Act, and had been sent in draft to all persons or organisations likely to be interested, without any objection being received. He then gave a rapid sketch of the rules.[1] Just what was accomplished by the passage of the rules in this perfunctory manner it is difficult to say. They were no more controversial than those contained in the Local Government Order; but even if they had been bristling with latent difficulties, there is no guarantee that the Lords would have spared the time to debate the whole code. The Lord Chancellor dwelt more on the elaborate safeguards to which the rules had been subjected before they came up to the House than on the contents; but a positive approval by the Houses of Parliament was meant to be an additional bulwark against a despotism believed to be more than a match for just those safeguards on which the Lord Chancellor placed his reliance. Perhaps the startling popularity of the new procedure — it was employed in nine statutes during the year 1930 — will not be maintained in the face of the apathy of the Commons, and the complexity of the questions presented for examination. If retained, however, it will serve as a useful reminder to the opponents of bureaucracy that Parliament cannot be in all places all the time, — and they will be less ready to make accusations where they have an opportunity for review, — and the necessity for a positive approval by Parliament will inevitably act as a deterrent on the departments from overstepping the limits of their powers, even by accident.

[1] 80 Lords Deb. (5th Series), p. 486, March 24, 1931.

EPILOGUE

I CANNOT close this essay without pointing out once more the very limited range of topics with which it deals. The powers herein discussed at length were chosen, not because they were typical of the functions of a department in 1931, certainly not to illustrate any deep-seated prejudice or novel suggestion, but for the simple reason that although the words "modification," "Henry VIII clause," formed the heavy artillery in the battle which has been and still is raging round the delegation of legislative power, they have made a noise out of all proportion to their size. It is trite learning that only for a trifling period of his working hours does the civil servant roll like Juggernaut across the stage of government. Is this mildly intellectual person ever a Juggernaut? That is the question which I have tried to answer by an examination of the most glittering trappings of the new despotism.

The English constitution did not reach ultimate perfection in 1688. The Bill of Rights put an end, it is true, to certain controversial claims of a strong executive, but it cannot be quoted as an inspired declaration of unalterable principles in good government. Since that date England has developed from a self-sufficient appendage to Europe of some ten million souls to a world power, from a simple organisation of rural communities to a teeming urban and industrial nation, and although the legal framework of government has undergone few changes, the difference in content is difficult to measure. Much is now expected of the State; it is no longer enough for it to keep the peace, it must watch over health, education, industry, transport, and many other social interests. With its vast reserves of coercive power and of wealth it can afford to disdain a short-sighted materialism, and with its far-reaching tentacles it can fasten upon sources of information which would be denied to private business operating for private gain. With the changing viewpoint of the State, — and it has so changed because the majority of voters so desired, — government naturally fell into the hands of officials whose function it is to build rather than to destroy.

I am not here concerned to paint a falsely glowing picture of some chimerical paradise of officialdom, but rather to suggest that it is only by means of the official that the vague yearnings of democracy can be converted into tangible improvements. Parliament is the heart, the Civil Service the head and hands, of our government. A legislature is always prone to be accused of "playing politics." There are from time to time movements to remove "politics" from government, to run a city or a country "on a business basis." But "politics," the clash of conflicting social philosophies, is of the very essence of democracy; what better justification can there be for legislative assemblies than to serve as a battleground for conflicting ideals of society? Nevertheless, when Parliament has made its choice, ideals are not enough: it is then time for administration, and — since administration involves interpretation — for interpretation, to begin. Who shall be the final interpreters of social legislation and in what spirit shall they approach the task?

At present most of the interpretation of such statutes is naturally done by the departments in their application to the facts. But this interpretation is not final; it is still open to any person who deems himself aggrieved by the practical interpretation placed thereon by an official to have recourse to the courts of Common Law on an allegation that the department placed a "wrong" construction on the Act. It may seem odd to reflecting persons that an overriding opinion may come from judges who are at best wholly dependent for their knowledge of the tacit assumptions involved in the legislation on the explanation of counsel specially briefed for the case, but it is good English law. Further, when such a case comes into court the English rules of statutory interpretation come into play. The Court must interpret the statute "according to the plain meaning of the words," is precluded from looking into its legislative history, may not hear evidence of the kind of evils it is designed to prevent or the kind of benefits it was passed to confer. Armed with a dictionary, the Court impartially construes the words, and since words have little meaning apart from an environment in which they are used, the Court, compulsorily ignorant of their true environment, must place them against the background of the Common Law, and replace the assumptions of 1931 by the assumptions of Lord Coke.[1]

No reflecting person, it may be said, would think this situation

---

[1] See Attorney-General *v.* Luncheon and Sports Club, [1929] A.C. 400, p. 406, per Lord Dunedin; Joint District School Board of Management *v.* Kelly, [1914] A.C. 667, p. 680, per Lord Loreburn.

odd; the purpose of judicial review is to prevent encroachment by the executive. Even granting that the genius of democracy demands that each arm of the State be at loggerheads with the others, a judge cannot say whether the executive has gone beyond the limits of its commission until he knows what those limits are; and if he is forced to decide the question by the arbitrary application of a long dead philosophy (with which he himself is probably quite out of sympathy), the result is not control of the executive but stultification of Parliament. That is the position in England today.

What is the solution? Administrative courts? Although such a course would involve yet another breach in the doctrine of Separation of Powers, the absence of control is in reality no objection. The doctrine of judicial self-limitation is well known: if the Common Law judges can decide against their own jurisdiction in matters strictly legal, it is reasonable to suppose that administrative judges will find themselves able and willing to do the same in their own field. One advantage that could not be gained by an adaptation of the existing procedure for the control of inferior bodies by the King's Bench Division would be the fresh start in a new field. The abolition of the prerogative writs and the substitution of a uniform appeal procedure cannot without more ado bring about a revolution from the restrictive methods of the law courts; a new system of government must be administered by those who do not draw their inspiration from Common Law analogies.

The control of delegated legislation may well be subjected to even more drastic reform. There is much to be said for giving conclusive effect to all rules issued by the departments after review by a committee of Parliament, subject perhaps to revocation by that committee if at any time subsequently they are found to work more injustice to individuals than they produce in benefit to the community at large.[1] Under the present system a rule which Parliament itself would never have dreamed of authorising may continue for years unchallenged, if technicalities or the poverty of persons aggrieved prevents the issue from being raised before a court, while a rule which to the eye of common sense is plainly within the purview of the Act may fall before an unsympathetic or misinformed tribunal. It is so haphazard. When a State may force its subject to obey rules made by its executive arm, and later

[1] Sir John Marriott's suggestion, in part.

through its judiciary mulct him for obeying what was held out to him as binding law, something is wrong.[1] A rule must be either legal or illegal. Why should the issue remain in doubt until it happens to be raised in the course of proceedings by an individual litigant, and then before a body which, as I pointed out above, is unsuited to the decision of questions of government?

[1] See Staffordshire Financial Co. Ltd. *v.* Valentine, [1910] 2 K.B. 233.

POSTSCRIPT

THE REPORT OF THE COMMITTEE ON
MINISTERS' POWERS

SINCE the completion of this essay the Committee on Ministers' Powers has reported,[1] and it has therefore become necessary to say something about its findings and recommendations. This Committee (referred to in the preceding chapters as the Donoughmore Committee after its original chairman, the Earl of Donoughmore) was the answer of the Government to the long series of criticisms which from 1920 onwards had been levelled with growing bitterness at the growing powers of the departments in the field of legislation and judicial decision. I have already traced the events and given examples of the public uneasiness which had by 1929 brought the issue of delegation into the forefront of the political stage, and I do not wish to repeat here what I have already laboured in the first chapter. There are, however, two points without a clear appreciation of which neither the findings nor the recommendations of the Committee can be properly understood: the academic manner in which the enemies of delegation had organised their attack, and the ultra-conservative attitude of its friends, the latter well illustrated by the Committee's terms of reference.

It was not because the Labour Government then in power was afflicted with a sense of guilt — indeed the Socialist ideal of government by the Civil Service is still remote enough to sound pleasantly romantic — that Lord Sankey set up the Committee, but for precisely the opposite reason: the chimerical bogey of the "new despotism," hinted at by the professors, outlined by the Press, and finally portrayed in fearsome detail by the authoritative pen of the Lord Chief Justice, had gained such a hold upon the imagination of English politicians and their constituents that deliberate obstruction to the most harmless measures was being greeted with applause. With the Statute Book, Statutory Rules and Orders, the circulars of the departments, and the Law Reports readily accessible, at least to those members of Parliament who were

[1] Cmd. 4060. Presented by the Lord Chancellor to Parliament in April, 1932.

lawyers, it might have been expected that some fearless knight would lay the ghost; but not one had the courage — or the industry — to arm himself with facts and strike. It was easier to bandy big words. And so the report of this Committee, dramatically appointed on the eve of the publication of *The New Despotism*, comes as an anti-climax. Founded as far as delegated legislation goes (and that is the only part of the report with which I am here concerned) on C. T. Carr's essay of 1921,[1] it reveals no abuses,[2] and is so far from being an indictment of the practice of delegating legislative power to the departments that the Committee sees in it "definite advantages, provided that the statutory powers are exercised and the statutory functions performed in the right way," [3] and concludes on this realistic note: "But in truth whether good or bad the development of the practice is inevitable. It is a natural reflection, in the sphere of constitutional law, of changes in our ideas of government which have resulted from changes in political, social and economic ideas, and of changes in the circumstances of our lives which have resulted from scientific discoveries." [4]

"But in truth whether good or bad the development of the practice is inevitable" — that is the soul of caution. Why, it may be asked, did a committee which fully recognised the decisive changes

---

[1] "Delegated Legislation." See the Report at pp. 15, 21, 23, 26, 47.

[2] After quoting a strong passage from The New Despotism (on the judicial powers of the departments), the Report goes on: "We regard this passage, and indeed the whole of the Lord Chief Justice's book, as a warning against possible dangers of great gravity towards which he discerns an existing tendency to drift. We are very much alive both to the presence of such dangers and to their gravity if not checked, and have considered them throughout our enquiry. But, as appears from our considered view in the next two sections of our Report, we see nothing to justify any lowering of the country's high opinion of its Civil Service or any reflection on its sense of justice, or any ground for a belief that our constitutional machinery is developing in directions which are fundamentally wrong." Report, p. 7.

See also Report, p. 59, for a long-overdue vindication of the motives of the Civil Service in securing the passage of Henry VIII clauses — "We dispose, in passing, of the suggestion, unsupported as it is by the smallest shred of evidence, that the existence of such provisions in certain Acts of Parliament is due directly or indirectly to any attempt or desire on the part of members of the permanent Civil Service to secure for themselves or for their Departments an arbitrary power. All that may be justly inferred from the facts is that Ministers have in certain instances regarded the inclusion of provisions of this kind as essential to the successful operation of measures which they were proposing to Parliament."

[3] Report, p. 4.   [4] Report, p. 5.

that have come about in the business of government confine their recommendations to the obvious, the amendment of the Rules Publication Act to catch all regulations and rules, the establishment of standing committees in both Houses "for the purpose of considering and reporting . . . on every regulation and rule made in the exercise of delegated legislative power, and laid before the House in pursuance of statutory requirement"? [1] Why have these Committees no teeth? Why was Mr. Robson's scheme of administrative courts nominated for oblivion? [2] Why did the Committee allow that delegation of legislative power was inevitable, and yet refuse to go further and assert with Miss Wilkinson that "the practice of Parliament delegating legislation and the power to make regulations, instead of being grudgingly conceded, ought to be widely extended, and new ways devised to facilitate the process"? [3] Professor Laski's note to Miss Wilkinson's note [4] suggests an answer to these questions, and brings out my second point, the restricted scope of the terms of reference.

The Committee was appointed "to consider the powers exercised by . . . Ministers of the Crown by way of . . . delegated legislation . . . and to report what safeguards are desirable or necessary to secure the constitutional principles of the sovereignty of Parliament and the supremacy of the Law." In the Never-never Land of legal formalism it may well be that phrases coined some fifty years ago by way of incisive generalisation for the use of undergraduates should pass as unalterable canons of good government. But to fetter thus the investigations of a committee appointed to probe behind legal fictions, to demand that whatever the evidence put before them, whatever the social requirements of the time, they should pay homage to a facile generalisation, is to determine beforehand both findings and recommendations. With such terms of reference constructive suggestion was not to be expected. Nevertheless, even if it has accomplished nothing else, the Committee has succeeded in bringing out the first thesis of any note in English administrative law.

I do not propose to discuss in detail the findings and conclusions of the Committee on what they call the "normal type" of delegated legislation, but rather to deal with those instances of the

[1] Report, pp. 67–68.   [2] Report, p. 110.

[3] Annex VI. Note by Miss Ellen Wilkinson on Delegated Legislation, Report, p. 137.

[4] Report, p. 138.

"exceptional type" described in the third and fifth chapters of this essay, and to take up the topic canvassed in the fourth chapter, private bill legislation by the departments. This last topic raised questions both of legislation and "quasi-judicial decision," and included elements more conveniently discussed in other connections, e. g. the exclusion of the jurisdiction of the Courts, and so, naturally, was given no separate treatment by the Committee.

To make clear what is meant by the "normal" and the "exceptional" type of delegated legislation, I cannot do better than quote the Report:

"The normal type of delegated legislation has two distinguishing characteristics: — one positive and the other negative.

"The positive characteristic is that the limits of the delegated power are defined so clearly by the enabling Act as to be made plainly known to Parliament, to the Executive, and to the Public, and to be readily enforceable by the Judiciary.

"The negative characteristic is that powers delegated do not include power to do certain things, namely:

"i. to legislate on matters of principle or to impose taxation;

"ii. to amend Acts of Parliament, either the Act by which the powers are delegated, or other Acts.

.   .   .   .

"There are, however, to be found on the Statute Book certain exceptional instances of delegated legislative powers, which may be conveniently classified as follows:

"i. Instances of powers to legislate on matters of principle, and even to impose taxation;

"ii. Instances of powers to amend Acts of Parliament, either the Act by which the powers are delegated, or other Acts;

"iii. Instances of powers conferring so wide a discretion on a Minister, that it is almost impossible to know what limit Parliament did intend to impose;

"iv. Instances where Parliament, without formally abandoning its normal practice of limiting delegated powers, has in effect done so by forbidding control by the Courts." [1]

It was only to classes ii and iv of the above classification that I gave full treatment in Chapters III and V of my essay. The field covered by classes i and iii I dealt with cursorily in a subdivision of Chapter III under the head of "Skeleton Legislation." My

[1] Report, pp. 30–31.

chief concern was to draw attention to three points at which the departments had begun to supplant Parliament, in the making of general laws (Chapter III), in the grant of special privileges over and above the general law (Chapter IV), and in the amendment of general laws already on the Statute Book (Chapter V). The making of general laws by the departments was in itself a subject so vast, and besides involved subsidiary questions of such interest to a student of litigation, that, perhaps wrongly, I did not probe as deeply as I might have done into the different types of general law which the departments were in effect permitted to make, but was content to show that they did on occasion make such laws, and that such laws once made were free from any control by the courts.

I have given in Chapter III the salient instances of the exercise of legislative power by the departments in matters of principle, D.O.R.A., the Emergency Powers Act, the Cremation Act, 1902, the Seeds Act, 1920, Section 136 of the Poor Law Act, 1930, and others; the Committee itself supplies as instances of delegation of the taxing power, instances very much in point, the succession of temporary Acts passed in the autumn of 1931 to meet the financial crisis in which England found herself,[1] and the Import Duties Act, 1932;[2] this last, if a novelty in England, is no novelty in the United States, where delegation is viewed with a suspicion far exceeding that of the most rigid legal theorist in England. On this division of the enquiry the Committee had no specific recommendation to make, but after a suggestion of doubt whether in the past Parliament had always been aware of the difference between its normal and its exceptional practice, they "ventured to express a hope that . . . Parliament will not depart from the normal into the exceptional type of delegated legislation without special need, nor without conscious consideration of the special grounds put forward as constituting the need; and that it will grant delegated powers of the exceptional type, — e. g. powers to legislate on matters of principle or to impose taxation — only on exceptional grounds."[3] Now in so far as this "hope" urges Parliament to be conscious of what it is doing, it is wholly good, but in so far as it makes excep-

[1] Gold Standard (Amendment) Act, National Economy Act, Foodstuffs (Prevention of Exploitation) Act, Abnormal Importation (Customs Duties) Act, Horticultural Products (Emergency Customs Duties) Act.

[2] The Committee regards this Act as "obviously one of the most important delegating enactments which Parliament has ever passed." Report, p. 36.

[3] Report, pp. 58–59.

tional the delegation of power to legislate on "matters of principle" without a hint of the meaning of that cryptic phrase, it must be regarded as a product of the terms of reference upon which I have already had some comments to make, and as an obstacle in the path of the evolution of governmental methods in England. The settlement of detail involving matters of principle — and much detail does involve such matters, e. g. prison and poor law regulations — is, it seems, for the future to be made by Parliament; Parliament is to reassert itself as the sole creator of new law, and is to suffer diminution of its sovereignty only for good cause specifically assigned.

The clearest justification for the employment of the exceptional type of delegated legislation is, of course, the existence of an emergency; but there still remains the difficult question of what is an emergency, a question discussed with some bitterness during the crisis of 1931. The Committee were fully conscious of the difficulty, and although they stated that "emergency and urgency are matters of degree," that "the measure of the need should be the measure alike of the power and of its limitation," they did not express an opinion how far the Acts of the autumn of 1931 measured up to their standards [1] (that would have been to enter upon politics), nor did they lay down any general rules about the delegation by Parliament to the executive of power to legislate on occasions of emergency.

In dealing with the other branch of "skeleton legislation," those enactments which leave everything to the Minister's discretion in plain but wide language, e. g. subsection 1 of section 1 of the Patents Designs and Trade Marks Act, 1888, "such rules as are in the opinion of the Board required for giving effect to the section," the Committee, softened by the kindly tolerance of Lords Herschell and Watson in *Lockwood's Case*, appeared to recognise the expediency of leaving a department free from the control of the courts where it is charged with the inauguration of a new social policy falling peculiarly within its province, e. g. the establishment of a register of patent agents by the Board of Trade or the regula-

---

[1] Report, p. 52: "The recent emergency statutes . . . afford other illustrations of the necessity of this method of legislation *where there is thought to be need* of giving to the Government power to take very rapid decisions which to be effective must possess the force of law." The italics are mine.

See also Report, pp. 51–54, for an excellent summary of the arguments for and against delegation of legislative power.

tion of public service vehicles by the Minister of Transport.[1] Their recommendations, however, do not go quite so far. Here again Parliament is to be fully conscious of its own intentions, and if it grants a discretion should clearly define the limits.[2]

The recommendations directed specifically to the controversial question of the exclusion of the jurisdiction of the courts are best treated closely with the findings and opinions on the "have effect as if enacted in the Act" and the "conclusive evidence" clauses. The Committee did not suffer from my perplexities and doubts upon the meaning of the first type of clause;[3] for them *Yaffe's Case* conveniently decides once and for all that a rule or order made under a "have effect as if enacted in the Act" clause remains open to question, i. e. that the clause is redundant and is merely a superfluous statement of the position at Common Law of a rule or order if intra vires. About the "conclusive evidence" clause they refused to be so positive: it has not yet been considered by the House of Lords. "It is, however, we think, plain that the protection afforded even by this clause is not limitless. If the Minister of Agriculture and Fisheries went out of his province altogether in confirming an "order" (i. e. a regulation) under section 39 of the Small Holdings and Allotments Act, 1908, — if, for example, he confirmed an order which provided for boiling the Bishop of Rochester's cook to death, — we doubt whether the order would be protected by the section, although, if a new Act of Parliament were to be passed expressly conferring such a power, the order would be unassailable."[4] I wholeheartedly agree; to that extent, at any rate, a departmental order sheltering beneath the "conclusive evidence" clause will be inferior to an Act of Parliament. But the words are plain enough, equally plain the fact that Parliament never intended them to protect an order such as that suggested. My agreement does not rest on an interpretation of the words of the clause in "their plain natural sense," the canon of statutory interpretation set up by the Committee.[5] I agree because I know that the judges, aided by their "inarticulate major premiss"[6] that "the Courts are the only refuge of the subject against departmental aggression," can here as ever surmount mere

[1] Report, pp. 38–39.   [2] Report, p. 65, Rec. II.
[3] See Chapter III, *passim*.   [4] Report, p. 40.
[5] Report, p. 56.
[6] Report, p. 135, Note by Professor Laski on the Judicial Interpretation of Statutes.

verbal obstacles in a statute falling to be construed by them. But they do not confine their acrobatics to cases like that suggested by the Committee.

"But the clause is objectionable," the Report continues,[1] and we doubt whether it is ever justified. In exceptional cases where Parliament may determine that it is necessary to confer on a Minister the power to make regulations whose validity is not to be open to challenge in the Courts, the enabling statute should declare this intention in clear and precise language." [2] A few pages later the Committee, ever mindful of the terms of reference, comes to this conclusion:

"The rule of law requires that all regulations should be open to challenge in the Courts except where Parliament deliberately comes to the conclusion that it is essential in the public interest to create an exception and confer on a Minister the power of legislating with immunity from challenge. We recognise that such exceptions must be created in cases where finality is desirable, e. g. where power is given to a Minister to make law upon the faith of which titles to property may be created [3] or money may be raised, e. g. Stock Regulations, or upon which marriages may be solemnized, e. g. Regulations under the Foreign Marriage Act, 1892. But we are of opinion that when for such reasons the regulations cannot remain indefinitely open to challenge, there should be an initial period of challenge of at least three months and preferably six months. Apart from emergency legislation, we hardly think there can be any case so exceptional in its nature, as to make it both politic and just to prohibit the possibility of challenge altogether." [4]

It would be more "politic and just" to devise some method of scrutiny which should forever supersede the chances of fortuitous litigation, to set up some permanent body clothed with power to review all delegated legislation as it issued and quash any that went beyond the statutory power; but that would cut into the sacred rule of law, in withdrawing from the ordinary courts the control of delegated legislation. And yet any suggestion that this

[1] Report, p. 41.

[2] E. g. "shall not be questioned in any legal proceedings whatever," as in Section 5 of the Extradition Act, 1870, Section 3 of the Parliament Act, 1911, Section 11 of the Housing Act, 1930, and a few other very recent Acts.

[3] E. g. schemes for the compulsory acquisition of land under the Small-holdings Act, 1908, the Housing Act, 1925, and others.

[4] Report, p. 61.

type of review should be undertaken by the courts offends against an equally sacred principle, heroically vindicated by all the legal genius of England in the debates on advisory opinions, that no issue shall come before a court for adjudication until there are found parties not only sufficiently aggrieved but sufficiently wealthy to run the risk of being mulcted in heavy costs.

The recommendation of the Committee that even in exceptional cases there should be an initial period of challenge of six months — at first sight a substantial safeguard — is apparently the result of the uncritical acceptance of section 11 of the Housing Act, 1930.[1] This section was designed to provide a method whereby opponents of schemes might challenge their legal validity; the scheme being settled in all its details, the claim is made by a person aggrieved that he is being deprived of his legal rights by an illegal decision of an inferior tribunal, here the quasi-judicial decision of a Minister. The nature of a scheme is such that all persons likely to be affected are kept well posted of its provisions; and since it involves a quasi-judicial decision by a department, the individual affected by it may at once petition for a writ to quash that decision and invoke in his favour the historic jurisdiction of the King's Bench to keep inferior tribunals in their place. It is here both sensible and just to grant only a limited time for objection.

With regulations it is quite otherwise. Like all general laws, they only affect the individual as a member of a class, usually large and often indeterminate; what assurance is there that he will become aware within six months that his rights are threatened? Even if he does become aware of the threat, he cannot question the regulation before a court unless the question of its validity necessarily arises in the course of litigation to which he is a party: the mere issuance of an ultra vires regulation, unlike the giving of an ultra vires quasi-judicial decision, is no ground for interference by the King's Bench. It is not only conceivable, but very probable, that no such litigation will arise within the statutory period. All that the citizen can do, therefore, is to sit in helpless silence while the period runs out. My conclusion? That Parliament would have done just as well to prohibit recourse to the courts from the beginning, indeed would have done better if it had foreborne to introduce the element of uncertainty by entertaining the possibility that a regulation might be upset if a lawsuit involv-

[1] See Report, p. 62, n. 184.

ing its validity chanced to be brought within six months of its promulgation.

The Committee does, it is true, advocate under this head the introduction of a simpler, cheaper, and more expeditious procedure;[1] but the context shows that they were thinking of the judicial review of schemes on the petition of an individual affected. That such a procedure as that provided by section 11 of the Housing Act, 1930, is inapplicable to the challenge of "general" regulations I have already pointed out. And it is unlikely, to say the least, that they intended in those few words to recommend a procedure whereby regulations could come up for review before any person had been adversely affected by them. If only the Committee had dared to make so "unconstitutional" a suggestion, or to give teeth to their Standing Committees of Parliament!

No special treatment is given in the Report to the power of a department to confirm schemes by order — what I have called "private bill legislation by a department." In Chapter IV, I laid stress on the history of the emergence of this power and showed how in this matter the committee of Parliament had become displaced by a department; with that in mind I expressed surprise not at those cases where the scheme is immune from challenge before the courts, but at those where it is not. Again, to my mind, despite the language of judicial decision in which the Acts tended to be cast, the process was preëminently legislative. That it has legislative elements the Committee were ready to admit,[2] but in their opinion (and behind them they have the body of legal doctrine) the making of an order by the Minister is not only cast in the form of, but is in analysis sufficiently like, the judgment of a court to be treated in Section III of the Report, which deals with judicial power, and not in Section II, which deals with legislative power. The term "quasi-judicial," helpful as it is to a court which, like the Court of Appeal in *R*. v. *Electricity Commissioners*,[3] wishes to extend its jurisdiction, carries no conviction when it is used by a committee with masterly powers of analysis and no axe to grind.[4]

[1] Report, p. 62.

[2] Report, p. 27; "Where the Minister of Health confirms . . . a town planning scheme proposed by a Local Authority he is exercising what is constitutionally a legislative function."

[3] [1924] 1 K.B. 171.

[4] It must be remembered, however, that the Committee had to attach some meaning to the phrase "quasi-judicial" in their terms of reference.

The "quasi" in "quasi-judicial" recognises that although in form the process is judicial, the determination of existing rights, the order itself approaches to an act of legislation: it is the product of a discretion granted to enable ideas of policy to be carried into effect. The order may, of course, create new law in different degrees. Some orders, e. g. an order, under section 19 of the Education Act, 1921, determining in case of dispute whether a school is necessary or not,[1] create new law to so small a degree that they are correctly classified under the penumbra of "judicial." But a scheme is a departmental private Act, its sole purpose is to grant new powers, and an order confirming it is the outcome of deliberations which resemble more closely the proceedings of a committee of Parliament than those of a court of law. To attach the name "quasi-judicial" to the deliberations of a minister "whether or not he was satisfied that the circumstances were such as to justify the making of the scheme and that the carrying into effect of the scheme, either absolutely or subject to conditions or modifications, would be beneficial to the health of the inhabitants of the area in question or of the neighbouring dwelling houses," [2] is to play with words.[3]

However that may be, the Committee did treat a confirming order as a quasi-judicial decision, and recommended that such decisions should ordinarily be assigned to a minister, subject to the supervisory jurisdiction of the High Court [4] — the present position, since *Yaffe's Case*. They went on to suggest, however, a simplification of the legal procedure, and recommended that it should provide for the limitation of the time within which an "appeal" might be brought, and for the hearing to take place before a single judge whose decision should normally be final [5] — a suggestion springing from section 11 of the Housing Act, 1930.

I cannot leave this topic without a reference to the local inquiry. The chief objections levelled at the present procedure are (1) that the inspector does not confine himself to hearing testimony at the inquiry, but is in the habit of investigating for himself, (2) that his report to the department is not available either for the parties

[1] Report, p. 91.   [2] Report, p. 92.

[3] The Committee were not unaware of this difficulty, and attempted to resolve it in a footnote (see Report, p. 39, n. 129). But the trouble is that few courts are able to prevent their ideas of what is good policy from influencing their decision upon the question of ultra vires. See Professor Laski's Note (Report, p. 135).

[4] Report, p. 116, Rec. III, and p. 117, Rec. VII (a).

[5] Report, p. 117, Rec. IX; and see Report, p. 62, n. 184.

or the Press, and (3) that no reasons are assigned by the Minister for his decision. The Committee were wholly opposed to formalising the local inquiry: "When a public local inquiry is held as a preliminary to a quasi-judicial decision by a Minister it is not reasonable or practicable that the inspector should be entirely bound by the practice of the courts of law. He is not inquiring solely into facts or law; he is not as a rule a lawyer, and while his main function is to ascertain facts, it is sometimes his duty to form his own views on public policy, or at any rate to weigh all the circumstances in terms of public policy. Although the final decision is not taken by him, to make the inspector's inquiry purely legal and formal might defeat its purpose"; but they thought that in all cases the reasons for the decision should be given to the parties affected. They also thought, but only after a careful appraisal of the arguments pro and contra, that the inspector's report, under present practice treated as confidential, should be made available to the parties and the Press, but not before the release of the reasoned decision. They were, however, quite clear that the Minister should not thereby be barred from giving a decision directly contrary to the findings in the report; the decision must still be his decision, although with the report available to the parties he is not likely to go contrary to it without assigning good reasons therefor in the decision. What is to be done with confidential matter? The Committee were of the opinion that in the interests of open procedure — vital in securing the public confidence — matters of law and fact should all without exception appear on the face of the report, but that advice on questions of ministerial policy might be confidentially communicated.[1]

The power to amend an Act of Parliament is only treated by the Committee in its most striking manifestation, the so-called Henry VIII clause;[2] they expressly exclude the power to add to or alter lists of subject matter contained in schedules;[3] they give instances of, but do not discuss, amendments which are purely verbal or "for conformity";[4] and they do not even mention the power to apply an Act to similar trades, areas, or circumstances

---

[1] See on the whole question Report, pp. 101–107. As to the possibility of libel actions see Report, p. 113.

[2] The Committee think the comparison "certainly far-fetched" (Report, p. 36). In the Acts themselves the clause appears as the "power to remove difficulties" (Report, pp. 123–127).

[3] Report, p. 41.   [4] Report, pp. 37–38.

"with modification." [1] In view of their recognition that the nine instances of the Henry VIII clause were transitory and "to enable minor adjustments of [Parliament's] own handiwork to be made for the purpose of fitting its principles into the fabric of existing legislation, general or local, and of meeting cases of hardship to Local Authorities," [2] and of their being aware of the anticlimax to the controversy over Section 130 of the Local Government Act, 1929,[3] it is a little surprising to see the clause discussed at comparative length.[4] The Committee, apprehensive perhaps of enthusiasts, were anxious to see the principle kept within narrow bounds, and it is only after meeting the arguments from convenience and from necessity arising in the course of the reorganisation of complicated systems of administrator, and after suggesting that the possible loss of public confidence is a heavy price to pay, that they concede that "the Henry VIII clause is a political instrument which must occasionally be used."

Meaning by this that where the moment is opportune for the passage of an Act involving some great change of policy, it would be senseless to ask the Government to hold back, and perhaps lose the tide, while anomalies of local machinery or local difficulties were being smoothed out in the bill. Even in that case the Committee were unwilling to recommend the use of the clause except for the purpose of bringing the Act into operation, and then only as limited to changes in machinery and subject to a maximum time limit of a year.

There can be no doubt that this, the most extreme instance of the power to modify, touches closely the sovereignty of Parliament, and with the recommendations, directed as they are to preserving that sovereignty unimpaired, I am not disposed to quarrel. They are a natural outcome of the essentially conservative attitude of the Committee.

One final word to prevent possible misconception of what I have written in this postscript. I have in general dealt only with Section II of the Report, "Delegated Legislation," and only with those portions of that section which take up the more extraordinary powers of the departments discussed in my essay. Far the greater part of the section is concerned with an analysis of the present position of the departments in legislation, and an exposure

---

[1] See Chapter V, *passim.*
[2] Report, p. 36.
[3] Report, p. 59, n. 178.
[4] Report, pp. 59–61.

of anomalies in terminology [1] and in methods of parliamentary control.[2] With the normal type of delegated legislation [3] the Committee was wholly in sympathy, provided it was made subject to scrutiny by the suggested standing committees of Parliament,[4] given antecedent publicity under an amended Rules Publication Act,[5] and never withheld from review by the courts. The exceptional type they were for confining within the narrowest possible limits. The attitude of the Committee on this matter may appear retrograde, — I beg leave to refer once more to the terms of reference, — but if adopted by Parliament it will have at least one clear advantage: any further step towards placing the departments in the position of Parliament must be taken consciously and deliberately. Evolution in that direction will no more be haphazard, dependent on the whim of the government of the day or of parliamentary counsel,[6] a perpetual ground therefore for public suspicion, but powers and procedure will be fitted to the needs to be supplied, and out of the present disorder will emerge a system of administrative — or, if you prefer it, departmental — law.

[1] See Report, pp. 16–20, pp. 26–28, and p. 64, Rec. I.
[2] See, as to the Rules Publication Act, Report, pp. 44–47, and p. 66, Rec. VIII, as to the laying of regulations before Parliament, Report, pp. 41–44 and pp. 62–64.
[3] Report, pp. 30–31.   [4] Report, pp. 67–70.
[5] Report, p. 66, Rec. VIII.   [6] See Report, p. 24.

APPENDIX

APPENDIX

I. Classified List of Statutes

This list of statutes which bear on the questions discussed in the last three chapters of this essay begins with the year 1850. The list does not purport to be exhaustive but does not, I hope, make too many omissions. Many of the statutes have already been noted or referred to in the text. It was found more convenient to classify the power to issue rules of statutory finality primarily with reference to the departments exercising it, and the other powers of "skeleton legislation," "the conclusive evidence clause," "scheme making," "the power to remove difficulties," and "modification," with reference to their subject matter. I have also appended a few instances chosen at random of the powers of addition and dispensation, and of "appointed day clauses," and a few of the innumerable instances of Provisional Order procedure.

A. *Rules expressed to have effect as if enacted in the Act.*
1. *Issuable by the judges* (after 1850 matters of practice and procedure are regulated wholly by the judges).

   Alterations in Pleadings Act, 1850. 13 & 14 Vict., c. 16. (Passed for five years only, but further extended by 18 & 19 Vict., c. 26.)

   Process and Practice (Ireland) Act, 1850. 13 & 14 Vict., c. 18, secs. 12 and 16.

   Court of Chancery Act, 1850. 13 & 14 Vict., c. 35, sec. 30.

   Court of Session Act, 1850. 13 & 14 Vict., c. 36, sec. 54.

   Court of Chancery (County Palatine of Lancaster) Act, 1850. 13 & 14 Vict., c. 43, sec. 1.

   Civil Bills (Ireland) Act, 1851. 14 & 15 Vict., c. 57, sec. 156.

   County Courts (Further Extension) Act, 1852. 15 & 16 Vict., c. 54, sec. 3.

   Common Law Procedure Act, 1852. 15 & 16 Vict., c. 76, sec. 230.

   Improvement of the Jurisdiction of Equity Act, 1852. 15 & 16 Vict., c. 86, sec. 63.

   Jurisdiction of Stannary Courts Amendment Act, 1855. 18 & 19 Vict., c. 32, sec. 23.

   Crown Suits Act, 1855. 18 & 19 Vict., c. 90, sec. 3.

   Settled Estates Act, 1856. 19 & 20 Vict., c. 120, sec. 30.

   Sale and Transfer of Land Act (Ireland), 1858. 21 & 22 Vict., c. 72, sec. 30.

   Petition of Right Act, 1860. 23 & 24 Vict., c. 34, sec. 15.

   Chancery Evidence Act, 1860. 23 & 24 Vict., c. 128, sec. 1.

Irish Land Act, 1870. 33 & 34 Vict., c. 46, sec. 31.

Municipal Corporations Act, 1882. 45 & 46 Vict., c. 50, sec. 100.

Arrears of Rent (Ireland) Act, 1882. 45 & 46 Vict., c. 47, sec. 23.

Parliamentary Registration Act, 1878. 41 & 42 Vict., c. 26, sec. 39.

Clergy Discipline Act, 1892. 55 & 56 Vict., c. 32, sec. 9.

The rules issued under Judicature Act, 1873. 36 & 37 Vict., c. 66, sec. 74, which regulate the practice and procedure of the High Court, are not clothed with statutory finality.

2. *Issuable by the Lord Chancellor* (other than rules of court).

Transfer of Land Act, 1862. 25 & 26 Vict., c. 53, sec. 125.

Court of Chancery Funds Act, 1872. 35 & 36 Vict., c. 44, secs. 18 and 19.

Judicature Act Amendment Act, 1875. 38 & 39 Vict., c. 77, sec. 26.

Registration of Trade Marks Act, 1875. 38 & 39 Vict., c. 91, sec. 7.

Land Titles and Transfer Act, 1875. 38 & 39 Vict., c. 87, secs. 106, 111, and 121.

Merchant Shipping Act, 1876. 39 & 40 Vict., c. 80, sec. 9. See also the Consolidating Act of 1894, sec. 479.

Bankruptcy Act, 1883. 46 & 47 Vict., c. 52, sec. 127.

Lunacy Acts Amendment Act, 1889. 52 & 53 Vict., c. 41, sec. 88. See also the Consolidating Act of 1890, sec. 338 (2).

3. *Issuable by the Master of the Rolls.*

Public Record Office (Amendment) Act, 1877. 40 & 41 Vict., c. 55, sec. 1.

4. *Issuable by the Lord Lieutenant and the Privy Council of Ireland.*

a. *Rules regulating the constitution and operation of courts.*

Assizes (Ireland) Act, 1850. 13 & 14 Vict., c. 85, sec. 2.

Chairmen's Jurisdiction Act, 1876. 39 & 40 Vict., c. 71, sec. 3.

Supreme Court of Judicature (Ireland) Act, 1877. 40 & 41 Vict., c. 57, secs. 30 and 32.

Supreme Court of Judicature (Ireland) Amendment Act, 1887. 50 Vict., c. 6, sec. 2.

b. *Emergency rules.*

Contagious Diseases (Ireland) Act, 1866. 29 & 30 Vict., c. 4, sec. 2.

Criminal Law and Procedure (Ireland) Act, 1887. 50 & 51 Vict., c. 20, sec. 15.

See also Cattle Disease (Ireland) Act, 1870. 33 & 34 Vict., c. 36, sec. 2.

c. *Financial rules.*

Irish Reproductive Loan Act, 1874. 37 & 38 Vict., c. 86, sec. 10.

Police Act (Ireland), 1919. 9 & 10 Geo. 5, c. 68, sec. 4 (1).

d. *Miscellaneous.*

Parliamentary Voters (Ireland) Act, 1850. 13 & 14 Vict., c. 68, sec. 22.

Alteration of Fair Days (Ireland) Act, 1868. 31 & 32 Vict.,
c. 12, sec. 2.

Irish Land Act, 1870. 33 & 34 Vict., c. 46, sec. 41.

5. *Rules and orders issuable by the Privy Council in England.*

   a. *Emergency rules.*[1]

   Restoration of Order in Ireland Act, 1920. 10 & 11 Geo. 5,
   c. 31.

   Emergency Powers Act, 1920. 10 & 11 Geo. 5, c. 55.

   b. *Rules to prevent the importation and spread of disease.*

   Contagious Diseases of Animals Act, 1848. 11 & 12 Vict.,
   c. 107, sec. 4. (The statutory effect of these rules was confirmed ab initio by 29 & 30 Vict., c. 15, sec. 4.)

   Contagious Diseases of Animals Act, 1869. 32 & 33 Vict.,
   c. 70, sec. 75.

   Contagious Diseases of Animals Act, 1878. 41 & 42 Vict.,
   c. 74, secs. 10 and 58 (2).[2]

   Anthrax Prevention Act, 1919. 9 & 10 Geo. 5, c. 23, sec. 1 (2).

   c. *Rules regulating the constitution and holding of courts, the status
   of prisons and the machinery of voting.*[3]

      i. *Courts.*

      Judicature Act, 1873. 36 & 37 Vict., c. 66, secs. 27 and 32.

      Judicature Act (Amendment) Act, 1875. 38 & 39 Vict.,
      c. 77, sec. 23.

      Winter Assizes Act, 1876. 39 & 40 Vict., c. 57, sec. 2.

      Juries Act, 1922. 12 & 13 Geo. 5, c. 11, sec. 6 (2).

      ii. *Prisons.*

      Trial of Offences Act, 1856. 19 & 20 Vict., c. 16, sec. 14.

      Jurisdiction in Homicides Act, 1862. 25 & 26 Vict., c. 65,
      sec. 18.

      iii. *Voting.*

      Elections Act, 1853. 16 & 17 Vict., c. 68, sec. 7.

      Representation of the People Act, 1918. 7 & 8 Geo. 5, c. 64,
      sec. 20 (3).

   d. *Rules altering standards.*

   Weights and Measures Act, 1878. 41 & 42 Vict., c. 49, secs. 5,
   8, 41, 47, and 63.

   Carriage Act, 1870. 33 & 34 Vict., c. 10, secs. 11 and 12.

   e. *Rules regulating shipping and fisheries.*

   Dockyard Regulation Act, 1865. 28 & 29 Vict., c. 125, secs. 3,
   5, 6, 7, and 11.

[1] For other very drastic emergency powers of the Council, see: Army Regulation Act, 1871. 34 & 35 Vict., c. 86, sec. 16; Militia Act, 1875. 38 & 39 Vict.,
c. 69, sec. 44; Customs Laws Consolidation Act, 1876. 39 & 40 Vict., c. 36,
sec. 138; and the series of Defence of the Realm Acts, 1914–1915.

[2] This power was transferred to the Board of Agriculture in the Act of 1894.

[3] The power of the Privy Council over the machinery of government is illustrated also by the Acts providing for the creation of new ministries during
and immediately after the World War.

Merchant Shipping Act, 1894. 57 & 58 Vict., c. 60, *passim.*
Sea Fisheries Act, 1868. 31 & 32 Vict., c. 45, sec. 23.
Sea Fishing Boats (Scotland) Act, 1886. 49 & 50 Vict., c. 53, sec. 14.

f. *Rules dealing with foreign affairs.*
Merchant Shipping (Colonial) Act, 1869. 31 & 32 Vict., c. 11, secs. 6 and 8 (3).
Colonial Prisoners Removal Act, 1884. 47 & 48 Vict., c. 31, sec. 12.
Foreign Marriage Act, 1892. 55 & 56 Vict., c. 23, sec. 21.
Behring Sea Award Act, 1894. 57 Vict., c. 2, sec. 3 (1).

g. *Miscellaneous.*
Midwives (Scotland) Act, 1915. 5 & 6 Geo. 5, c. 91, sec. 4.
Midwives (Ireland) Act, 1918. 7 & 8 Geo. 5, c. 59, sec. 4.
Midwives Act, 1918. 8 & 9 Geo. 5, c. 43, sec. 1.
Naval Savings Bank Act, 1866. 29 & 30 Vict., c. 43, sec. 5.
Crown Office Act, 1877. 40 & 41 Vict., c. 41, sec. 2.

6. *Rules issuable by a secretary of state.*
Army Enlistment Act, 1870. 33 & 34 Vict., c. 67, sec. 16.
Military Tramways Act, 1887. 50 & 51 Vict., c. 65, sec. 8.
Naturalisation Act, 1870. 33 & 34 Vict., c. 14, sec. 11.
Metropolitan Police Superannuation Act, 1875. 38 & 39 Vict., c. 28, sec. 1.
Coal Mines Regulation Act, 1887. 50 & 51 Vict., c. 58, sec. 51 (1).
Coal Mines Act, 1911. 1 & 2 Geo. 5, c. 50, sec. 86.
Factory & Workshop Act, 1901. 1 Ed. 7, c. 22, sec. 126 (2).
Shops Act, 1912. 2 Geo. 5, c. 3, sec. 6 (3).
Cremation Act, 1902. 2 Ed. 7, c. 8, sec. 7.
Air Navigation Act, 1919. 9 Geo. 5, c. 3, sec. 1.
Poor Law Act, 1927. 17 & 18 Geo. 5, c. 14, sec. 12 (1), (election of guardians).

7. *Rules issuable by the Treasury.*[1]
Public Offices Fees Act, 1879. 42 & 43 Vict., c. 58, sec. 3.
Savings Banks Act, 1920. 10 & 11 Geo. 5, c. 12, sec. 1 (2).
Savings Banks Act, 1887. 50 & 51 Vict., c. 40, sec. 2.
Perhaps also Registry of Works (Ireland) Act, 1832. 2 & 3 Wm. 4, c. 87, sec. 35.

8. *Rules issuable by the Local Government Board and the Ministry of Health.*[2]
Public Libraries (Ireland) Act, 1894. 57 & 58 Vict., c. 38, sec. 11.

---

[1] The instances where the approval of the Treasury is necessary for rules of statutory finality issued by other departments are not included here. Cf. Post Office Savings Banks Act, 1861. 24 & 25 Vict., c. 14, sec. 11; Government Annuities Act, 1864. 27 & 28 Vict., c. 43, sec. 6.

[2] The few occasions on which the Ministry of Health, the most powerful of the departments, is empowered to issue final statutory rules is interesting for the light it throws on the comparative unimportance of the grant of this power.

Local Government (Allotments) (Ireland) Act, 1917. 7 & 8 Geo. 5, c. 30, sec. 1.

Agricultural Rates Act, 1896. 59 & 60 Vict., c. 16, sec. 6 (3).

Poor Law Act, 1927. 17 & 18 Geo. 5, c. 14, secs. 73 (1) and 211 (2).

National Health Insurance Act, 1924. 14 & 15 Geo. 5, c. 38, sec. 93 (1).

9. *Rules issuable by the Board of Trade.*

   a. *Procedural rules.*

      Patents and Designs Act, 1907. 7 Ed. 7, c. 28, sec. 86 (1) (a Consolidating Act: see Patents Act, 1883. 46 & 47 Vict., c. 57, sec. 101).

      Railway and Canal Traffic Act, 1888. 51 & 52 Vict., c. 25, sec. 35.

      National Insurance Act, 1911. 1 & 2 Geo. 5, c. 55, sec. 91.

      Electric Lighting Act, 1882. 45 & 46 Vict., c. 56, sec. 5.

      Electricity Supply Act, 1919. 9 & 10 Geo. 5, c. 100, sec. 34.

      Profiteering Act, 1919. 9 & 10 Geo. 5, c. 66, sec. 2 (2).

   b. *Technical rules.*

      Merchant Shipping (Life Saving Appliances) Act, 1888. 51 & 52 Vict., c. 24, sec. 3 (1).

      Merchant Shipping (Fishing Boats) Act, 1887. 50 Vict., c. 4, sec. 10 (1).

      Merchant Shipping (Load Line) Act, 1890. 53 Vict., c. 9, sec. 2 (2).

   c. *Orders granting permissions.*

      Railways (Extension of Time) Act, 1868. 31 & 32 Vict., c. 18, sec. 13.

      Railways Act, 1903. 3 Ed. 7, c. 30, sec. 1 (1).

   d. *Important legislative orders.*

      Pilotage Act, 1913. 2 & 3 Geo. 5, c. 31, sec. 7.

      Safeguarding of Industries Act, 1921. 11 & 12 Geo. 5, c. 47, sec. 2.

      Abnormal Importations Act, 1931.

10. *Rules issuable by the Postmaster-General* (purely procedural).

Post Office Savings Banks Act, 1861. 24 & 25 Vict., c. 14, sec. 11.

Savings Banks Act, 1887. 50 & 51 Vict., c. 40, sec. 1.

Savings Banks Act, 1920. 10 & 11 Geo. 5, c. 12, sec. 6 (1).

Government Annuities Act, 1864. 27 & 28 Vict., c. 43, sec. 16.

Electric Telegraphs Act, 1868. 31 & 32 Vict., c. 110, sec. 23.

11. *Rules issuable by the Board of Education.*

Education Act, 1870. 33 & 34 Vict., c. 75, sec. 74.

Education Act, 1921. 11 & 12 Geo. 5, c. 51, sec. 46.

12. *Rules issuable by the Board of Agriculture.*

Diseases of Animals Act, 1894. 57 & 58 Vict., c. 57, sec. 49 (2).

Milk and Dairies Act, 1914. 4 & 5 Geo. 5, c. 49, sec. 2.

13. *Rules issuable by the Ministries of Labour, Transport, Pensions, and the Registrar-General of Ireland.*

Unemployment Insurance Act, 1920. 10 & 11 Geo. 5, c. 30, sec. 35 (Labour).

War Pensions Act, 1921. 11 & 12 Geo. 5, c. 49, sec. 9. (Pensions.)

Bridges Act, 1929. 19 & 20 Geo. 5, c. 33, sec. 10 (1). (Transport.)

Births and Deaths Registration (Ireland) Act, 1863. 26 & 27 Vict., c. 11, sec. 6. (Registrar-General.)

14. *Rules issuable by commissioners and miscellaneous ad hoc bodies.*

Trinity House — Pilotage Act, 1853. 16 & 17 Vict., c. 129, sec. 23.

Oxford University Commissioners — Oxford University Act, 1860. 23 & 24 Vict., c. 23.

Inclosure Commissioners — Improvement of Land Act, 1864. 27 & 28 Vict., c. 114, sec. 90.

Loan Commissioners — Public Works Loans Act, 1875. 38 & 39 Vict., c. 89, sec. 41.

Lunacy Commissioners — Lunacy Acts Amendment Act, 1889. 52 & 53 Vict., c. 41, sec. 88.

Railway Commissioners — Railway and Canal Traffic Act, 1888. 51 & 52 Vict., c. 25, sec. 20.

Insurance Commissioners — National Insurance Act, 1911. 1 & 2 Geo. 5, c. 55, sec. 65.

Annuity Commissioners — Government Annuities Act, 1929. 19 & 20 Geo. 5, c. 29, sec. 52 (2).

Metropolitan Board of Works — Metropolitan Board of Works (Money) Act, 1878. 41 & 42 Vict., c. 37, sec. 18.

"Governing bodies" — Government of Oxford Act, 1854. 17 & 18 Vict., c. 81, sec. 35.

— Public Schools Act, 1868. 31 & 32 Vict., c. 118, sec. 8 (4).

Pharmaceutical Society of Ireland — Pharmacy (Ireland) Act, 1875. 38 & 39 Vict., c. 57, sec. 16.

Chairman of Committees in the House of Lords with the Chairman of Ways and Means in the House of Commons — Private Legislation Procedure (Scotland) Act, 1899. 62 & 63 Vict., c. 47, sec. 15.

15. *Rules issuable by Private Bodies.*

Bank of England — National Debt Act, 1870. 33 & 34 Vict., c. 71, sec. 39.

— Stock Certificate Act, 1863. 26 & 27 Vict., c. 28, sec. 10.

— India Stock Act, 1863. 26 & 27 Vict., c. 73, sec. 9.

B. *The "conclusive evidence" clause.*

1. *Orders issuable by the Lord Lieutenant in Ireland.*

a. *Emergency provisions.*

Peace Preservation (Ireland) Act, 1870. 33 & 34 Vict., c. 9, sec. 21.

Protection of Person and Property (Ireland) Act, 1881.
44 Vict., c. 4, sec. 1 (1).

b. *Reorganisation of the machinery of government.*
Registration (Ireland) Act, 1873. 36 Vict., c. 30, sec. 4.
Marshalsea (Dublin) Discontinuance Act, 1874. 37 & 38 Vict., c. 21, sec. 4.
Local Bankruptcy (Ireland) Act, 1888. 51 & 52 Vict., c. 44, sec. 18.

c. *Miscellaneous.*
Towns Improvement Act (Ireland), 1854. 17 & 18 Vict., c. 103, sec. 15.

2. *Orders of the Privy Council and the departments in England.*

a. *General legislative orders.*
Extradition Act, 1870. 33 & 34 Vict., c. 52, sec. 5.
Explosive Substances Act, 1875. 38 Vict., c. 17, sec. 83.
London Traffic Act, 1924. 14 & 15 Geo. 5, c. 34, sec. 10 (6).
Parliament Act, 1911. 1 & 2 Geo. 5, c. 13, sec. 3. (Certificate of the Speaker.)

b. *Legislative orders in the nature of private bills.*
i. *Schemes.*
Labourers' (Ireland) Act, 1906. 6 Ed. 7, c. 37, sec. 6 (4).
Light Railways Act, 1896. 59 & 60 Vict., c. 48, sec. 10.
Local Government Act, 1894. 56 & 57 Vict., c. 73, sec. 42.
Educational Endowments (Scotland) Act, 1928. 18 & 19 Geo. 5, c. 30, sec. 30.
ii. *Orders for the compulsory acquisition of land.*
Local Government Act, 1894. 56 & 57 Vict., c. 73, sec. 9 (7) (c).
Small Holdings and Allotments Act, 1907. 7 Ed. 7, c. 54, sec. 26 (3).
Housing Act, 1909. 9 Ed. 7, c. 44, Sched. I, 2. (See also Sched. III, 2, of the Act of 1925.)
Education Act, 1921. 11 & 12 Geo. 5, c. 51, Sched. 5 (2).
Salmon and Freshwater Fisheries Act, 1923. 13 & 14 Geo. 5, c. 16, sec. 16.

c. *Judicial orders in the nature of private bills.*
Drainage & Maintenance (Ireland) Act, 1866. 29 & 30 Vict., c. 49, sec. 20.
Improvement of Land Act, 1864. 27 & 28 Vict., c. 114, sec. 55.
Valuation of Property (Metropolis) Act, 1869. 32 & 33 Vict., c. 67, sec. 45.
Shannon Navigation Act, 1874. 37 & 38 Vict., c. 60, sec. 18.
Railway and Canal Traffic Act, 1873. 36 & 37 Vict., c. 48, sec. 29.
Housing Act, 1925. 15 Geo. 5, c. 14, sec. 32 (2).

d. There are strangely enough a good many instances where the "conclusive evidence clause" is used to protect rules of procedure.

E. g.:
   Public Works Loans Act, 1875. 38 & 39 Vict., c. 89, sec. 41.
   Gas and Waterworks Facilities Act Amendment Act, 1873.
      36 & 37 Vict., c. 89, sec. 14.
   Tramways Act, 1870. 33 & 34 Vict., c. 78, sec. 64 (4).

C. *Skeleton Legislation* (only the most striking instances of what is now
   an everyday practice are here set out).

   1. *Where the general policy of an Act is declared and it is left to the
      executive to decide in exactly what cases it is to apply.*
      Prevention of Crimes Act Amendment Act, 1876. 39 & 40 Vict.,
         c. 23, sec. 2.
      Seeds Act, 1920. 10 & 11 Geo. 5, c. 54, sec. 7 (1).

   2. *Where a scheme is sketched out and the details are left to be done by
      order.*
      Bishopric of St. Albans Act, 1875. 38 & 39 Vict., c. 34, sec. 9.
      Newcastle Chapter Act, 1884. 47 & 48 Vict., c. 66, sec. 3 (5).
      Ministry of Munitions and Shipping (Cessation) Act, 1921.
         11 Geo. 5, c. 8, sec. 1.
      Treaties of Peace Act, 1920. 10 Geo. 5, c. 7, sec. 1 (1).

   3. *Where the rules are to be based on the report of a departmental
      committee.*
      Cotton Cloth Factories Act, 1897. 60 & 61 Vict., c. 58, sec. 1.
         (See also the Acts of 1911. 1 & 2 Geo. 5, c. 21, sec. 1 (1), and of
         1929. 19 & 20 Geo. 5, c. 15, sec. 1.
      Intermediate Education (Ireland) Act, 1900. 63 & 64 Vict., c. 43,
         sec. 1 (1).

   4. *Where the executive is left to draw up a code on a subject best treated
      by experts.*
      Railway Employment Act, 1900. 63 & 64 Vict., c. 27, sec. 1.
      Cremation Act, 1902. 2 Ed. 7, c. 8, sec. 7.
      Motor Car Act, 1903. 3 Ed. 7, c. 36, secs. 2 and 7.

   5. *Where although general rules are laid down for ordinary cases, special
      rules are to be made for special cases.*
      Process and Practice (Ireland) Act, 1850. 13 & 14 Vict., c. 89,
         sec. 31.
      Factories Act, 1916. 6 & 7 Geo. 5, c. 31, sec. 7 (1).

D. *The making of schemes.*

   1. *Grants of rights over quasi-public property.*
      Fisheries Act, 1877. 40 & 41 Vict., c. 42, sec. 7.
      Sea Fisheries (Clam and Bait Beds) Act, 1881. 44 Vict., c. 11,
         sec. 4.

   2. *Schemes of fiduciary bodies with respect to property under their
      control.*
      Lunatics Act (Amendment) Act, 1862. 25 & 26 Vict., c. 111,
         sec. 4.

Endowed Schools Act, 1869. 32 & 33 Vict., c. 56, secs. 35 to 39.

Educational Endowments (Scotland) Act, 1882. 45 & 46 Vict., c. 59, secs. 21–32.

City of London Parochial Charities Act, 1883. 46 & 47 Vict., c. 36, sec. 34.

Educational Endowments (Ireland) Act, 1885. 48 & 49 Vict., c. 78, sec. 29.

Educational Endowments (Scotland) Act, 1928. 18 & 19 Geo. 5, c. 30, sec. 30.

3. *Confirmation of voluntary agreements which require governmental assent.*

   a. *Between railways* (before the date of the Railway Commission).
      Railway Companies (Powers) Act, 1864. 27 & 28 Vict., c. 120, secs. 4–17.
      Railways Construction Facilities Act, 1864. 27 & 28 Vict., c. 121, secs. 6–17.

   b. *Creditors Schemes.*
      Railway Companies Act, 1867. 30 & 31 Vict., c. 127, secs. 6–18.
      Railway Companies (Scotland) Act, 1867. 31 & 32 Vict., c. 126, secs. 6–18.
      Liquidation Act, 1868. 31 & 32 Vict., c. 68, sec. 10.

   c. *Agreements for the transfer of powers.*
      London Electric Lighting Act, 1904. 4 Ed. 7, c. 13, sec. 4.
      Land Drainage Act, 1930. 20 & 21 Geo. 5, c. 44, sec. 40.

4. *Schemes setting up new bodies to exercise powers usually granted only by private bill.*

   Tramways Construction Act (Ireland), 1860. 24 & 25 Vict., c. 102, sec. 9.
   Light Railways Act, 1896. 59 & 60 Vict., c. 48, secs. 7–9.
   Municipal Corporations Act, 1882. 45 & 46 Vict., c. 50, sec. 213.
   Education Act, 1902. 2 Ed. 7, c. 42, sec. 21 (3).
   Salmon and Freshwater Fisheries Act, 1923. 13 & 14 Geo. 5, c. 16, sec. 38.
   See also:
   Land Drainage Act, 1918. 8 & 9 Geo. 5, c. 17, Sched. I, Part I.
   Truro Chapter Act, 1878. 41 & 42 Vict., c. 44, secs. 8–9.
   Bishoprics Act, 1878. 41 & 42 Vict., c. 68, secs. 7–9.

5. *Redistricting and reorganisation schemes.*

   Union of Contiguous Benefices Act, 1855. 18 & 19 Vict., c. 127, secs. 2–7.
   Municipal Corporations Act, 1882. 45 & 46 Vict., c. 50, sec. 30.
   Ministry of Transport Act, 1919. 9 & 10 Geo. 5, c. 50, sec. 3 (1) (d).

6. *Schemes carrying into effect social improvements that involve compulsory acquisition of, or dealings with, land.*

   Landowners (Ireland) Amendment Act, 1885. 48 & 49 Vict., c. 77, sec. 12.

Military Tramways Act, 1887. 50 & 51 Vict., c. 65, sec. 10 (3).
Local Government Act, 1894. 56 & 57 Vict., c. 73, sec. 9.
Public Health (Scotland) Act, 1897. 60 & 61 Vict., c. 38, sec. 145 (5), (6), and (8).
Housing of the Working Classes Act, 1890. 53 & 54 Vict., c. 70, sec. 39.
Housing Act, 1903. 3 Ed. 7, c. 39, sec. 5.
Housing Act, 1909. 9 Ed. 7, c. 44, sec. 24.
Housing Act, 1919. 9 & 10 Geo. 5, c. 35, sec. 11 (2) (3).
Housing Act, 1925. 15 Geo. 5, c. 14, secs. 35–40.
Housing Act, 1909. 9 Ed. 7, c. 44, sec. 54.
Town Planning Act, 1925. 15 Geo. 5, c. 16, sec. 2.

7. *Schemes carrying into effect social improvements that require no dealings with land.*
Electricity Supply Act, 1919. 9 & 10 Geo. 5, c. 100, sec. 7.
Unemployment Insurance Act, 1920. 10 & 11 Geo. 5, c. 30, sec. 18.
War Pensions Act, 1921. 11 & 12 Geo. 5, c. 49, sec. 1. (Establishment of committees.)
Mining Industry Act, 1926. 16 & 17 Geo. 5, c. 28, sec. 7 (4).
Coal Mines Act, 1930. 20 & 21 Geo. 5, c. 34, sec. 1.
Agricultural Marketing Act, 1931. 21 & 22 Geo. 5, c. 42, sec. 1.

8. *Pension schemes by departments affecting their employees only.*
Education (Scotland) Act, 1908. 8 Ed. 7, c. 63, sec. 14 (4), and sec. 16 (2).
See also Education (Scotland) (Superannuation) Act, 1919. 9 & 10 Geo. 5, c. 17, sec. 8.

NOTE. Only schemes expressed to "have effect as if enacted in the Act" or protected by the "conclusive evidence" clause are included in this list. Schemes of limited application, e. g. that in section 47 of Workmen's Compensation Act, 1925, are also omitted.

E. *The power to remove difficulties and the power to modify.*

1. *The power to remove difficulties.*

   a. *Where the occasion for its use is strictly defined in the Act.*
   Local Government Act, 1888. 50 & 51 Vict., c. 41, sec. 108.
   Local Government Act, 1894. 56 & 57 Vict., c. 73, sec. 80 (1).
   Education (Scotland) Act, 1918. 8 & 9 Geo. 5, c. 48, Sched. II, 15 (5).
   Metropolitan Water Act, 1902. 2 Ed. 7, c. 41, sec. 51 (1), (2).
   Local Government (Ireland) Act, 1919. 9 & 10 Geo. 5, c. 19, sec. 10 (2).
   Poor Law Act, 1927. 17 & 18 Geo. 5, c. 14, sec. 13.

   b. *Where the occasion for its use is more laxly defined.*
   National Insurance Act, 1911. 1 & 2 Geo. 5, c. 55, sec. 78.

Military Service Act, 1916. 5 & 6 Geo. 5, c. 104, Sched. II, 6.

Unemployment Insurance Act, 1920. 10 & 11 Geo. 5, c. 30, sec. 45.

Widows Orphans and Old Age Contributory Pensions Act, 1925. 15 & 16 Geo. 5, c. 70, sec. 36.

Rating and Valuation Act, 1925. 15 & 16 Geo. 5, c. 90, sec. 67 (1).

Local Government Act, 1929. 19 Geo. 5, c. 17, sec. 130.

2. *The power to modify an Act of Parliament.*

    1. *Power to modify an Act other than the Act granting the power.*

        i. *Power to modify a public general Act.*

            (a) *Substituting new principles and new standards for the old.*

Courts of Justice Salaries Act, 1869. 32 & 33 Vict., c. 91, sec. 14.

Factory Acts (Extension) Act, 1867. 30 & 31 Vict., c. 103, sec. 14.

Registration of Births and Deaths Act, 1874. 37 & 38 Vict., c. 88, sec. 44.

Judicature Act Amendment Act, 1875. 38 & 39 Vict., c. 77, sec. 24.

Motor Car (International Circulation) Act, 1909. 9 Ed. 7, c. 37, sec. 1.

London Traffic Act, 1924. 14 & 15 Geo. 5, c. 34, sec. 10 (2).

            (b) *Modifications necessary on the application of an old Act to new circumstances.*

Elementary Education (Scotland) Act, 1876. 39 & 40 Vict., c. 79, sec. 16.

Day Industrial Schools (Scotland) Act, 1893. 56 Vict., c. 12, sec. 3 (9).

Local Government (Ireland) Act, 1898. 61 & 62 Vict., c. 37, sec. 104 (1).

Local Government (Scotland) Act, 1929. 19 & 20 Geo. 5, c. 25, sec. 76 (1).

Local Government Act, 1929. 19 Geo. 5, c. 17, sec. 138 (3).

            (c) *Modifications necessary on the transfer of the powers and duties of an old authority to a new.*

Ministry of Pensions Act, 1916. 6 & 7 Geo. 5, c. 65, sec. 2 (1).

Air Force Act, 1917. 7 & 8 Geo. 5, c. 51, sec. 8 (4).

Scottish Board of Health Act, 1919. 9 & 10 Geo. 5, c. 20, sec. 4 (4).

Ministry of Health Act, 1919. 9 & 10 Geo. 5, c. 21, sec. 3 (2), (3), (4), and sec. 8 (2), (3).

Forestry (Transfer of Woods) Act, 1923. 13 & 14 Geo. 5, c. 21, Sched. (1).

ii. *Power to modify local Acts.*

    (a) *Modification of statutory charges.*

        Turnpike Acts Continuance Act, 1850. 13 & 14 Vict., c. 79, sec. 3.

        Statutory Undertakings (Temporary Increase of Charges) Act, 1918. 8 & 9 Geo. 5, c. 34, sec. 1.

        Gas Regulation Act, 1920. 10 & 11 Geo. 5, c. 28, sec. 1 (1), (2).

        Water Undertakings (Modification of Charges) Act, 1921. 11 & 12 Geo. 5, c. 44, sec. 2.

        Harbours (Temporary Increase of Charges) Act, 1920. 10 & 11 Geo. 5, c. 21, sec. 1 (1).

        Housing (Financial Provisions) Act, 1924. 14 & 15 Geo. 5, c. 35, sec. 5.

    (b) *Modifications of provisions other than those imposing statutory charges.*

        Metropolis Local Management Act, 1855. 18 & 19 Vict., c. 120, sec. 247.

        Special Acts (Extension of Time) Act, 1915. 5 & 6 Geo. 5, c. 72, sec. 1.

        Road Traffic Act, 1930. 20 & 21 Geo. 5, c. 43, sec. 91 (3).

        Bridges Act, 1929. 19 & 20 Geo. 5, c. 33, sec. 3 (2) (e).

    (c) *Modifications necessary on the coming into force of a new Act.*

        Education (Scotland) Act, 1918. 8 & 9 Geo. 5, c. 48, Sched. V (6).

        Gas Regulation Act, 1920. 10 & 11 Geo. 5, c. 28, sec. 10 (1), (2) (h).

        Rating and Valuation Act, 1925. 15 & 16 Geo. 5, c. 90, sec. 66.

        Local Government (Ireland) Act, 1898. 61 & 62 Vict., c. 37, sec. 104 (2) (d).

        Public Health Act, 1925. 15 & 16 Geo. 5, c. 71, sec. 6.

        Gas Undertakings Act, 1929. 19 & 20 Geo. 5, c. 24, sec. 1 (3).

2. *Power to modify the Act which grants the power.*

    i. *Power to alter forms and fees.* (This is a very normal head of executive action and is also not easy to distinguish from the powers of addition and suspension. A few instances only are given.)

    Companies Act, 1862. 25 & 26 Vict., c. 89, sec. 71.

    Hackney Carriage (Dublin) Act, 1853. 16 & 17 Vict., c. 112, secs. 7 and 48.

    Births and Deaths Registration (Ireland) Act, 1880. 43 & 44 Vict., c. 13, sec. 34.

    ii. *Power to alter standards set up by the Act.*

    Sea Birds Preservation Act, 1869. 32 & 33 Vict., c. 17, sec. 3.

    Wild Fowl Preservation Act, 1876. 39 & 40 Vict., c. 29, sec. 3.

Chain Cables and Anchors Act, 1871. 34 & 35 Vict., c. 101, sec. 6.

Weights and Measures Act, 1878. 41 & 42 Vict., c. 49, sec. 41.

Factory and Workshop Act, 1901. 1 Ed. 7, c. 22, sec. 3 (2).

iii. *Power to modify the provisions of the Act in order to incorporate the determinations of experts or new special conditions.*

Merchant Shipping Act, 1854. 17 & 18 Vict., c. 104, sec. 371.

Metropolitan Buildings Act, 1855. 18 & 19 Vict., c. 122, sec. 55.

Merchant Shipping Acts Amendment Act, 1862. 25 & 26 Vict., c. 63, sec. 25.

Explosives Act, 1875. 38 Vict., c. 17, sec. 33.

Representation of the People Act, 1918. 7 & 8 Geo. 5, c. 64, sec. 13 (2).

West Indian Encumbered Estates Act, 1854. 17 & 18 Vict., c. 117, sec. 66.

Vaccination (Scotland) Act, 1863. 26 & 27 Vict., c. 108, sec. 12.

Police Act, 1910. 10 Ed. 7 & 1 Geo. 5, c. 13, sec. 1 (2).

Workmen's Compensation Act, 1925. 15 & 16 Geo. 5, c. 84, sec. 43 (3).

Peterhead Harbour of Refuge Act, 1886. 49 & 50 Vict., c. 49, sec. 20 (3).

F. *The "appointed day" clause and the powers of addition and dispensation.*

1. *The "appointed day" clause. This clause is now employed in most statutes.*

Copyright Amendment Act, 1852. 15 & 16 Vict., c. 12, sec. 2.

Fugitive Offenders Act, 1881. 44 & 45 Vict., c. 69, sec. 12.

Local Government (Ireland) Act, 1898. 61 & 62 Vict., c. 37, sec. 124 (1).

Land Transfer Act, 1897. 60 & 61 Vict., c. 65, sec. 20 (1).

Improvement of Live Stock (Licensing of Bulls) Act, 1931. 21 & 22 Geo. 5, c. 43, sec. 13 (1).

Companies Act, 1928. 18 & 19 Geo. 5, c. 45, sec. 118 (4).

2. *The power of adding to the list of situations as to which the Act has effect.* (Selections.)

Salmon Fisheries (Scotland) Act, 1863. 26 & 27 Vict., c. 50, sec. 4.

Sale of Poisons Act, 1868. 31 & 32 Vict., c. 121, sec. 2.

Carriage of Dangerous Goods Act, 1866. 29 & 30 Vict., c. 69, sec. 9.

Public Health Act, 1875. 38 & 39 Vict., c. 55, sec. 276.

Contagious Diseases of Animals Act, 1886. 49 & 50 Vict., c. 32, sec. 3.

Foreign Jurisdiction Act, 1890. 53 & 54 Vict., c. 37, sec. 5 (1).

National Insurance Act, 1916. 6 & 7 Geo. 5, c. 20, sec. 2 (1).

Trade Boards Act, 1918. 8 & 9 Geo. 5, c. 32, sec. 1 (2).
Public Health (Smoke Abatement) Act, 1926. 16 & 17 Geo. 5, c. 43, sec. 4.

3. *The power of dispensation.* (All the instances which I have discovered.)

White Herring Fishery (Scotland) Amendment Act, 1861. 24 & 25 Vict., c. 72, sec. 5.
Burials (Ireland) Act, 1868. 31 & 32 Vict., c. 103, sec. 4.
Coal Mines Regulation Act, 1872. 35 & 36 Vict., c. 76, sec. 22 (2).
Pollution of Rivers Act, 1876. 39 & 40 Vict., c. 75, sec. 3.
Factory and Workshop Act, 1878. 41 Vict., c. 16, sec. 43.
Merchant Shipping (Fishing Boats) Act, 1883. 46 & 47 Vict., c. 41, sec. 3.
Weights and Measures Act, 1889. 52 & 53 Vict., c. 21, sec. 30.
Copyhold Act, 1894. 57 & 58 Vict., c. 46, sec. 12 (1).
Collecting Societies and Industrial Assurance Companies Act, 1896. 59 & 60 Vict., c. 26, sec. 11.
Truck Act, 1896. 59 & 60 Vict., c. 44, sec. 9.
Factory and Workshop Act, 1901. 1 Ed. 7, c. 22, sec. 36.
Coal Mines Regulation Act, 1908. 8 Ed. 7, c. 57, sec. 4.
Official Secrets Act, 1911. 1 & 2 Geo. 5, c. 28, sec. 11.
Merchandise Marks Act, 1926. 16 & 17 Geo. 5, c. 53, sec. 1 (3).
Moneylenders Act, 1927. 17 & 18 Geo. 5, c. 21, sec. 11 (1).

4. *A few instances of Provisional Order Procedure.*

Public Health Act, 1848. 11 & 12 Vict., c. 63, sec. 10.
Public Health (Scotland) Act, 1867. 30 & 31 Vict., c. 101, sec. 90.
Drainage of Land Act, 1861. 24 & 25 Vict., c. 133, sec. 21.
Pilotage Act, 1862. 25 & 26 Vict., c. 63, sec. 40.
Fishery Harbours Act, 1915. 5 & 6 Geo. 5, c. 48, sec. 2 (3).
Port of London Act, 1908. 8 Ed. 7, c. 68, sec. 6 (2).
Local Government Act, 1926. 16 & 17 Geo. 5, c. 38, sec. 2.

II. LITERATURE

MOST of the material for this essay was drawn direct from the statutes 1848–1931, the volumes of Statutory Rules and Orders, the departmental circulars contained in the Local Government Reports, the Parliamentary Debates and the Law Reports.

On the more general aspects of delegation of legislative power the following works and articles were referred to:

Delegated Legislation (1921). C. T. Carr.
Administrative Law (1929). F. J. Port.
The New Despotism (1929). Lord Hewart.
Law in the Making — Chapter VII, Subordinate and Autonomic Legislation (1927). C. K. Allen.
Bureaucracy Triumphant (1931). C. K. Allen.

The Crisis of English Liberty, Prologue (1930). Sir John Marriott.
Vinogradoff, Collected Papers, Vol. II, p. 381.
How Britain is Governed (1929). Ramsay Muir.
Advisory Committees in British Administration (1926). J. A. Fairlie. 20 Am. Pol. Sci. Rev. 812.
The Development of Administrative Law in England. Dicey. 31 L.Q.R. 148 (1915).
Introduction to Second Edition of Law and Opinion (1914). Dicey.
Introduction to Eighth Edition of the Law of the Constitution (1923). Dicey.
The Rhodes Lecture (1918), 34 L.Q.R. at 130. Sir T. E. Scrutton.
The Rule of D.O.R.A. (1919), 1 J.S.C.L. (3rd Ser.), Part I, 37.
A Review of the New Despotism in 1 Political Quarterly 127 (1930).

The most valuable periodical literature is:

The annual review of the legislation of the United Kingdom in J.S.C.L.,

and the following articles in the Journal of Public Administration:

Recent Tendencies towards the Devolution of Legislative Functions to the Administration. Stamp. 2 J.P.A. 23 (1924).
Powers of Public Departments to Make Rules Having the Force of Law. Gwyer. 5 J.P.A. 404 (1927).
Legislative Powers of Public Authorities. Potter. 6 J.P.A. 32 (1928).
Bureaucracy. Anderson. 7 J.P.A. 3 (1929).
The Legislature and the Administration. Christie. 8 J.P.A. 367 (1930).
The Legislative Functions of Government Departments. Laing. 8 J.P.A. 335 (1930).
The Method of Social Legislation. Cole. 9 J.P.A. 4 (1931).

The following works were referred to before embarking on Chapter IV:

The First (1925), Second (1928), and Final (1929) Reports of the Royal Commission on Local Government — also the Minutes of Evidence.
May's Parliamentary Practice (13th Edition) (1924).
Williams' Private Bill Legislation (1927).
Introduction to Hill's The Complete Law of Housing (1931).
Law Making by Government Departments. Macassey. 5 J.S.C.L. (3rd Ser.), Part I, 73 (1923).
A City Council from Within. E. D. Simon. (1926.)

INDEX

INDEX

NOTE. No Acts of Parliament are listed except those fully discussed in the text.